Bloom's Modern Critical Interpretations

Bloom's Modern Critical Interpretations

James Joyce's
ULYSSES

Edited and with an introduction by
Harold Bloom
Sterling Professor of the Humanities
Yale University

CHELSEA HOUSE
PUBLISHERS
A Haights Cross Communications Company
Philadelphia

©2004 by Chelsea House Publishers, a subsidiary of
Haights Cross Communications.

A Haights Cross Communications ◀── Company

Introduction © 2004 by Harold Bloom.

Printed and bound in Malaysia.

10 9 8 7 6 5 4 3 2 1

Library of Congress Cataloging-in-Publication Data
Ulysses / edited and with an introduction by Harold Bloom.
        p. cm. -- (Bloom's modern critical interpretations)
Includes bibliographical references and index.
  ISBN 0-7910-7576-1
  1. Joyce, James, 1882-1941. Ulysses. 2. Dublin (Ireland)--In
literature. I. Bloom, Harold. II. Series.
  PR6019.O9U748 2003
  823'.912--dc21

                                        2003006928

Contributing editor: Janyce Marson

Cover design by Terry Mallon

Cover: © Richard Cummins/CORBIS

Layout by EJB Publishing Services

Chelsea House Publishers
1974 Sproul Road, Suite 400
Broomall, PA 19008-0914

http://www.chelseahouse.com

Contents

Editor's Note

My Introduction is a Bloomian excursus upon the Jewishness of the other Bloom, who is not Talmudically Jewish, since both his maternal grandmother and his mother were Irish Catholics. But Poldy identifies with his father, Virag, a Hungarian Jew. Joyce's aesthetic contest with Shakespeare is seen as flowering out of Bloom, who is identified both with Joyce and with Shakespeare.

Richard Ellmann, Joyce's best biographer, sketches the literary and the Dublin backgrounds of *Ulysses*, while Wolfgang Iser outlines the reader's share in "The Oxen of the Sun" episode.

The "Ithaca" episode is charted by A. Walton Litz, after which Robert D. Newman analyzes the roles of Hermetic messengers in *Ulysses*, with their parodistic style a kind of recall of Giordano Bruno, the beacon of Renaissance Hermeticism.

Marylu Hill examines the Telemachiad episode and subtly establishes Joyce's precarious balance between patriarchy and the powerful selfhood of woman, particularly as the figure of the mother, while Nicholas A. Miller gives a Freudian reading of the "Ithaca" section. Weldon Thornton emphasizes Joyce's powerfully archaic assumption of authorial omniscience.

The Ovidian element in *Ulysses* is uncovered by José Lanters, while Joley Wood examines Plato's influence upon *Ulysses*. In the penultimate essay, Sara Danius juxtaposes Proust and Joyce, the two great novelists of their century.

In this volume's final essay, Eric D. Smith traces Joyce's aesthetic maturation that results sublimely in *Ulysses*.

HAROLD BLOOM

Introduction

I.

It is an odd sensation to begin writing an introduction to a volume of Joyce criticism on June 16, particularly if one's name is Bloom. Poldy is, as Joyce intended, the most *complete* figure in modern fiction, if not indeed in all of Western fiction, and so it is appropriate that he have a saint's day in the literary calendar: Bloomsday. He is, thankfully, no saint, but a mild gentle sinner; in short, a good man. So good a man is he that even the critic Hugh Kenner, who in his earlier commentary saw Poldy as an instance of modern depravity, an Eliotic Jew as it were, in 1980 could call Joyce's hero "fit to live in Ireland without malice, without violence, without hate." How many are fit to live, in fact or fiction, in Ireland or America, without malice, without violence, without hate? Kenner, no sentimentalist, now finds in Poldy what the reader must find: a better person than oneself.

Richard Ellmann, Joyce's biographer, shrewdly says of Poldy that "he is not afraid that he will compromise his selfhood." Currently fashionable criticism, calling itself "Post-Structuralist Joyce," oddly assimilates Joyce to Barthes, Lacan, Derrida; producing a Poldy without a self, another floating signifier. But Joyce's Poldy, as Ellmann insists, is heroic and imaginative; his mimetic force allies him to the Wife of Bath, Falstaff and Sancho Panza, and like them his presence is overwhelming. Joyce's precursors were Dante and

Shakespeare, and Poldy has a comprehensiveness and immediacy worthy of his ancestry. It is good to remember that, after Dante and Shakespeare, Joyce cared most for Wordsworth and Shelley among the poets. Wordsworth's heroic naturalism and Shelley's visionary skepticism find their way into Poldy also.

How Jewish is Poldy? Here I must dissent a touch from Ellmann, who says that when Poldy confronts the Citizen, he states an ethical view "more Christian than Judaic." Poldy has been unbelieving Jew, Protestant and Catholic, but his ethical affirmations are normative Jewish, as Joyce seems to have known better than Ellmann does. When Poldy gazes upon existence, he finds it good. The commonplace needs no hallowing for Poldy. Frank Budgen, taking the hint from Joyce, emphasizes how much older Poldy seems than all the other inhabitants of Joyce's visionary Dublin. We do not think of Poldy as being thirty-eight, prematurely middle-aged, but rather as living in what the Hebrew Bible called *olam*: time without boundaries. Presumably, that is partly why Joyce chose to make his Ulysses Jewish rather than Greek. Unlike a modern Greek, Poldy is in surprising continuity with a lineage of which he has little overt knowledge. How different would the book have been if Joyce had centered on a Greek living in Dublin? The aura of exile would not be there. Joyce the Dubliner in exile, tasting his own stoic version of a Dantesque bitterness, found in Poldy as wandering Jew what now seems his inevitable surrogate. Poldy, not Stephen, is Joyce's true image.

Yet Poldy is certainly more like Homer's Ulysses than like the Yahwist's Jacob. We see Poldy surviving the Cyclops, but not wrestling with one among the Elohim in order to win a name for himself. Truly Jewgreek, Poldy has forsworn the Covenant, even if he cannot escape from having been chosen. Joyce, too, has abandoned the Church, but cannot escape the intellectual discipline of the Jesuits. Poldy's sense of election is a little more mysterious, or perhaps it is Joyce's sense of his hero's election that is the true mystery of the book. At the end of the Cyclops episode, Joyce evidently felt the necessity of distracting himself from Poldy, if only because literary irony fails when confronted by the heroic pathos of a creation that defies even Joyce's control.

> —Are you talking about the new Jerusalem? says the citizen.
> —I'm talking about injustice, says Bloom.
> —Right, says John Wyse. Stand up to it then with a force like men.

But that is of course not Poldy's way. No interpolated sarcasm, however dramatically wrought, is able to modify the dignity of Poldy's rejoinder:

—But it's no use, says he. Force, hatred, history, all that. That's not life for men and women, insult and hatred. And everybody knows that it's the very opposite of that that is really life.
—What, says Alf.
—Love, says Bloom. I mean the opposite of hatred.

Twelve delirious pages of hyperbole and phantasmagoria follow, detailing the forced exit of the noble Poldy from the pub, and ending in a grand send-up indeed:

When, lo, there came about them all a great brightness and they beheld the chariot wherein He stood ascend to heaven. And they beheld Him in the chariot, clothed upon in the glory of the brightness, having raiment as of the sun, fair as the moon and terrible that for awe they durst not look upon Him. And there came a voice out of heaven, calling: *Elijah! Elijah!* And he answered with a main cry: *Abba! Adonai!* And they beheld Him even Him, ben Bloom Elijah, amid clouds of angels ascend to the glory of the brightness at an angle of forty-five degrees over Donohoe's in Little Green Street like a shot off a shovel.

It is all in the juxtaposition of "ben Bloom Elijah" and "like a shot off a shovel," at once a majestic deflation and a complex apotropaic gesture on Joyce's own part. Like Falstaff and Sancho Panza, Poldy runs off with the book, and Joyce's strenuous ironies, dwarfing the wit of nearly all other authors, essentially are so many reaction-formations against his love for (and identity with) his extraordinary hero. Homer's Ulysses may be as complete as Poldy, but you wouldn't want to be in one boat with him (you would drown, he would survive). Poldy would comfort you in every sorrow, even as he empathizes so movingly with the pangs of women in childbirth.

Joyce was not Flaubert, who at once was Madame Bovary and yet was wholly detached from her, at least in aesthetic stance. But how do you maintain a fixed stance toward Poldy? Falstaff is the monarch of wit, and Sancho Panza the Pope of innocent cunning. Poldy's strength, as Joyce evidently intended, is in his completeness. "The complete man" is necessarily a trope, but for what? On one side, for range of affect, like Tennyson's Ulysses, Poldy is a part of all that he has met. His curiosity, his susceptibility, his compassion, his potential interest—these are infinite. On another side, for cognitive activity, Poldy, unlike Stephen, is certainly not brilliant, and yet he has a never-resting mind, as Ulysses must have. He can be said to have a Shakespearean mind, though he resembles no one in Shakespeare (a comparison of Poldy and Shylock is instructive). Poldy is neither Hamlet nor Falstaff, but perhaps he is Shakespeare, or Shakespeare reborn as James Joyce, even as Stephen is the younger Dante reincarnated as Joyce. We can think of Poldy as Horatio to Stephen's Hamlet, since Horatio represents us, the audience, and we represent Shakespeare. Poldy is our representative, and it is Joyce's greatest triumph that increasingly we represent him, as we always have and will represent Shakespeare.

Post-Structuralist Joyce never wearies of reminding us that Poldy is a trope, but it is truer to say that we are tropes for Poldy, who as a supermimesis of essential nature is beyond us. I may never recover from a walk through a German park with a dear friend who is the most distinguished of post-structuralists. When I remarked to him, in my innocent cunning, that Poldy was the most loveable person in Western fiction, I provoked him to the annoyed response that Poldy was not a person, but only language, and that Joyce, unlike myself, knew this very well. Joyce knew very well that Poldy was more than a person, but only in the sense that Poldy was a humane and humanized God, a God who had become truly a bereft father, anguishing for his lost Rudy. Poldy is not a person only if God is not a person, and the God of the Jews, for all his transcendental sublimities, is also very much a person and a personality, as befits his immanent sublimities. Surely the uniqueness of Yahweh, among all the rival godlings, is that Yahweh is complete. Yahweh is the complete God, even as Poldy is the complete man, and God, after all, like Poldy, is Jewish.

II

French post-structuralism is of course only a belated modernism, since everything from abroad is absorbed so slowly in xenaphobic Paris. French Hegel, French Freud, French Joyce are all after the event, as it were, just as French romanticism was a rather delayed phenomenon. French Joyce is about as close to the text of *Ulysses* and *Finnegans Wake* as Lacan is to the text of *Three Essays on the Theory of Sexuality* or Derrida to Hegel and Heidegger. Nor should they be, since cultural belatedness or Alexandrianism demands the remedy of misprision, or creative misreading. To say that "meaning" keeps its distance from Poldy is both to forget that Poldy is the Messiah (though which Messiah is not clear) and that one name (Kabbalistic) for Yahweh is "language." The difference between Joyce and French Joyce is that Joyce tropes God as language and the belated Parisians (and their agents) trope the Demiurge as language, which is to say that Joyce, heroic naturalist, was not a Gnostic and Lacan was (perhaps unknowingly).

As a knowing Gnostic, I lament the loss of Joycean heroic naturalism and of Poldy's natural heroism. Let them deconstruct the Don Quixote; the results will be as sorrowful. Literary criticism is a mode which teaches us not to read Poldy as Sancho Panza and Stephen as the Don, but more amiably takes us back to Cervantes, to read Sancho as Poldy. By a Borgesian blessing in the art of mistaken attribution, we then will learn to read not only *Hamlet* and the *Inferno* as written by Joyce, but *Don Quixote* as well, with the divine Sancho as an Irish Jew!

Joyce necessarily is closer to Shakespeare than to Cervantes, and Joyce's obsession with *Hamlet* is crucial in *Ulysses*. His famous reading of Hamlet, as expounded by Stephen, can be regarded as a subtle coming-to-terms with Shakespeare as his most imposing literary father in the English language. Ellmann, certainly the most reliable of Joyce scholars, insisted that Joyce "exhibits none of that anxiety of influence which has been attributed to modern writers ... If Joyce had any anxiety, it was over not incorporating influences enough." This matter is perhaps more dialectical than Ellmann realized. Not Dante, but Shakespeare is Joyce's Virgil, as Ellmann also notes, and just as Dante's poetic voice matures even as Virgil fades out of the *Commedia*, so Shakespeare had to fade out of *Ulysses* even as Joyce's voice matured.

In Stephen's theory, Shakespeare is the dead king, rather than the young Hamlet, who becomes the type of the Romantic artist, Stephen himself. Shakespeare, like the ghost, has been betrayed, except that Anne Hathaway went Gertrude one better, and cuckolded the Bard with both his brothers. This sexual defeat has been intensified by Shakespeare's loss of the dark lady of the sonnets, and to his best friend, a kind of third brother. Shakespeare's revenge is to resurrect his own dead son, Hamnet, who enters the play as Prince Hamlet, with the purpose of vindicating his father's honor. Such a resurrected son appears to be free of the Oedipal ambivalences, and in Joyce's view does not lust after Gertrude or feel any jealousy, however repressed, for the dead father. So Stephen and Poldy, as two aspects of Shakespeare/Joyce, during the "Circe" episode gaze into a mirror and behold a transformed Shakespeare, beardless and frozen-faced ("rigid in facial paralysis"). I do not interpret this either as the view that Poldy and Stephen "amount only to a paralytic travesty of a Shakespeare" (W.M. Schutte) or that "Joyce warns us that he is working with near-identities, not perfect ones" (Ellmann). Rather, I take it as a sign of influence-anxiety, as the precursor Shakespeare mocking the ephebe Joyce: "Be like me, but you presume in attempting to be too much like me. You are merely a beardless version, rigid in facial paralysis, lacking my potency and my ease of countenance."

The obscene Buck Mulligan, Joyce's black beast weakly misreads *Hamlet* as masturbation and Poldy as a pederast. Joyce himself, through Stephen, strongly misreads *Hamlet* as the cuckold's revenge, a play presumably likelier to have been written by Poldy than by Stephen. In a stronger misreading still, I would suggest that Joyce rewrites *Hamlet* so as to destroy the element in the play that most menaces him, which is the very different, uncannily disinterested Hamlet of act 5. Stephen quotes the subtle Sabellian heresy that the Father was Himself His Own Son. But what we may call the even subtler Shakespearean heresy (which is also Freudian) holds rather that the Son was Himself His Own Father. This is the Hamlet of act 5, who refers to his dead father only once, and then only as the king. Joyce's Hamlet has no Oedipus complex. Shakespeare's Hamlet may have had one, but it passes away in the interval between acts 4 and 5.

Stephen as the Prince does not convince me; Poldy as the ghost of the dead king, and so as Shakespeare/Joyce, is rather more troublesome. One wishes the ghost could be exorcised, leaving us with the fine trinity of Shakespeare/Poldy/Joyce, with Poldy as the transitional figure reconciling forerunner and latecomer, a sort of Messiah perhaps. Shakespeare is the original Testament or old aesthetic Law, while Joyce is the belated Testament or new aesthetic dispensation. Poldy is the inner-Testamentary figure, apocryphal and apocalyptic, and yet overwhelmingly a representation of life in the here and now. Joyce went on to write *Finnegans Wake*, the only legitimate rival to Proust's vast novel in the Western literature of our time. More than the difficulties, both real and imaginary, of the *Wake* have Joyce's common readers centered upon *Ulysses*. Earwicker is a giant hieroglyph; Poldy is a person, complete and loving, self-reliant, larger and more evocative even than his book.

RICHARD ELLMANN

The Backgrounds of Ulysses

Then, pious Eneas, conformant to the fulminant firman which enjoins on the tremylose terrain that, when the call comes, he shall produce nichthemerically from his unheavenly body a no uncertain quantity of obscene matter not protected by copyright in the United Stars of Ourania or bedeed and bedood and bedang and bedung to him, with this double dye, brought to blood heat, gallic acid on iron ore, through the bowels of his misery, flashly, faithly, nastily, appropriately, this Esuan Menschavik and the first till last alshemist wrote over every square inch of the only foolscap available, his own body, till by its corrosive sublimation one continuous present tense integument slowly unfolded all marryvoising moodmoulded cyclewheeling history (thereby, he said, reflecting from his own individual person life unlivable, transaccidentated through the slow fires of consciousness into a dividual chaos, perilous, potent, common to allflesh, human only, mortal) but with each word that would not pass away the squidself which he had squirtereened from the crystalline world waned chagreenold and doriangrayer in its dudhud. This exists that isits after having been said we know.

—*Finnegans Wake* (1.85–6)

Joyce had been preparing himself to write Ulysses since 1907. It grew steadily more ambitious in scope and method, and represented a sudden outflinging of all he had learned as a writer up to 1914. Its use of many styles

7

was an extension of the method of *A Portrait of the Artist*, where the style, at first naive, became romantic and then dramatic to suit Stephen's ontogeny. Now Joyce hit upon the more radical device of the undependable narrator with a style adjusted to him. He used this in several episodes of *Ulysses*, for example in *Cyclops*, where the narrator is so obviously hostile to Bloom as to stir up sympathy for him, in *Nausicaa*, where the narrator's gushiness is interrupted and counteracted by Bloom's matter-of-fact reporting, and in *Eumaeus*, where the narrator writes in a style that is constabular. The variety of these devices made T. S. Eliot speak of the 'anti-style' of *Ulysses*, but Joyce does not seem to oppose style so much as withdraw it to a deeper level. His ebullient hand shows through its concealments.

The most famous of the devices of *Ulysses*, the interior monologue,[1] was also the result of earlier experiments. Joyce had been moving rapidly towards a conception of personality new to the novel. Unlike Henry James, who worked by analysis of great trends in moral life, he had begun to evolve in *Dubliners* and *A Portrait* a synthetic method, the construction of character by odds and ends, by minutiae. He did not allow his characters the sudden, tense climaxes towards which James ushered the people of his books, and preferred instead to subdue their dramas. His protagonists moved in the world and reacted to it, but their basic anxieties and exaltations seemed to move with slight reference to their environment. They were so islanded, in fact, that Joyce's development of the interior monologue to enable his readers to enter the mind of a character without the chaperonage of the author, seems a discovery he might have been expected to make.[2]

He had observed approaches to the interior monologue in Dujardin, George Moore, Tolstoy, even his brother's journal. He had toyed with Freud's theories of verbal association; his notes to *Exiles* first list a group of words: 'Blister-amber-silver-oranges-apples-sugarstick-hair-spongecake-ivy-roses-ribbon,' and then proceed to gloss them: 'The blister reminds her of the burning of her hand as a girl. She sees her own amber hair and her mother's silver hair....' The notion of dispensing with the gloss and slightly elaborating the key words, as if a multitude of small bells were ringing in the mind, was close at hand. Joyce's first interior monologue was inserted at the end of *A Portrait of the Artist*, where however he makes it seem less extraordinary by having Stephen write it in a journal. It had a dramatic justification there in that Stephen could no longer communicate with anyone in Ireland but himself. But it was also a way of relaxing by sentence fragments and seemingly casual connections among thoughts the more formal style of most of the narrative:

March 21, morning. Thought this in bed last night but was too lazy and free to add it. Free, yes. The exhausted loins are those of Elizabeth and Zacchary. Then he is the precursor. Item: he eats chiefly belly bacon and dried figs. Read locusts and wild honey. Also, when thinking of him, saw always a stem severed head or death mask as if outlined on a grey curtain or veronica. Decollation they call it in the fold. Puzzled for the moment by saint John at the Latin gate. What do I see? A decollated precursor trying to pick the lock....

March 22. In company with Lynch, followed a sizable hospital nurse. Lynch's idea. Dislike it. Two lean hungry greyhounds walking after a heifer.

March 23. Have not seen her since that night. Unwell? Sits at the fire perhaps with mamma's shawl on her shoulders. But not peevish. A nice bowl of gruel? Won't you now?

Having gone so far, Joyce in *Ulysses* boldly eliminated the journal, and let thoughts hop, step, jump, and glide without the self-consciousness of a journal to account for their agitation.

Another formative element in *Ulysses*, the counterpoint of myth and fact, was begun when Joyce first evolved the name and character of Stephen Dedalus, when he allowed the imagery of Calvary to play over the last scene in 'The Dead,' when he parodied Dante's division into three parts in 'Grace.' In his notes to *Exiles* Joyce constantly compares his characters to Biblical ones: Robert Hand is the elder brother in the parable of the Prodigal Son; Bertha's state at one point is 'like that of Jesus in the garden of olives,' and she is also like Isolde, her 'sister-in-love.' And Richard and Robert are Sacher-Masoch and Sade. In *Ulysses* Joyce uses not only the Homeric and post-Homeric legend, but a variety of other identifications: Stephen is not only Daedalus but Icarus, Hamlet, Shakespeare, Lucifer. But the principal task in the book was to find a pagan hero whom he could set loose in a Catholic city, to make Ulysses a Dubliner. Stephen Dedalus could not take this role, for he was Joyce's immature *persona*; as a mature *persona* Joyce chose Leopold Bloom. Stephen and Bloom came from opposite ends of his mind and life, but there were necessarily many resemblances, which Joyce emphasized and justified by making the older man like a father to Stephen.

This counterpoint, which Joyce from the first intended, enabled him to secure the same repetition with variations that he had obtained in *A Portrait*.

In the earlier book he had conceived of the whole work as a matrix in which elements of Stephen's being might form and reform; in *Ulysses* he plays Stephen's youthful point of view against Bloom's mature point of view, often confronting them with the same places and ideas. So the two traverse at different times the same parts of Dublin, or think of like things at the same moment. They repeat each other, and then the events are recapitulated on a deeper level in the *Circe* episode, and again, in wider contexts, in the last two episodes, *Ithaca* and *Penelope*.[3] The enclosing framework in *Ulysses* is in part the body, which supplies an organ to preside over each episode, but it is also the day, which interacts with the minds of the characters, certain hours encouraging certain moods. In the end the whole day seems to terminate in Molly Bloom's nocturnal mind; life returns to its source.

Joyce did not have his book all in mind at the beginning. He urged a friend later not to plan everything ahead, for, he said, 'In the writing the good things will come.' He knew his modern Ulysses must go through Dublin in a series of episodes like those of the Odyssey. The narrative coalesced excitingly: the Cyclops as a nationalist, Circe as madam of a brothel, were principal connections with Homer, and soon there were more subtle relationships as well. The Trojan horse, for example, is scarcely mentioned in Homer, but Joyce remembered that Dante made it the reason for Ulysses' being in hell. He turned this Odyssean adventure into Bloom's misadventure in volunteering an unconscious tip about the prospects of a dark horse in the races. Joyce's high spirits made him see many parallels of this kind: in the *Cyclops* episode, as Stuart Gilbert notices, the cigar Bloom keeps brandishing in front of the citizen is like the spear Ulysses uses to blind the Cyclops; the post-Homeric legend tells how Ulysses stole the statue of Pallas Athena, and in Joyce's book Bloom takes an erotic, profane look at the goddesses in the National Museum. The many light-hearted cross-references of this kind have lent support to the idea that *Ulysses* is a great joke on Homer, but jokes are not necessarily so simple, and these have a double aim. The first aim is the mock-heroic, the mighty spear juxtaposed with the two-penny cigar. The second, a more subtle one, is what might be called the ennoblement of the mock-heroic. This demonstrates that the world of cigars is devoid of heroism only to those who don't understand that Ulysses' spear was merely a sharpened stick, as homely an instrument in its way, and that Bloom can demonstrate the qualities of man by word of mouth as effectively as Ulysses by thrust of spear.

Joyce's version of the epic story is a pacifist version. He developed an aspect of the Greek epic which Homer had emphasized less exclusively, namely, that Ulysses was the only good *mind* among the Greek warriors. The brawny men, Achilles and Ajax and the rest, relied on their physical strength, while Ulysses was brighter, a man never at a loss. But of course Homer represents Ulysses as a good warrior, too. Joyce makes his modern Ulysses a man who is not physically a fighter, but whose mind is unsubduable. The victories of Bloom are mental, in spite of the pervasive physicality of Joyce's book. This kind of victory is not Homeric, though Homer gestures toward it; it is compatible with Christianity, but it is not Christian either, for Bloom is a member of a secular world. Homer's Ulysses has been made less athletic, but he retains the primary qualities of prudence, intelligence, sensitivity, and good will. Consequently Joyce, as might be expected, found the murder of the suitors at the end of the book to be too bloody as well as too grand, so he has Bloom defeat his rival, Blazes Boylan, in Molly Bloom's mind by being the first and the last in her thoughts as she falls off to sleep. In the same way Joyce enabled Richard Rowan in *Exiles* to defeat Robert Hand in Bertha's mind.

Another aspect of his hero Joyce borrowed as much from Dante as from Homer. In Dante Ulysses makes a voyage which Homer does not mention, a voyage which expresses his splendid lust for knowledge. In Canto XXVI of the *Inferno*, Ulysses says: 'Neither fondness for my son, nor reverence for my aged father, nor the due love that should have cheered Penelope, could conquer in me the ardor that I had to gain experience of the world, and of human vice and worth.' This longing for experience, for the whole of life, is related to that of Stephen crying at the end of *A Portrait*, 'Welcome, O life,' but Bloom is able, with the persistent, ruminative curiosity which is his middle class correlative for Ulysses' lust, to cover even more of life and the world in his thoughts than Stephen is. He does so, too, without the element of ruthlessness that Dante, modifying Homer's picture of a less hasty hero, criticizes in Ulysses, and which is also prominent in the Stephen of *A Portrait*.

The relationship of Bloom and Ulysses has sometimes been thought to be more tenuous than this: Ezra Pound, for example, insists that the purpose of using the Odyssey is merely structural, to give solidity to a relatively plotless work. But for Joyce the counterpoint was important because it revealed something about Bloom, about Homer, and about existence. For Bloom is Ulysses in an important sense. He is by no means a Babbitt. Our contemporary notion of the average man, *l'homme moyen sensuel*, is a notion conditioned by Sinclair Lewis and not by Joyce. It is not a notion which is congenial in Ireland. Irishmen are gifted with more eccentricities than Americans and Englishmen. To be average in Ireland is to be eccentric. Joyce knew this, and moreover he believed that every human soul was unique. Bloom is unusual in his tastes in food, in his sexual conduct, in most of his interests. A critic has complained that Bloom has no normal tastes, but Joyce would undoubtedly reply that no one has. The range of Bloom's peculiarities is not greater than that of other men.

At the same time, Bloom maintains his rare individuality. His responses to experience are like other people's, but they are wider and cleverer. Like Ulysses, though without his acknowledged fame, he is a worthy man. Joyce does not exalt him, but he makes him special. Aldous Huxley says that Joyce used to insist upon a 'thirteenth-century' etymology for the Greek form of Ulysses' name, Odysseus; he said it was a combination of *Outis*—nobody, and *Zeus*—god. The etymology is merely fanciful, but it is a controlled fancy which helps to reinforce Joyce's picture of the modern Ulysses. For Bloom is a nobody—an advertisement canvasser who, apart from his family, has virtually no effect upon the life around him—yet there is god in him. By god Joyce does not intend Christianity; although Bloom has been generously baptized into both the Protestant Church and the Catholic Church, he is obviously not a Christian. Nor is he concerned with the conception of a personal god. The divine part of Bloom is simply his humanity—his assumption of a bond between himself and other created beings. What Gabriel Conroy has to learn so painfully at the end of 'The Dead,' that we all—dead and living—belong to the same community, is accepted by Bloom from the start, and painlessly. The very name Bloom is chosen to support this view of Bloom's double nature. Bloom is, like Wallace Stevens's Rosenbloom, an ordinary Jewish name, but the name also means flower, and Bloom is as integral as a flower. Lenehan in the book comments about him, 'He's not one of your common or garden ... he's a cultured allround man, Bloom is.' He achieves this distinction in part by not belonging in a narrow sense, by ignoring the limits of national life; he is not so much an Irishman as a man.

The desire Joyce has that Bloom be respected encourages him to give Bloom the power that he has himself, to infuse common things with uncommonness.[4] Bloom's monologue is a continuous poetry, full of phrases of extraordinary intensity. In the first chapter in which he appears, his mind wanders to thoughts of the East; he imagines himself walking by mosques and bazaars, and says to himself, 'A mother watches from her doorway. She calls her children home in their dark language.' Passing Larry O'Rourke's public house, he says, 'There he is, sure enough, my bold Larry, leaning against the sugarbin in his shirtsleeves watching the aproned curate swab up with mop and bucket.' Or, when he considers the cattlemarket where he once worked, be says to himself, 'Those mornings in the cattlemarket the beasts lowing in their pens, branded sheep, flop and fall of dung, the breeders in hobnailed boots trudging through the litter, slapping a palm on a ripemeated hindquarter, there's a prime one, unpeeled switches in their hands.' Or when he thinks of modern Palestine: 'A barren land, bare waste. Volcanic lake, the dead sea: no fish, weedless, sunk deep in the earth. No wind could lift those waves, grey metal, poisonous foggy water. Brimstone they called it raining down: the cities of the plain: Sodom, Gomorrah, Edom. All dead names. A dead sea in a dead land, grey and old. Old now. It bore the oldest, the first race. A bent hag crossed from Cassidy's clutching a naggin bottle by the neck. The oldest people. Wandered far away over all the earth, captivity to captivity, multiplying, dying, being born everywhere.'

It might be supposed that this is Joyce talking for Bloom, and not Bloom's way of thinking at all, that just as the scullions in Shakespeare speak like poets, so does everyone in Joyce. But this is not so. Stephen and Molly, it is true, have their own particular forms of eloquence, although Molly's is limited in scope and Stephen's is hyperconscious; Bloom's surpasses theirs. But there are other examples of interior monologue in *Ulysses* which show none of this disparity between conversation and inward thought. In the *Wandering Rocks* episode, Father Conmee is on his way to the Artane orphanage to arrange to have one of Dignam's children admitted there, and Joyce writes: 'The Superior, the Very Reverend John Conmee S.J. reset his smooth watch in his interior pocket as he came down the presbytery steps. Five to three. Just nice time to walk to Artane. What was that boy's name? Dignam, yes. *Vere dignum et iustum est.* Brother Swan was the person to see. Mr. Cunningham's letter. Yes. Oblige him, if possible. Good practical catholic: useful at mission time.'

And here is another example, of the Dignam boy himself: 'Master Dignam walked along Nassau street, shifted the porksteaks to his other hand. His collar sprang up again and he tugged it down. The blooming stud was too small for the buttonhole of the shirt, blooming end to it. He met schoolboys with satchels. I'm not going tomorrow either, stay away till Monday. He met other schoolboys. Do they notice I'm in mourning? Uncle Barney said he'd get it into the paper tonight. Then they'll all see it in the paper and read my name printed and pa's name.' Bloom differs from lesser Dubliners in that his internal poetry is continual, even in the most unpromising situations. It is one of the primary indications of the value Joyce attaches to him.

The verisimilitude in *Ulysses* is so compelling that Joyce has been derided as more mimic than creator, which charge, being untrue, is the greatest praise of all. After his death, when the British Broadcasting Corporation was preparing a long program about him, its representatives went to Dublin and approached Dr. Richard Best to ask him to participate in a radio interview. 'What makes you come to me?' he asked truculently. 'What makes you think I have any connection with this man Joyce?' 'But you can't deny your connection,' said the men of the B.B.C., 'After all, you're a character in *Ulysses*.' Best drew himself up and retorted, 'I am not a character in fiction. I am a living being.' The incident is a useful warning. Even with a *roman à clef*, which *Ulysses* largely is, no key quite fits. Art lavishes on one man another's hair, or voice, or bearing, with shocking disrespect for individual identity. Like Stephen in the *Circe* episode, art *shatters* light through the world, destroying and creating at once. So, when Dubliners asked each other in trepidation after the book appeared, 'Are you in it?' or 'Am I in it?' the answer was hard to give. A voice sounded familiar for an instant, a name seemed to belong to a friend, then both receded into a new being. For instance, the name of Mrs. Purefoy, whose labor pains end in the *Oxen of the Sun* episode with the birth of a boy, comes appropriately enough from Dr. R. Damon Purefoy, in 1904 Dublin's leading obstetrician. As, *Finnegans Wake* insists, 'The traits featuring the chiaroscuro coalesce, their contrarieties eliminated, in one stable somebody.' Even the personages who retain their actual names, like Dr. Best himself, are often altered; so Best is depicted as saying ceaselessly, 'Don't you know?' not because this was one of his expressions, which it was not, but because it seemed to Joyce the sort of expression that the fictional Best should use.

Still Joyce made Stephen Dedalus emphasize in *Ulysses* that the artist and his life are not distinct. Stephen fabricates Shakespeare's personal development from the evidence of his work. *Venus and Adonis* demonstrates for him that Shakespeare was seduced by Anne Hathaway, like Venus, an older woman; the gloomy *Richard III* and *King Lear* testify that Anne betrayed her husband with his two brothers-in-law Richard and Edmund, whose names Shakespeare accordingly attributes to the villains of those plays; the late plays show by their lightened feelings that the birth of a granddaughter had reconciled Shakespeare to his lot.

This theory, which according to friends Joyce took more seriously than Stephen,[5] suggests that *Ulysses* divulges more than an impersonal and detached picture of Dublin life; it hints at what is, in fact, true: that nothing has been admitted into the book which is not in some way personal and attached. In *Finnegans Wake* Joyce goes so far as to say of Shem the Penman that, like a spider, he produced 'from his unheavenly body a no uncertain quantity of obscene matter' and 'with this double dye ... wrote over every square inch of the only foolscap available, his own body....' Instead of being creation's god, the artist, Joyce now says, is its squid. Of course Joyce was both.

The daughters of memory, whom William Blake chased from his door, received regular employment from Joyce, although he speaks of them disrespectfully. His work is 'history fabled, not only in *A Portrait* but in

Ulysses as well. He was never a creator *ex nihilo*; he recomposed what he remembered, and he remembered most of what he had seen or had heard other people remember. The latter category was, in a city given over to anecdote, a large one. For the main body of his work Joyce relied chiefly upon his early life in Dublin and the later visits he had made there.[6] Certain comic material was ready at hand, and, in thinking back upon his native city, he prepared his great convocation of the city's eccentrics. There was Professor Maginni, the dark, middle-aged dancing master of North Great George's Street. Everyone knew his costume of tailcoat and dark grey trousers, silk hat, immaculate high collar with wings, gardenia in buttonhole, spats on mincing feet, and a silver-mounted, silk umbrella in hand. There were also Mrs. M'Guinness the queenly pawnbroker, and the five Hely's sandwichmen, each bearing a letter of the name; there was 'Endymion' Farrell, who carried two swords, a fishing rod, and an umbrella, who wore a red rose in his buttonhole, and had upon his head a small bowler hat with large holes for ventilation; from a brewer's family in Dundalk, he was said to have fallen into a vat and never recovered. Then there was the one-legged beggar known as 'The Blackbird,' who used to sing and to curse under his breath if he got nothing for it.

Less known than these, but familiar to Joyce or his family, was a cluster of other characters. When Molly Bloom objects to the singing of Kathleen Kearney, the name is a modification of that of Olive Kennedy, who appeared on a concert program with Joyce in 1902. Other names brought up by Molly had a similar basis in fact; Tom Devin's two sons were friends of the Joyces, and Connie Connolly was the sister of his Belvedere classmates Albrecht and Vincent Connolly. Even the dog Garryowen was not made up of stray barks and bites, but belonged to the father of Joyce's Aunt Josephine Murray, whom Gerty McDowell accurately identifies as 'Grandpapa Giltrap.' To find some of his characters Joyce went among the dead, the best example being Pisser Duff, whose name he delicately altered to Pisser Burke. Duff looked harmless, but was a violent man who hung around the markets, brushing down horses while their owners drank at pubs. He was beaten to death by the police in Gardiner Street about 1892, but Joyce evoked him to be a friend of the equally vicious narrator of the *Cyclops* episode. One of the most curious composites is Lenehan, the parasite who speaks French. The name is borrowed from Matt Lenehan, a reporter on the *Irish Times*, but the personality Joyce took from a friend of his father named Michael Hart, who was dead by about 1900. Mick Hart, because of his habit of speaking French, was called Monsart (that is, Monsieur Hart). He worked, as Joyce implies, for a racing paper called *Sport*, and always attended the races in flashy attire. 'Lenehan' makes his first appearance in Joyce's work in 'Two Gallants,' when he is depicted accurately as longing to marry a rich girl. For this purpose Hart paid court for a time to the daughter of Joseph Nagle, one of the three brothers who kept a big public house in Earl Street; but nothing came of it. He knew a great deal about racing and was fond of writing doggerel; his greatest day was that, still recalled by Dubliners, when he 'tipped the double' in verse; that is, he predicted the winners of both the Lincolnshire Handicap and the Grand National Steeplechase.

Not long after this triumph he went downhill, and spent his later days in 'knocking around on the hard.' He continued to write verse; Joyce gives one of his less successful productions, a limerick, in the *Aeolus* episode.[7] Yet, as if to belie his reincarnation in *Ulysses*, Joyce includes Michael Hart in a list of Bloom's friends who are now dead.

Joyce's surface naturalism in Ulysses has many intricate supports, and one of the most interesting is the blurred margin. He introduces much material which he does not intend to explain, so that his book, like life, gives the impression of having many threads that one cannot follow. For example, on the way to the funeral, the mourners catch sight of Reuben J. Dodd, and Mr. Dedalus says, 'The devil break the hasp of his back.' This reaction seems a little excessive unless we know that Dodd had lent money to Joyce's father, and that the subsequent exactions were the efficient cause of Mr. Dedalus's irritation. In the *Circe* episode Mulligan says, 'Mulligan meets the afflicted mother,' a remark based upon a story current in Dublin that Gogarty, returning home late one night during his medical course, staggered up the steps of his home on Rutland Square, reciting a station of the Cross at each step until, as he reached the top of the stairs and his worried mother opened the door, he concluded, 'Gogarty meets the afflicted mother.' Stephen's allusions to 'The Tinahely twelve' and 'Cranly's eleven true Wicklowmen to free their sireland' refer to a remark that J. F. Byrne had made to George Clancy; they agreed that twelve men with resolution could save Ireland, and Byrne said that he thought he could find twelve such men in Wicklow. With numerous truncated references of this sort Joyce edged his book.

The *Circe* episode offers an extended instance of Joyce's merging observations and reading into a new form. There was, to begin with, the necessity of finding an adequate setting. Following a long series of Homeric commentators who have moralized Circe's den as a place of temptation where the bestial aspects of men emerge, Joyce decided on the red-light district of Dublin for his scene. The word 'Nighttown' he had picked up from Dublin journalists, who always spoke of the late shift as 'Nighttown.' Joyce used it instead of the customary word for the brothel area, 'Monto,' so called from Montgomery Street. Monto was labeled about 1885 by the Encyclopaedia Britannica as the worst slum in Europe. It was concentrated chiefly in Mecklenburg Street, which became Tyrone Street and is now a dreary Railway Street, the name having been changed twice as part of an effort, vain until recently, to change its character. The street is made up of eighteenth-century houses; while some of these had by 1900 decayed into tenements, others, the 'flash houses,' were kept up beautifully by women who appeared in full evening dress before their select clientele.

Horse Show week in August was especially grand in Monto. The British officers arrived in numbers for the event, and the Monto ladies sent their cards at once to the officers' mess. The ladies drove to the races in pony traps, and afterwards a procession of innumerable cabs followed them back to Monto. The Boer War also proved a great boon to their business. In 1902 the Irish Battalion of Yeomanry returned from South Africa, and a dull-witted society paper published an anonymous poem sentimentally celebrating the heroes' return, in which however the first letter of each line formed the acrostic sentence, 'Whores will be busy.' This poem, which was quickly comprehended, killed the paper. It was usually attributed to Gogarty, then a medical student.

Joyce's knowledge of Monto was of course as complete as his knowledge of the *Evening Telegraph*, which he used in the *Aeolus* episode. He does not have Bloom and Stephen patronize the lower numbers of Mecklenburg Street, near Mabbot Lane, since these were usually patronized by English 'tommies'; these houses were full of religious pictures, behind which the ladies kept 'coshes,' pieces of lead pipe, to prevent trouble. Joyce asked one of his visitors in the 'thirties to secure a complete list of the names and addresses on Mecklenburg Street, and seems to have retained his interest in them. A lady appropriately named Mrs. Lawless lived at No. 4; her neighbour, at No. 5, was Mrs. Hayes, a grandmotherly type. But at the upper end of the street were the principal houses. Bloom, searching for Stephen at Mrs. Cohen's (No. 82), knocks first by mistake at No. 85, but is told that this is Mrs. Mack's house. Actually Mrs. Mack kept two houses, No. 85 and No. 90, and was so well known that the whole area was sometimes called 'Macktown.'[8]

As for Mrs. Cohen, she was older than Mrs. Mack, and by 1904 had either retired or died, but Joyce restored her in business because her name suited the Jewish themes in the book. Her girls were probably modelled on contemporary prostitutes. Florry Talbot, for instance, was probably Fleury Crawford.[9] The description of another girl, Kitty Ricketts, suggests Becky Cooper, probably the best known among Dublin prostitutes from the beginning of the century until the 'twenties.[10] Joyce was probably familiar also with Lady Betty and May Oblong (Mrs. Roberts); he reserved the latter's name for *Finnegans Wake*, where all Dublin is *d'Oblong*.

Yet the deeper problem of *Circe* was to relate Bloom and Stephen on the unconscious level, to justify the father–son theme that Joyce had made central in his book. He does so chiefly in terms of one trait which the two men share, their essentially inactive roles. Joyce is quite earnest about this. He has shown Bloom throughout as the decent man who, in his pacific way, combats narrowmindedness, the product of fear and cruelty, which Stephen combatted in *A Portrait* and still combats. Once it is understood that Joyce sympathizes with Bloom and Stephen in their resistance in terms of mind rather than body, an aspect of the library episode becomes less baffling. Stephen Dedalus asserts there that Shakespeare was not Hamlet but Hamlet's father. Since Stephen in so many ways resembles Hamlet, and since be obviously thinks of himself as like Shakespeare, this identification may seem capricious. But it fits Joyce's notion both of the artistic temperament and of the desirable man. Joyce, Stephen, and Bloom share the philosophy of passivity in act, energy in thought, and tenacity in conviction. Hamlet, on the other hand, is the hero of a revenge-play; however unwittingly and fumblingly, be sheds a great deal of blood. Joyce does not encourage this view of the artist, and so he relates Shakespeare to the suffering father, the victim, rather than to the avenging son. The artist endures evil—he doesn't inflict it. 'I detest action,' says Stephen to the soldiers. Because he takes this position, he belongs, in the extended metaphor which underlies all *Ulysses*, to the family of Bloom,[11] who tells the Citizen, 'It's no use.... Force, hatred, history, all that. That's not life for men and women, insult and hatred.' They are son and father mentally, if not physically, and both of them argue that what is physical is incidental.

The kinship of Stephen and Bloom, on the surface so unlikely, is established with great adroitness. Joyce makes use of two sources to aid him, both literary; the first is Leopold von Sacher-Masoch, the second is William Blake. In the worst light Bloom's passivity in the face of Boylan's advances to Molly, and his rejection of force in the *Cyclops* episode, seem part of a willing submission comparable to that of Sacher-Masoch. In the best light they are Blake's rejection of the corporeal.

While writing the *Circe* episode Joyce drew heavily upon Sacher-Masoch's book, *Venus im Pelz*.[12] Much of the material about flagellation is derived from it. *Venus in Furs* tells of a young man named Severin who so abases himself before his mistress, a wealthy woman named Wanda, and so encourages her cruelty toward him, that she becomes increasingly tyrannical, makes him a servile go-between, and then, in a rapturous finale, turns him over to her most recent lover for a whipping. There are many similarities to *Circe*. The society ladies who appear to Bloom, Mrs. Yelverton Barry (a name modified from that of a suspected transvestist) and Mrs. Bellingham (an actual name), are as fond of wearing furs as Wanda. Mrs. Bellingham recounts accusingly of Bloom, 'He addressed me in several handwritings[13] with fulsome compliments as a Venus in furs and alleged profound pity for my frost-bound coachman Balmer while in the same breath he expressed himself as envious of his earflaps and fleecy sheepskins and of his fortunate proximity to my person, when standing behind my chair wearing my livery and the armorial bearings of the Bellingham escutcheon garnished sable, a buck's head couped or.' The hero of *Venus in Furs* wears his lady's livery, has to follow her at ten paces, and suffers luscious indignities comparable to those of Balmer.

Like Severin too, Bloom is depicted as welcoming his being birched, as even requesting this privilige. Wanda, reluctant at first to yield to her lover's strange importunities, is gradually attracted by them: 'You have corrupted my imagination and inflamed my blood,' she tells him; 'Dangerous potentialities were slumbering in me, but you were the first to awaken them.' Mrs. Mervyn Talboys puts it more ludicrously in *Ulysses*, 'You have lashed the dormant tigress in my nature into fury.' Severin asks to be allowed to put on his mistress's shoes, and is kicked for performing the task too slowly. Bloom is similarly set to lacing the shoes of Bella Cohen, and fears she will kick him for his ineptitude. The more fearful and hateful Bella is, the more Bloom admires her; so Bella, like Wanda, puts her foot on Bloom's neck. The willing slavery of Severin to Wanda, which is sealed by an agreement she makes him sign, is echoed in Bloom's promise never to disobey Bella, and in her announcement to him, 'What you longed for has come to pass. Henceforth you are unmanned and mine in earnest, a thing under the yoke.'

The degradation of Bloom continues. Like Severin he is forced to usher in Bella's new lover, Blazes Boylan. A scene in *Venus in Furs*, in which Severin attends Wanda at her bath, is reflected in an equivalent scene in *Ulysses*. And the climax of Sacher-Masoch's book, when Wanda, pretending affection, coyly persuades Severin to let her bind him against a pillar, and then turns him over to her new lover for a merciless flogging, is echoed in Bella's pretense of affection which facilitates her pulling Bloom's hair. Even the references to the marble statuette that Bloom takes home in the rain, and to the nymph, 'beautiful immortal,' whose 'classic curves' are pictured above his bed, are paralleled in the 'stonecold and pure' plaster cast of Venus to which Severin prays in *Venus in Furs*.

Closely as he followed his source, Joyce made two major modifications. First, his version of Sacher-Masoch is a vaudeville version; and second, Bloom's masochistic fantasies occur in his unconscious mind; he berates himself, and makes himself worse than he is, because he is *conscious* of having allowed too much in reality. Then masochism is modified by Blakeism.

Several references are made to Blake in the *Circe* episode, the most important at its end. There Stephen falls out with two soldiers, who accuse him of attacking the king because of his declaration, 'But in here it is I must kill the priest and the king.' Joyce has in mind here an incident that occurred during Blake's stay at Felpham, when he put two soldiers out of his garden in spite of their protests that as soldiers of the king they should not be handled so. He replied to them, or was alleged to have replied, 'Damn the king,' was therefore haled up for treason, and barely got off. (In *Finnegans Wake* the two soldiers become three, and have an equally unpleasant role to play.) Stephen does not put the soldiers to flight; rather, to parody Blake as well, they knock *him* down, but not before he has stated his contention that the authorities, religious and secular, must be defeated in spiritual rather than. corporeal warfare. This is Blake's central conception of the conquest of tyranny by imagination.[14]

Having displayed the body's defeat and the spirit's victory in both their ridiculous and noble aspects, Joyce brings about the mental purgation of Bloom and Stephen at the end of the episode. They are purged in a surprising way, for so reserved a book, that is, by love. The theme of family love, the love of parent for child and of child for parent, runs covertly throughout *Ulysses*. Molly Bloom's thoughts return to the lambswool sweater she knitted for her son Rudy, who died when he was only eleven days old. The hyperborean Stephen, who claims to have denied his family, almost yields to affection when he comes upon his sister reading Chardenal's French primer, and remorse over his treatment of his mother accounts for his vision of her at the end of *Circe*. But Bloom emerges even more decisively from the Circean sty with his vision of Rudy as he might be now:

> Against the dark wall a figure appears slowly, a fairy boy of eleven, a changeling, kidnapped, dressed in an Eton suit with glass shoes and a little bronze helmet, holding a book in his hand. He reads from right to left inaudibly, smiling, kissing the page.
>
> BLOOM
> (Wonderstruck, calls inaudibly.) Rudy!
>
> RUDY
> (Gazes unseeing into Bloom's eyes and goes on reading, kissing, smiling. He has a delicate mauve face. On his suit he has diamond and ruby buttons. In his free left hand he holds a slim ivory cane with a violet bowknot. A white lambkin peeps out of his waistcoat pocket.)

Tenderness is not contrary to Joyce's temperament. This is the vision of a fond father, colored as such visions are; and the sentimental coloring is offset by the bizarre attire and the detachment of the child, both of which establish a sense of distance and estrangement from Bloom. The relation of Bloom and Rudy, as of Molly and Rudy, is profoundly moving; so is the relation of Bloom to his own father, who committed suicide by taking aconite poison.[15] Joyce deliberately says nothing about its emotional quality, but he has Bloom at one point recall a few snatches from the letter found at his father's bedside: 'To my dear son Leopold. Tomorrow will be a week that I received ... it is no use Leopold to be ... with your dear mother ... That is not more to stand ... to her ... all for me is out ... be kind to Athos, Leopold ... my dear son ... always ... of me ... das Herz ... Gott ... dein....' Paternity is a more powerful motif in the book than sexual love.

The phrase, 'Be kind to Athos,' refers to Bloom's father's dog—and kindness to animals, who are so much like children, and can repay affection only with affection, is another of those quite ordinary and undistinguished aspects of human nature that Joyce underlines. Even the Citizen, like Homer's Cyclops, is good to Garryowen. The kindness of Bloom on June 16, 1904, begins with animals and ends with human beings. So he feeds his cat in the morning, then some sea gulls, and in the *Circe* episode a dog. He remembers his dead son and dead father, he is also concerned about his living daughter, and he never forgets his wife for a moment. He helps a blind man cross a street. He contributes very generously—beyond his means—to the fund for the children of his friend Dignam who has just died; and, when he begins to see Stephen as a sort of son, he follows him, tries to stop his drinking, prevents his being robbed, risks arrest to defend him from the police, feeds him too, and takes him home in what Joyce calls, half-humorously, 'orthodox Samaritan fashion.' Stephen will not stay the night with Bloom—the barrier between man and man breaks down only occasionally and usually only a little, and the barrier quickly reforms—but in the temporary union of the two Joyce affirms his perception of community.

The relation of Bloom and Stephen confirms Joyce's point of view in another way: Bloom's common sense joins Stephen's acute intelligence; Stephen Dedalus, the Greek-Christian-Irishman, joins Bloom Ulysses, the Greek-Jewish-Irishman; the cultures seem to unite against horsepower and brutality in favor of brainpower and decency. The two men are contrasted in the book with those who are strong: Stephen can't swim while Mulligan swims beautifully; Bloom is only a Walker, while the Citizen is the holder of the shotput record for all Ireland; and Bloom is a cuckold while Blazes Boylan is the loud-mouthed adulterer; but we spend most of the book inside

Bloom's consciousness, and never enter Boylan's, as if coarseness had no consciousness. It is true that Mulligan is clever as well as strong, but it is a cleverness that goes with brutality. Stephen and Bloom, the mental men, are ranged against Mulligan and Boylan, the burly men, and Joyce's partisanship is clear.

The scheme of value of *Ulysses* comes closer to explicit expression in the *Circe* episode than it does anywhere else. It is buttressed by another passage in the *Ithaca* episode. When Bloom and Stephen are walking home to 7 Eccles Street from the cabman's shelter, they discuss a great many things, and Joyce notes, with some understatement, that their views were on certain points divergent. 'Stephen,' he writes, 'dissented openly from Bloom's view on the importance of dietary and civic selfhelp while Bloom dissented tacitly from Stephen's views on the eternal affirmation of the spirit of man in literature.' While the loftiness of Stephen's statement is mocked, that literature embodies the eternal affirmation of the spirit of man is not a crotchet of Stephen but a principle of Joyce, maintained by all his books. It is no accident that the whole of *Ulysses* should end with a mighty 'yes.'[16]

In making his hero Leopold Bloom, Joyce recognized implicitly what he often spoke of directly, his affinity for the Jews as a wandering, persecuted people. 'I sometimes think,' he said later to Frank Budgen, 'that it was a heroic sacrifice on their part when they refused to accept the Christian revelation. Look at them. They are better husbands than we are, better fathers and better sons.'[17] No doubt the incongruity of making his good Dubliner a Jew, and one so indifferent to all religious forms as to have sampled (without accepting) both Protestantism and Catholicism, attracted him with its satirical possibilities. But he must have been affected also by the Dreyfus uproar in Paris, which continued from 1892 to 1906; it had reached one of its crises in September 1902, just before Joyce's arrival in Paris, when Anatole France, a writer he respected, delivered his eloquent oration at the funeral of Zola, whose *J'accuse* was still stirring up Europe. A connection between the Jew and his artist-defender may have been fixed in Joyce's mind by the connection between Zola, France, and Dreyfus. When he returned to Dublin in 1903, he was in time for one of the rare manifestations of anti-Semitism in Ireland, a boycott of Jewish merchants in Limerick that was accompanied by some violence.

Joyce was not a propagandist for better treatment of minorities. The conception of the likable Jew attracted without overwhelming him. He decided to make Bloom amiable and even noble in a humdrum sort of way, but to save him from sentimentality by making him also somewhat absurd as a convert, a drifter, a cuckold. His remarks make clear that the two characteristics of the Jews which especially interested him were their chosen isolation, and the close family ties which were perhaps the result of it.

These characteristics he saw in himself as well, and they gave him a sense of affinity. A great deal of his own experience became Bloom's. He not only took over the theme of adultery and the address of 7 Eccles Street from his 1909 trip to Dublin; he surrounded his hero with a Joycean atmosphere. For example, the Joyce family in Dublin employed for a time a charwoman, Mrs. Fleming; in *Ulysses* she works in a similar capacity for the Blooms. The name of the Joyces' midwife was Mrs. Thornton; it is she who is credited with having delivered both the Blooms' children. Joyce was born at Brighton Square, and the Blooms lived there shortly after their marriage. While at Belvedere, Joyce took part in a dramatized version of Anstey's *Vice Versa*; Bloom acted in this as a boy also, though not in the same role. Both Joyce and Bloom took out books from the Capel Street Library. They shared an admiration for the poetry of Byron, and Bloom gave Molly a copy of his works during their courtship. Not all these details were unique, but their accumulation is important. Sometimes Joyce mocks himself, as in the *Nausicaa* episode, where Bloom's contemplation of Gerty MacDowell parodies the stages of Stephen's (and Joyce's own) vision of the girl at the seashore in *A Portrait*. Stephen's revulsion against his body during the retreat in *A Portrait* is paralleled in *Ulysses* by many examples of Bloom's fastidiousness. Molly's proposed concert tour of English watering places parodies Joyce's plans to buy a lute and sing Dowland's songs in the same area. This technique of self-depreciation is used especially in the swelling and ridiculing of the *Cyclops*, *Nausicaa*, and *Oxen of the Sun* episodes, but it operates less conspicuously throughout the book. Like Shem in *Finnegans Wake*, Joyce is 'for ever cracking quips on himself.'

But Bloom is more (and less) than Joyce. He had at least one Triestine prototype, for, when Dr. Daniel Brody asked Joyce later, 'Mr. Joyce, I can understand why the counterpart of your Stephen Dedalus should be a Jew, but why is he the son of a Hungarian?' Joyce, taking off his glasses and looking at him casually yet with an air of pronouncement, replied, 'Because he was.' This prototype was probably Teodoro Mayer, the publisher of the *Piccolo della Sera*, whose father like Bloom's was a Hungarian peddler, and who wore the moustache that Joyce gave to Bloom. Ettore Schmitz also contributed details. He said once to Stanislaus, 'Tell me some secrets about Irishmen. You know your brother has been asking me so many questions about Jews that I want to get even with him.' The difference in age between Schmitz and Joyce was, as Harry Levin points out, roughly the same as that between Bloom and Stephen, and Stanislaus Joyce thought there was a resemblance, although Signora Schmitz always denied it. Schmitz was in many ways quite different from Bloom; but he had married a Gentile, he had changed his name (though only for literary purposes), he knew something of Jewish customs, and he shared Bloom's amiably ironic view of life. Joyce could not abide the inner organs of animals and fowl, while Schmitz, like Bloom, loved them.[18] Some of these are small similarities, but Joyce had a spider's eye.

Several Dubliners helped Joyce to complete his hero. The first was the man named Hunter, about whom he had asked Stanislaus: and, later, his Aunt Josephine Murray to send him all the details they could remember. But in making Bloom an advertisement canvasser Joyce had someone else in mind. This man is first mentioned in the story 'Grace' under the name of C. P. M'Coy, and is identified there as having been a clerk in the Midland Railway, a canvasser for advertisements for the *Irish Times* and *Freeman's Journal*, a town traveler for a coal firm on commission, a private inquiry agent, a clerk in the office of the sub-sheriff, and secretary to the City Coroner. His wife had been a soprano and still taught young children to play the piano at low terms. These facts all point to M'Coy's actual prototype, Charles Chance, whose wife sang soprano at concerts in the 'nineties under the name of Madame Marie Tallon. In the variety of his jobs, in the profession of his wife, Chance fitted the description of Bloom; and that Joyce intended to combine him with Hunter is suggested by the juxtaposition of 'Charley Chance' with 'Mr. Hunker' in *Finnegans Wake*.

'Leopold Bloom' was named with due deliberation. Leopold was the first name of Signorina Popper's father in Trieste; Bloom was the name of two or three families who lived in Dublin when Joyce was young. One Bloom, who was a dentist, had been converted to Catholicism in order to marry a Catholic woman; they had five children, including a son, Joseph, who also became a dentist and practiced like his father on Clare Street in 1903 and 1904. The son was renowned for his wit. Joyce deliberately confuses Joseph Bloom the dentist with Leopold in one chapter, and in another he lists as one of Leopold's old addresses 38 Lombard Street, which was actually Joseph Bloom's address. Joyce no doubt also knew of another Bloom, who was committed in Wexford early in the century for the murder of a girl who worked with him in a photographer's shop. He had planned a double suicide; after having killed her and, as he thought, himself, he scrawled the word LOVE (but misspelt it as LIOVE) with his blood on the wall behind him. He was let off on mental grounds and, after some time in an institution, left the country. This incident presumably gave Joyce the plan of establishing Bloom's daughter Milly as an apprentice in a photographer's shop. He put the shop in Mullingar because he remembered that there was such a shop there when he visited the town with his father in 1900 and 1901.

The concert name of Mrs. Charles Chance, 'Madame Marie Tallon,' bears a deliberate resemblance to Madame Marion Tweedy, Mrs. Bloom's concert name. In using the Chances Joyce neatly concealed their identity, however; he prevented anyone's supposing they were the Blooms by introducing them into his book as the M'Coys, and by inventing a professional rivalry between Mrs. M'Coy and Mrs. Bloom. The character which he attributes to Mrs. Bloom is also unlike that of Mrs. Chance, whom he probably did not know; it is closer to that of the buxom wife of a fruit store owner named Nicolas Santos, with whom he was acquainted in Trieste and in Zurich. Signora Santos stayed indoors all day to preserve her complexion, for which she mixed her own creams. That Mrs. Santos had a share in Mrs. Bloom was an open secret in the Joyce family later. But the seductiveness of Molly came, of course, from Signorina Popper. For the Spanish quality in her Joyce drew upon one of the many daughters of Matt Dillon, an old friend of his family who is mentioned in Ulysses too. This daughter had been in Spain, smoked cigarettes, and was considered a Spanish type.

If bits and pieces of Mrs. Chance, Signora Santos, Signorina Popper, and Matt Dillon's daughter helped Joyce to design the outer Molly Bloom, he had a model at home for Molly's mind. Nora Joyce had a similar gift for concentrated, pungent expression, and Joyce delighted in it as much as Bloom did. Like Molly she was anti-intellectual; and like Molly she was attached to her husband without being awestruck. The rarity of capital letters and the run-on sentences in Molly's monologue are of course related to Joyce's theory of her mind (and of the female mind in general) as a flow, in contrast to the series of short jumps made by Bloom, and of somewhat longer ones by Stephen. But he had in mind as well Nora's carelessness in such matters.

Joyce also returns to the subject that had so bothered him in his early years of living with Nora, her refusal to recognize a difference between him and the other young men she had known. Bloom recognizes this characteristic in Molly, but Molly manifests it independently as well. Throughout her monologue Joyce lets her refer to various men she has known chiefly as 'he,' with only occasional indication of a change of the person involved. Her husband and her past lovers, among whom Mulvey of Galway makes an unexpected appearance, are speedily interchanged in her mind. At the end of her monologue she remembers the supreme moment in Bloom's courtship of her, when

> he asked me to say yes and I wouldnt answer first only looked out over the sea and the sky I was thinking of so many things he didnt know of Mulvey and Mr Stanhope and Hester and father and old captain Groves ... and Gibraltar as a girl where I was a Flower of the mountain yes when I put the rose in my hair like the Andalusian girls used or shall I wear a red yes and how he kissed

me under the Moorish wall and I thought well as well him as
another and then I asked him with my eyes to ask again....

The 'he' who kissed her under the Moorish wall was not Bloom but Mulvey;
but it is Bloom of whom she says, 'I thought well as well him as another.'
Molly, like Nora, fails to differentiate, though she is paradoxically aware that
Bloom is rather special.[19] Joyce attributes to his heroine the character of
woman as Nora had shown it to him, not the character, so often presumed
by novelists, of an irresponsible, passionate, romantic creature. As he told
Frank Budgen, Molly was intended to represent 'perfectly sane full amoral
fertilisable untrustworthy engaging shrewd limited prudent indifferent
Weib.' The last adjective is, appropriately, *indifferent*. If Joyce was wrong in
this analysis, the error was not for lack of observation.

Apart from her prototypes, Molly is a woman who has been much
misunderstood. The celebrated monologue in which 'flesh becomes word'
does not deserve its reputation as the summit of promiscuity nor does it fit
its description, by some writers, as the summit of cruel, unfair, and anti-
feminine dissection. If Molly were really promiscuous in her conduct, Joyce
would not have used her for heroine, for he needed an everyday woman to
counterpoise Bloom's oddities. It is true that Bloom, and critics after him,
lists no less than twenty-five lovers of Molly. But on examination the list
contains some extraordinary names: there are two priests, a lord mayor, an
alderman, a gynecologist, a bootblack, a professor. In the book it is clear that
she has confessed to the priests, consulted the gynecologist, and coquetted
with the rest. But only the most rigorous interpretation of infidelity—a
burlesque of Richard Rowan's interpretation in *Exiles*—could include these
episodes.

The two lovers Molly has had since her marriage are Bartell D'Arcy
and Boylan. While adultery is not excused by its infrequence, her behavior is
not unpredictable in view of the fact that for eleven years, since she was
twenty-two, her husband has not had adequate sexual relations with her.
Most of her internal monologue is devoted to her reminiscences of love-
making before her marriage, but even these are on examination less
glamorous, and much less numerous, than usually recognized. It is suggested
that she was a demi-vierge when she was married. The impression of
voluptuousness remains, but is based more on her longings or potentialities
than on her activities. Joyce delights in heightening her into someone
beyond herself, and then in pulling her back to 7 Eccles Street.

There is no reason to exalt her, because she is earthy, into an earth
goddess. She has had two children, a boy and a girl, but the boy died shortly
after birth. Her motherhood was only an aspect of that femininity which

Joyce was trying to report. It may be objected that if she has not engendered everything, at least she accepts everything. Actually she does not. She is dissatisfied with the coarseness of Blazes Boylan, and beyond that, seems dissatisfied with the male body and with the consummation of physical love. She remains a wife more than a goddess of acquiescence; married to Bloom, she will remain married, even if dissatisfied with him too. For Molly also acknowledges, though with considerable reluctance and appropriate feminine indirection, the importance of mind as opposed to body, the importance of decency, and the bonds of the family. The virile Boylan is nothing but a shell, while the much less virile Bloom is, with all his shortcomings, a man of both intellect and body.

In forming the character of Boylan, Joyce made his villain the negative reproduction of his hero. Joyce's notes for *Exiles* show that he regarded the relation of protagonist and antagonist as complicated by admiration as well as repugnance for each other. The mindless swagger of Boylan has an air about it. While Joyce's clear preference is for the mental men, the Shems, he may have had a sneaking regard for those burly men, the Shauns, with whom Boylan belongs.

The models for Boylan had to be opposite to Bloom in their manner of dress and speech, in their conduct of life. *Ulysses* supplies a few particulars, that Boylan's father was a horse dealer off Island Bridge who sold horses to the British during the Boer War, that Boylan is a flashy dresser, especially notable for his straw hat, and that he has just managed a prize fighter. The horse dealer who had his premises off Island Bridge was James Daly, who does not fit the other details except that, like all other horse dealers in Dublin, he sold horses to the British during the Boer War. There was, however, a horse dealer during the 'nineties who bore the name Boylan, and had Blazes or Blazer for a nickname. Joyce took his name, and perhaps borrowed the occupation and appearance of the character from another man named Ted Keogh. Keogh ran a junk shop under Merchant's Arch in almost exactly the same location as the hawker's car where Bloom buys *The Sweets of Sin* for Molly. He did not know Joyce personally; his only connection with the family, he declared, was that as a boy he shot a peashooter at John Joyce's top hat and hit it. Keogh in 1909 was, like his father, a horse dealer; he dressed expensively, and habitually wore a straw hat; and when Joyce visited Dublin Keogh was managing a well known prize fighter. Keogh's character was not, however, what Joyce needed for Boylan's. Some of Boylan's flashiness and breeziness may have come from Prezioso.

Boylan's first name is not Blazes, as he is always called, but Hugh; and the provenance of this name is diverting. It is likely that Joyce had in mind his classmate at University College, Dublin, the prim and proper Hugh

Boyle Kennedy. Kennedy was later to become Chief Justice of the High Court, and Joyce must have keenly enjoyed his little private joke.

Joyce had fixed upon June 16, 1904, as the date of *Ulysses* because it was the anniversary of his first walk with Nora Barnacle. He was able to obtain, perhaps on his last visit to Dublin, copies of the newspapers of that day. In his book, Bloom's fondest memory is of a moment of affection plighted among the rhododendrons on Howth, and so is Mrs. Bloom's; it is with her recollection of it that the book ends. In this sense *Ulysses* is an epithalamium; love is its cause of motion. The spirit is liberated from its bonds through a eucharistic occasion, an occasion characterized by the joy that, even as a young man, Joyce had praised as the emotion in comedy which makes it a higher form than tragedy. Though such occasions are as rare as miracles, they are permanently sustaining; and unlike miracles, they require no divine intercession. They arise in quintessential purity from the mottled life of everyday.

The theme of *Ulysses* is simple, and Joyce achieves it through the characters of Bloom, Molly, and Stephen. Casual kindness overcomes unconscionable power. Stephen's charge against Mulligan is that Mulligan is brutal and cruel;[20] Molly's complaint against Boylan is again on the score of brutality, of animal sensuality without feeling. Bloom is allowed to formulate this theme of the book, though in comic circumstances, when he defends love to the Cyclops, and defines it meekly but deftly as 'the opposite of hatred.' It is opposite also to chauvinism and force. So in the *Penelope* episode, Molly, faithful in spite of herself, ends the day by yielding once more to her husband and dismissing Boylan as inconsequential. In Joyce's work the soul—a word which he never renounced—carries off the victory.

Whatever else about the book was unclear to Joyce in 1914, as he set himself for what he knew would be a long period of work, this point of view was firm. All the trivia of Dublin and many of Trieste must be conscripted to express it. In his art Joyce went beyond the misfortune and frustration he had grown accustomed to regard as the dominant notes of his life, and expressed his only piety, a rejection, in humanity's name and comedy's method, of fear and hatred.

NOTES

1. Stuart Gilbert argues persuasively that 'silent monologue' would be a more accurate translation of *monologue intérieur*.

2. Other writers, like Dorothy Richardson, achieved a different kind of monologue for different reasons.

3. There is also a repetition of incidents from *A Portrait*, often with parodic changes. Stephen's vision of the girl at the seashore, with its stages of excitement carefully

delineated, is parodied in *Nausicaa* by Bloom's orgasmic but equally detached contemplation of Gerty MacDowell. In the same way, Stephen's announcement, while walking with Cranly in *A Portrait*, that he is leaving the Church in favor of art, is parodied by Bloom's announcement to his friends Mastiansky and Citron that he is giving up religion for Darwinism. See also note, p. 49.

4. Bloom's rather fatuous conversation in the *Eumaeus* episode must be understood in terms of the time of day and his physical exhaustion. As Stuart Gilbert writes, 'The *Eumaeus* episode—I remember Joyce's insisting on this point—was meant to represent the intercourse and mental state of two fagged-out men. Stephen is suffering from a mild hangover and inclined to be snappish, while Bloom, half asleep, rambles on—perhaps even intending his talk to have a mildly sedative effect on his young protégé. Bloom can talk and think intelligently when he makes an effort, but he's too tired to make an effort. Personally I find him rather endearing in this episode, and so I think did Joyce.'

5. Stephen says he does not believe his own theory, but means perhaps only that he believes in nothing. The theory nevertheless suits him.

6. An amusing use of later information is Bloom's advocacy of the Poulaphouca reservoir scheme, which, as Joyce knew, was later adopted, and his prediction that Nannetti would be Lord Mayor of Dublin before long, as indeed he became in 1906.

7. Most of Hart's poems had to do with attempts to get money and credit; one was entitled, 'On Looking for the Loan of a Tanner [sixpence]'; another dealt with his effort to obtain a pint of stout at Darden's Public House:

> One day I asked a pint on tick
> From Mr. Darden, who
> In lordly accents told me
> 'Twas a thing he didn't do.

> In Fanning's I owed threepence,
> In Bergin's one and four,
> In McGuire's only sixpence
> For they wouldn't give me more.

> When makes* is gone and nothing's left
> To shove into the pawn,
> I ramble up to Stephen's Green
> And gaze on Ardilaun.**

(*Makes* are halfpence.
**Ardilaun* is the statue of a member of the Guinness family, who made porter.)

8. The medical students had a bawdy song that began:

> O there goes Mrs. Mack;
> She keeps a house of imprudence,
> She keeps an old back parlor
> For us poxy medical students.

9. This young woman's father had a political job as scrivener in the Education Board. A priest came to see him to ask that he do something about his daughter; but Mr. 'Crawford' twirled his villainous moustaches and replied, 'Well, the girl appears to be enjoying herself, and besides, she's a source of income to me.'

10. Becky Cooper was noted for the prodigality of her charities as well as for her favors; young men who took her fancy were the surprised and sometimes embarrassed recipients of gifts of money and new clothes. A familiar song about her celebrated not her generosity, however, but her accessibility:

> Italy's maids are fair to see
> And France's maids are willing
> But less expensive 'tis to me:
> Becky's for a shilling.

11. This method of reinforcing his theme by multiplying instances of similar behavior becomes even more prominent in *Finnegans Wake*.

12. W. Y. Tindall first pointed out an allusion to this book. Joyce had several of Sacher-Masoch's books in his library.

13. See p. 463 for Joyce's use of a special handwriting.

14. Joyce said to Stanislaus as early as October 1, 1901, 'Cruelty is weakness.'

15. His death is made to take place at the Queen's Hotel in Ennis because Joyce remembered a suicide that occurred there early in the century.

16. For Joyce's use of this final word, see p. 353 and pp. 531, 536.

17. He was interested too, in the way that, as he said, 'A Jew is both king and priest in his own family.'

18. So did John Joyce.

19. So Nora Joyce acknowledged in later life to Carola Giedion-Welcker, 'I don't know whether my husband is a genius, but I'm sure of one thing, there is nobody like him.'

20. Joyce completed in this character his analysis of Gogarty. He had written it long before for *A Portrait*, but had put it aside. The earlier version was much more essaylike:

> 'Doherty's gibes flashed to and fro through the torpor of his mind and he thought without mirth of his friend's face, equine and pallid, and of his pallid hair, grained and hued like oak. He had tried to receive coldly these memories of his friend's boisterous humour, feeling that his coarseness of speech was not a blasphemy of the spirit but a coward's mask, but in the end the troop of swinish images broke down his reserve and went trampling through his memory, followed by his laughter...'

WOLFGANG ISER

Patterns of Communication in Joyce's Ulysses

I
Myth and Reality

Joyce called his novel *Ulysses* after Homer's hero, though the latter never
appears in the book. Instead Joyce deals with eight different aspects of a
single day in Dublin, mainly following the involvement of two characters—
Leopold Bloom and Stephen Dedalus—in events that take place between
early morning and late at night. What, then, is the connection between the
Odyssey and June 16, 1904? Most answers to this question try to join these
two poles of the novel through the 'tried and tested' ideas of the recurrence
of archetypes, or the analogy between the ideal and the real.[1] In the first case,
the explanation is provided by the permanent nature of basic human
conduct—and so *Ulysses* has its roots in things we already know; the second,
Platonizing interpretation claims that the basic idea of the *Odyssey* is a
homecoming, while that of Bloom's wanderings is just a copy of a
homecoming: for Ulysses this means release from his sufferings, but for
Bloom it is merely a critical moment in the restless monotony of everyday
life.

Although one is reluctant to dispute these lines of interpretation, they
certainly suffer from the fact that not a single character from the *Odyssey*
actually appears in *Ulysses*—in contrast to many modern texts, where the

From *The Implied Reader: Patterns of Communication in Prose Fiction from Bunyan to Beckett.* ©
1974 by The Johns Hopkins University Press.

31

return of mythical figures is a fundamental theme—and Joyce's deliberate allusions to Homeric heroes and epic events show them in a different light from that with which we are familiar through the *Odyssey*. The permanence idea gets into difficulties here, as it is never clear what is to be equated with what, and who with whom. There are similar objections to the analogy thesis, which postulates a sort of declivity from Homer to the present. One simply does not have the impression that everyday life in Dublin has been conceived as the woeful decline of an ideality that existed in the past. And again there is no clear parallel between past and present. Nevertheless, one can understand why the permanence and analogy theories have proved so attractive to those trying to combine past and present in a single vision: they do, after all, offer a means of organizing the seemingly opaque chaos of everyday life by referring it back to meanings drawn from Homer. The solution is convincing by virtue of its simplicity—but from an esthetic point of view it is quite inadequate. Joyce himself once said, ironically, of his novel: "I've put in so many enigmas and puzzles that it will keep the professors busy for centuries arguing over what I meant, and that's the only way of insuring one's immortality."[2] If for a moment one examines this statement with a little more seriousness than was perhaps intended, one is faced with the question of what actually gives rise to this preoccupation with the enigmas. Is it the enigmas themselves, or is it perhaps the critical armory which the professors are constantly dipping into as they try to solve the riddles? Whichever it may be, the parallelism indicated by the title of the novel compels one to see Dublin and Homer in conjunction, principally because one is anxious to extract some kind of meaning from the apparent senselessness of everyday life. But, like all compulsions, this makes one blind to certain not insignificant facts: one of these is the peculiar nature of the two poles that constitute the novel.

No Homeric figures actually appear in *Ulysses*, and yet the novel cannot be described as a realistic depiction of ordinary life in Dublin, despite the vast number of verifiable details that run right through it. We have since learned that a great deal of this material was drawn from Dublin address books, topographical descriptions, and the daily press of that time, so that an astonishing wealth of names, addresses, local events, and even newspaper cuttings can actually be identified,[3] though in the text they frequently form a montage that is stripped of its context. Sometimes these details vanish away into the impenetrable private sphere of Joyce himself, and sometimes they seem to lead the reader into a veritable labyrinth when he attempts to collate them. In searching for and visualizing connections, he often loses the organizing principle of those connections he thought he had discovered. And frequently it seems as though the many details are simply there for their own sake and, through sheer weight of numbers, more or less deliberately blur the outline of events in the narrative.

The effect of all this is somewhat paradoxical, for it runs completely contrary to the expectations that the realistic novel had established in its readers. There, too, one was confronted with a wealth of details which the reader could see reflected in his own world of experience. Their appearance in the novel served mainly to authenticate the view of life offered.[4] But in *Ulysses* they are, to a great extent, deprived of this function. When details no longer serve to reinforce probability or to stabilize the illusion of reality, they must become a sort of end in themselves, such as one finds in the art-form of the collage. The unstructured material of *Ulysses* is taken directly from life itself, but since it no longer testifies to the author's preconception of reality, it cannot be taken for life itself. Thus the details illustrate nothing; they simply present themselves, and since they bear witness to nothing beyond themselves, they revoke the normal assumption that a novel represents a given reality. It is not surprising, then, that one is constantly returning to the title in order to try to create—through recourse to the *Odyssey*—some sort of frame of reference that will bring this chaos of detail under control and will endow everyday life with a pattern, with meaning, and with significance.

We now have a double frustration of our expectations: not only do the Homeric figures fail to appear in *Ulysses* but also the many details are deprived of their usual function. As a result, our attention is drawn to the evocative nature of the novel. We realize that all these details constitute a surplus that projects far beyond any organizational schema that the novel may offer us. And so each reading gives us a new chance to integrate the details in a different way—with the result, however, that each form of integration brings about a sort of kaleidoscopic reshuffling of the material excluded.

By giving his novel this structure—whether consciously or unconsciously—Joyce was complying with a basic disposition of the reader, described by Northrop Frye as follows: "Whenever we read anything, we find our attention moving in two directions at once. One direction is outward or centrifugal, in which we keep going outside our reading, from the individual words to the things they mean, or, in practice, to our memory of the conventional association between them. The other direction is inward or centripetal, in which we try to develop from the words a sense of the larger verbal pattern they make."[5] These two tendencies seem to take the reader of *Ulysses* in completely different directions, which are divergent rather than convergent. As he reads, he finds that everyday life in Dublin is, so to speak, continually breaking its banks, and the resultant flood of detail induces the reader to try and build his own dams of meaning—though these in turn are inevitably broken down. Even the signal contained in the title seems to dispel rather than fulfill one's hopes of controlling the material, for the central frame of reference that one would so like to deduce from the *Odyssey* is never formulated anywhere in the text. According to whether one reads the novel from the Dublin viewpoint or from that of the *Odyssey*, one will get quite different 'images'. In the first case, the apparent lack of connection between the many details creates the impression of a thoroughly chaotic world; in the second, one wonders what the return of Ulysses in modern trappings is supposed to signify. Both approaches are, in themselves, relatively flabby, and the task of stiffening them up, and indeed bringing them together, is what the novel sets its reader.

Soon after the publication of *Ulysses*, Eliot and Pound both described the interaction of the two constituent poles of the novel, each using different metaphors. In his discussion of *Ulysses*, Eliot saw in the novel's references to tradition a demand that was to be made of all literature: "In using the myth, in manipulating a continuous parallel between contemporaneity and antiquity, Mr. Joyce is pursuing a method which others must pursue after him. They will not be imitators, any more than the scientist who uses the discoveries of an Einstein in pursuing his own, independent, further investigations. It is simply a way of controlling, of ordering, of giving a shape and a significance to the immense panorama of futility and anarchy which is contemporary history."[6] According to this, the mythic parallel is meant to give a constant outline to an order that is to be read into the events in Dublin. But this cannot mean—at least for Joyce—that the chaotic and enigmatic present is measured against the significance of Homeric archetypes. It would be closer to the truth to say that the mythic parallel offers patterns of perception, though what is perceived never conforms completely to these patterns. Indeed, the revelation of the irreducible differences is what constitutes the real function of the mythical patterns through which we are to look upon the modern world. The very fact that these cannot incorporate everything endows the nonintegrated material with the necessary degree of live tension to make us immediately aware of it. It is not by chance that Eliot refers back to Einstein in order to indicate how the 'discovery' of Joyce is to be evaluated and handled. The mythic parallel here is more in the nature of an explanatory hypothesis, and is scarcely to be interpreted as the return of the myth. It is simply a repertoire of patterns serving an overall strategy through which the present-day world is to be presented.

Ezra Pound, on the same subject, writes: "These correspondences are part of Joyce's mediaevalism and are chiefly his own affair, a scaffold, a means of construction, justified by the result, and justifiable by it only. The result is a triumph in form, in balance, a main schema, with continuous inweaving and arabesque."[7] Pound sees in the mythical correspondences nothing but preconditions for the construction of the novel—the scaffolding round the shell of the building to be erected. But the novel itself is more than the sum of its preconditions, and is in no way reducible to this sum. Ultimately, the network of mythical correspondences forms nothing but a framework of presentation, which is so clearly delineated in the novel in order to draw attention to the limitations of all such organizational patterns. This applies in equal measure to the recognizable archetypes, but the question then arises as to what such limitations actually are meant to achieve.

II
Experiments in Style

The Homeric allusions in *Ulysses* open up an horizon which is certainly not identical to that of the modern "World-Weekday,"[8] for between the present and the archetypes of the Homeric epic lies the whole of history, which could only be passed over if *Ulysses* were concerned with nothing but the return of archetypes. One should not forget, when considering the Homeric parallel, that Joyce permeated his novel with just as many Shakespearean allusions as Homeric. And even if one tries to equate Shakespeare's presence in *Ulysses* with the return of the archetypes, nevertheless there is no denying the fact that Joyce was obviously more interested in the various manifestations of such archetypes than in merely establishing their return. This certainly indicates that for him the archetype was, at most, a vehicle, but not a subject. The history of its manifestations takes precedence over its mythical nature. But what is this history, and in what form is it reflected in the novel?

Our answer to this question can, perhaps, best proceed from the experiments in style. These in themselves are an innovation, insofar as the eighteen chapters of the novel present the narrative through eighteen differently structured perspectives. Normally, when reading a novel, we are asked only once to adopt the author's chosen standpoint in order to fulfill his intentions—but here the same demand is made of us no less than seventeen extra times, for each chapter is written in a different style. Style, according to John Middleton Murry, "is a quality of language which communicates.... a system of emotions or thoughts, peculiar to the author."[9] We can talk of style when systematic viewpoints bring about a frame of reference that is to direct the reader's observations by selecting which facts are or are not to be presented.

This function of style is both its strength and its weakness, for inevitably it must restrict the field of observation. The meaning that it is to express can only take its shape through the process of selecting particular aspects of the phenomena to be presented, and so phenomena are reproduced mainly for the sake of what they will communicate to the reader. As style imposes a specific meaning and edits reality to coincide with this meaning, it reveals itself to be a "mythical analogue,"[10] which—as Clemens Lugowski has shown—not only implies a particular conception of reality but is also the agent that actually forms it. Although this "'mythical artifice' ... is the result of a deeply unconscious and indirect act of interpretation,"[11] for this very reason it will freeze the historical conditions under which such acts of interpretation came into being.

In *Ulysses* Joyce shows up these limitations by thematizing the capacity of style itself. By constantly changing the perspective through the eighteen chapters, he draws attention to the normative pressure caused by the modes of observation inherent in any one style, thus revealing the extreme one-sidedness of each individual "act of interpretation." While the change of styles shows up these limitations, the process is underlined in the individual chapters by the surplus of nonintegrated, unstructured material. This, too, makes one aware of the limitations of the style in question, so that it often seems more real than the view of reality being presented at the time.

And so we have changes of style and nonintegrated material to show up the limitations of each style, and in addition to these two factors, there is even a kind of authorial commentary[12] which has these very limitations as its subject. This is the case in "The Oxen of the Sun," which Joyce critics have always approached with a kind of embarrassment.[13] T. S. Eliot had the impression that this chapter showed the "futility of all the English styles,"[14] and this must certainly have been at least one of the effects that Joyce was aiming at.

In this display of individual and period styles, we are made aware of the various assumptions that condition the different presentations of the theme. By parodying the styles, Joyce makes sure that we do not overlook the 'interpretative' nature of the forms of presentation. Leopold Bloom finds himself transformed into a variety of figures, in accordance with the particular style used: the medieval "traveller Leopold" changes into the Arthurian knight "Sir Leopold," who in turn leaps into a new context as "childe Leopold."[15] The reader cannot help being aware of the one-sidedness of all these characterizations, as he has already become familiar in the preceding chapters with the many-sidedness of Bloom's character. This same one-sidedness is equally evident in the central theme of the chapter. This does not deal with love, but only with the way in which Malory, Bunyan, Addison and the other writers conceived of love. The basically comic effect arises out of the impression one has that the views, expressed in such a variety of styles, exclude rather than supplement one another. With each author the main theme takes on a different shape, but as each style automatically and unquestioningly assumes that it has captured the reality of the phenomenon, a latent naiveté comes to the surface. The question arises as to which of these individual views comes closest to the truth, but even then we realize that the individual authors, precisely through their selection of a particular means of presentation, have in fact edited the subject to form a single meaning and a single evaluation. The very fact that these meanings and evaluations seem to assume a normative validity makes us aware of the extent to which they depend on the historical situation from which they have sprung. If "The Oxen of the Sun" is taken, then, as the author's own 'commentary' on his work, one can scarcely expect him to organize his novel as yet another "act of interpretation." It is the *presentation* of everyday life that concerns him, and not the evaluation.

However, such a presentation also requires a form, and inevitably any form that Joyce chose would automatically foreshorten the phenomenon to be presented. And so one might assume that the chapters of the novel were organized, each as a sort of rebuttal to the others, with their respective *principium stilisationis*. The consequences of this principle of construction are very far-reaching. Joyce could parody the different styles in order to show the limitations of their capacity, but if he applied this technique to the whole novel, it would mean that in trying to present the events, etc., of June 16, 1904, he would have to parody himself continually. There are certainly traces of this in the text, but a constant self-parody would ultimately distract the reader from coming to grips with the events of June 16, 1904. And would this not in turn—like all parodies—lead primarily to a negative evaluation, as limited in its own way as the evaluations of the authors parodied? Such a form would itself constitute an "act of interpretation."

Is it possible for anything to be presented, and yet at the same time for the "act of interpretation" to be suspended without the object of presentation becoming incomprehensible? *Ulysses* is the answer to this question. In order to moderate, if not actually to neutralize, the interpretative nature of style, Joyce called upon virtually every stylistic mode that the novel had evolved during its comparatively short history. These he enriched with a whole armory of allusions and with the recall of archetypes. The multiplicity of these schemata, together with the complexity of their interrelationships, results in a form of presentation that in fact presents each incipient meaning simultaneously with its own diffusion. Thus the novel does not paint a picture of the "World-Weekday"—which means, ultimately, that it does not 'present' anything in the conventional sense—but, through the great variety of its perspectives, it offers possibilities for conceiving or imagining the "World-Weekday." These possibilities must be fulfilled by the reader himself, if he wants to make contact with the reality of the novel. One must therefore differentiate between 'presentation' (i.e., by the author) and 'imagination' (on the part of the reader). Of course, even if the 'interpretative acts' of the novel are obvious, the reader still has to imagine things for himself. But he will only conduct these 'interpretative acts' if the system of presentation leaves out the coordinating elements between observable phenomena and situations. In *Ulysses* this is brought about mainly through the overprecision of the system, which presents more conceivable material than the reader is capable of processing as he reads. And so it is not the style of the novel but the overtaxed reader himself that reduces the amount of observable material to manageable proportions. In doing so, he can scarcely avoid equating this reduced amount with the meaning. If one considers reactions to *Ulysses* over the last forty years—insofar as these can be gauged by the different interpretations offered—one can see how historically conditioned such meanings are. At the same time, it cannot be denied that the many possible permutations of meaning in *Ulysses* act as a constant inducement to the reader to formulate a meaning—and in doing so, he is forced to enter into the action of the novel.

The individual chapters of *Ulysses* act, to a greater or lesser degree, as signposts that point the way through the "World-Weekday," rather than guidebooks that impose on the reader a specific interpretation of the regions they represent. If we want to get a proper understanding of the function of the patterns of presentation, the allusions, and also the archetypes, it might be as well first to examine one or two concrete examples.

The novel begins with the parody of a church ritual. Mulligan, the medical student, holds his shaving-bowl aloft at the top of the Martello tower, and intones: *Introibo ad altare Dei*.[16] If this little curtain-raiser is a sign of what is to come, then we appear to be due for one long parody. At first this impression seems to be confirmed by the subsequent conversation between Mulligan and Stephen, for as he talks the former jumps abruptly from one stylistic level to another, everyday slang alternating with scholarly allusions to Greece, Irish mythology, and even Zarathustra.[17] Indeed individual allusions are sometimes broken up and even corrupted. Are we now to have a series of parodied stylistic levels? If so, there would be a danger of the tension soon flagging, for a parody of stylistic levels here might seem trivial after the initial 'exposing' of the mass. Moreover, it is scarcely possible to find a *tertium comparationis* for the various intersecting levels of Mulligan's speech.

It is also impossible to establish a purpose for such a parody, unless one wanted to conclude from the diffusion of stylistic levels that Joyce was advocating a purist use of language—an idea that is hardly worth considering. In fact, one gets the impression that what is stated is nothing but a stimulus to call forth its own reversal. Thus the profane distortions of the ritual of the mass take on a significance other than that of mere parody. Like the subsequent conversation, they point up the limitations of all clearly formulated statements and induce the reader to supply his own connections between the segmented stylistic levels. As the text offers no point of convergence for the phenomena it sets before him, the reader tends to load each detail with meaning, and since the meaning cannot be fully realized, there arises a latent tension between the unconnected phenomena. This basic pattern, with a few variations, runs right through the first chapter, which Joyce called "Telemachus."[18] The most important type of variation is the abrupt switch of narrator. In the middle of a third-person narrative we are suddenly confronted with statements in the first person,[19] which strike the reader so forcibly that he soon becomes more conscious of narrative patterns than of things narrated. And so here, as elsewhere in the novel, one gets the impression that one must constantly differentiate between the linguistic possibilities of style and the possible nature of the phenomena concerned.

The predominant pattern of reversal in this first chapter reduces all that is clear and concrete to a mere position in life, but life itself goes far beyond such positions. The next chapter, originally called "Nestor," reveals the implications of this fact, and naturally another collection of stylistic patterns is necessary to uncover these hidden consequences. Stephen's interior monologue is the dominant pattern in this chapter, but it is broken up by authorial passages, direct speech, and also quotations from Milton's *Lycidas*,[20] all set against and arising out of the background of the morning lesson. They lead to reflections on history and man's possible place in history:

> For them too history was a tale like any other too often heard, their land a pawnshop. Had Pyrrhus not fallen by a beldam's hand in Argos or Julius Caesar not been knifed to death? They are not to be thought away. Time has branded them and fettered they are lodged in the room of the infinite possibilities they have ousted. But can those have been possible seeing that they never were? Or was that only possible which came to pass? Weave, weaver of the wind.... It must be a movement then, an actuality of the possible as possible.[21]

It is not insignificant that this reflection on the possible is inspired specifically by historical processes in which everything appears to be so irrevocably fixed. Is this determinacy ultimately to be seen only as one possibility among many? What about the existences of historical individuals? If, through their deeds and sufferings, they stepped outside the jurisdiction of infinite possibilities, why should they now fall back into it? It seems almost like a sophism when Stephen asks whether Pyrrhus and Caesar even considered the possibility, when they were alive, that one day they would not be there, or that they would end as they did. Although he himself considers such thoughts to be mere speculations, they do not stop him from concluding that real life can only be understood as an actuality of one possibility among many. But if what happened did not happen inevitably, then the real is nothing but a chance track left by the possible. And if reality is nothing but one chance track, then it pales to insignificance beside the vast number of unseen and unfulfilled possibilities; it shrinks to the dimensions of a mere curiosity. The tendency apparent in these reflections of Stephen's runs parallel to that at the beginning of the novel, where whatever was said pointed the way to its own reversal, and whatever possibilities were excluded by each utterance were brought out by another.

The children are bored by the history lesson, and want Stephen to tell them a story: "Tell us a story, sir.—Oh, do, sir. A ghoststory."[22] Stephen himself has just had the impression that, when one thinks about it, history changes into a ghost story, albeit a different type from the one the children would like to hear. Bored by the factual, they are now asking for the fantastic, without realizing how much incomprehensibility lies in the factual. The text, of course, does not state this, but the manner in which the different perspectives are thrust against one another compels the reader to search for a link between them. The text offers him no guide as to how the different standpoints might be evaluated, and at best he can only orientate himself through the next perspective which, like that of the children, is inserted into Stephen's monologue. There is no ghost story; instead, the children begin to read verses from Milton's *Lycidas*—those lines where the mourning shepherd is consoled with the assurance that the dead do not perish. Evidently only poetry eternalizes; but poetry is fiction.

In this comparatively short section of text, there are three different intersecting patterns: interior monologue, direct speech, and literary quotations—all focused upon a relatively uniform theme which, however, takes on three different forms as it is presented to the reader. For Stephen reality is so overshadowed by the possible that it is deprived of its unique significance. The children are bored by what has been and want the titillation of the unreal. The literary quotation shows clearly that eternalization only exists in the medium of fiction. The text does not say how these three viewpoints are to be joined together, but simply offers three different possibilities for relating the real to the unreal. As the individual stylistic patterns intersect within the text, there is no hierarchic construction. The reflections of the inner monologue point inevitably to the private nature of the opinion expressed; the desires of the school children appear as something spontaneous and naive and the quotation as a kind of insurance without any reality. Although this need not be regarded as the only possible interpretation of the different patterns of the text, the conditions are certainly there for such an interpretation. Since these patterns are without a point of convergence, their meaning arises out of their interaction—a process which is set in motion by the reader himself and which will therefore involve him personally in the text.

Apart from the patterns we have mentioned, this process is encouraged above all by the end of the chapter, which deals with a conversation between Stephen and the headmaster, Mr. Deasy. The headmaster gives Stephen a letter which he wants published in the *Evening Telegraph*, because it contains his (Deasy's) solution to an important problem: foot-and-mouth disease. "I have put the matter into a nutshell, Mr Deasy said. It's about the foot and mouth disease. just look through it. There can be no two opinions on the matter."[23]

For Mr. Deasy there can be no two opinions about this or about a number of other political problems in Ireland. But now the segmented text pattern of Stephen's history lesson becomes the background to Mr. Deasy's unequivocal utterances, through which he seeks once and for all to set right existing realities. Again the text says nothing about any relationship between these two passages, but the reader will soon find a relatively straightforward way to bridge this gap. Viewed against the background of infinite possibilities, Mr. Deasy's self-confidence appears absurdly narrow-minded, and so the reader will most likely come to two conclusions: first, that Mr. Deasy is a pompous ass; second, and far more important, that any claim to knowledge is an automatic reduction of the infinite and discounts above all the changeability of phenomena. However, let it be emphasized once again—this interpretation will be the reader's, for there is no such statement in the text itself.

As regards the original chapter heading—"Nestor"—this offers yet another perspective, insofar as the reader will try to link the wisdom of Nestor with the pretension of Mr. Deasy. He will probably find that not only does Mr. Deasy suffer from the comparison, but so, too, does Nestor. For if, in Mr. Deasy's case, claims to knowledge presuppose unawareness of the changeability of phenomena, then the mythical wisdom of Nestor is open to re-evaluation by the reader.

The third chapter, originally called "Proteus," takes the experiment in yet another direction, at the same time bringing to a close the sections grouped under the heading "Telemachia," which deal with Stephen's inner situation before the appearance of Bloom. In comparison with the preceding chapters, one is struck by the relative uniformity of the stylistic pattern used here. Stephen's monologue forms the dominant *principium stilisationis*, though there are occasional traces of the authorial narrator. These latter, however, are of a special nature. Instead of relating the monologue to an overall situation, the author's voice here seems to be unable to keep up with Stephen's reflections and is virtually swamped by them. It no longer acts as a mediator between the context and the narrated situation; instead the monologue seems to abstract itself even, from the authorial medium. With the authorial narrator thus deprived of his normal function, we are left with a gap between monologue and overall situation and, as always when such gaps arise, the reader is stimulated into forming his own connections. But in this case, his task is made doubly difficult by the fact that Stephen's monologue has no consistent pattern. At one moment it seems like a stream of consciousness, stirring up the past, the next it is a mere recording of observations on the beach at Sandymount, and then it is like a soliloquy or an introspective reflection which—unlike the conventional interior monologue—is not concerned with memory or observation, but with the conditions that initially give rise to memory and observation.

In the very first sentence of the monologue, we are made aware of the peculiar nature of Stephen's reflections: "Ineluctable modality of the visible: at least that if no more, thought through my eyes. Signatures of all things I am here to read, seaspawn and seawrack, the nearing tide, that rusty boot. Snotgreen, bluesilver, rust: coloured signs. Limits of the diaphane."[24]

Stephen tries to show the consequences that arise out of his inescapable restriction to his own perceptions. This is apparently only possible through concrete consideration of the actual mode of perception. If observation automatically involves so many preconceptions, then how is one to read the signatures of things? At best, seawrack and tide might be described as colors, but such a reduction not only impoverishes them—it also leads one swiftly to the borderline at which they resist perception and retreat into total opacity. It is perception itself that ultimately produces this opacity, which in turn appears to be a characteristic of the object which is to be perceived. Thus for Stephen, the subject under discussion is the frame of reference of perception itself. Perhaps this frame is such that in approaching objects, it changes them in order to make them accessible to one's comprehension.

Stephen tries to test this idea; he closes his eyes in order to 'see' if such a change really is produced by vision. He opens them again with the statement:

"See now. There all the time without you: and ever shall be, world without end."[25] Obviously, things exist independently of one's comprehension and observation of them, and if this comprehension is, in turn, to be comprehended, it must be through the idea that the act of seeing is what produces the opacity of things. The monologue that follows is like an attempt to give form to this idea. Stephen's reflections on the limitations of observation culminate in a welter of fragmentary situations, images, characters, and contexts. The reader is perplexed, not least because this is not what he expects from analytical reflection in a novel. Normally, the aim of this sort of reflection should be progress toward clarity and truth—it should enlighten and not obscure.[26]

The perplexing effect of the monologue derives mainly from the fact that the individual sentences or passages, which all deal with recognizable but unrelated themes, are simply set side by side without any apparent connection. Thus the vacant spaces in the text increase dramatically in number. These may irritate the reader—but as far as the intention of the monologue is concerned, they are perfectly consistent. They prevent the reader from correlating what he observes, with the result that the facets of the external world—as evoked by Stephen's perception—are constantly made to merge into one another. However, the perplexity that this process causes in the reader cannot be the sole purpose of the text, if one considers Stephen's preceding train of thought. Here, as elsewhere, perplexity should be regarded rather as a stimulus and a provocation—though, of course, the reader is not obliged to take the bait and will, indeed, ignore it if he feels himself to be overtaxed. The point is that one can read something into this fragmentary text. Stephen's reflections on his acts of perception reveal a state of consciousness which has been described, in a different context, by Cassirer as follows: "The further consciousness progresses in its formation and division, and the more 'meaningful' its individual contents become—i.e., the more they take on the power to 'adumbrate' others—the greater is the freedom with which; through a change of 'viewpoint,' it can transform one gestalt into another."[27] It is this disposition of consciousness that is brought out through the ceaseless transformation of 'gestalten' in the monologue. But it should be added that the transformation is effected primarily by the way in which Stephen varies the distance between the observed reality and himself as the conscious observer. This variation ensures that the world which is open to perception cannot be confined to any one conscious frame of reference. A vital element of it is the continual retraction of each adopted attitude to everything that occurs on the beach at Sandymount, and the whole process functions through the gaps, interrupting the images formed by acts of perception, thus focusing the reader's attention on the interaction between perception and reality.

The text also offers indications of this process: "I throw this ended shadow from me, manshape ineluctable, call it back. Endless, would it be mine, form of my form? Who watches me here?"[28] This awareness of the necessity to separate modes of perception from the thing perceived, so that the observed world can take on its inherent multifariousness, is conveyed in the text through the gaps which prevent us from connecting the phenomena processed by observation. And so the monologue appears to release all the observed and recorded details from any overriding structure.

In the face of this impression, one might be tempted to regard this chapter as offering a focus for the whole manner of presentation of the "World-Weekday." Stephen's reflections on his own mode of observation, self-observation as a constant check on things observed, and the liberation of things perceived from the clutches of perception—these could easily be taken for the basic schema of the novel. But if this were so, Joyce would fall victim to his own trap. For then he would simply be replacing the styles he parodies with another of his own. For this very reason it is essential not to overlook the demarcation points through which he indicates the limitations of the mode of presentation in this chapter. First, we have nothing but the view of one character in the novel. The perspective is offered in the form of a monologue which sometimes seems to lose its way in the impenetrable individuality of the person delivering it. Second, even if one can follow these reflections, the very form of the monologue emphasizes the private nature of the ideas expressed, for the interior monologue is a private form of presentation, the ego addressing itself. And, finally, elsewhere in the novel Joyce gives certain indications as to how Stephen's cogitations are to be judged. Much later in the book—352 pages to be precise—in the chapter on the parody of styles (nota bene!), Stephen's introspective searchings are labeled "perverted transcendentalism."[29] Of course the Joyce reader needs a very good memory (and usually hasn't got one good enough) to recall all such indications, but even an average, if overburdened, memory will record enough to show that the mode of presentation in the "Proteus" chapter is to be seen only as a facet of and not as a paradigm for the presentation of everyday life.

We might add one more reflection on this chapter, and that concerns the Homeric parallel. Joyce called the chapter "Proteus," and we know from the *Odyssey* that Proteus keeps escaping from Menelaus and transforming himself into different shapes, because he does not want to yield the secret of how Menelaus can best get home. But Menelaus has been warned in advance not to be put off by these changes of form, because it is his courage that will compel Proteus to give away the vital secret. The transformations brought about by Stephen's thinking are somewhat different. Certainly it seems as though a secret is being kept from him, but, in contrast to the Homeric story, he is producing this secret himself. He knows he is inescapably restricted to observation, and he knows that things change the moment one observes them. Every approach changes them into something different. And so the 'courage' of knowing just what it is that we can see and understand, actually blocks the way to the secret. The act of knowing itself produces the secret of things that change when they are observed. While the Homeric world order enabled Menelaus to learn the secret he coveted, the modern world uses its knowledge to reveal the fact that there is a secret—the indeterminate nature of all phenomena. As far as Menelaus is concerned, the knowledge wrested from Proteus leads directly to action; for Stephen, the knowledge that he is bound to his own forms of perception leads to an endless delving into the ultimate constitution of the world.

As it would be beyond the scope of this essay to deal with all the experiments of style in *Ulysses*, we shall confine ourselves to those that evince the most striking variations. One of these is undoubtedly the "Aeolus" chapter, which is especially relevant to our discussion, as in many respects it forms a contrast to the "Proteus" chapter. Bloom's visit to the newspaper office provides the framework for a curiously patterned form of narration. Analysis reveals two separate levels of the text, which one might call, for the sake of convenience, the micro- and the macrostructure of the chapter. The microstructural level consists of a large number of allusions which basically can be divided into three different groups: (1) those dealing with the immediate situation, Bloom's effort to place an advertisement at the newspaper office and the events connected with it; (2) those referring to completely different episodes outside the chapter itself, sometimes relating to incidents already described and sometimes anticipating things; (3) those passages which seem to slide into obscurity when one tries to work out exactly where they might be heading. However, as these allusions are not distinctly separated, but are in fact woven into an intricate pattern, each one of them tends to entice the reader to follow it. Thus the allusions themselves turn into microperspectives which, because of their very density, simply cannot be followed through to the end. They form abbreviated extracts from reality which inevitably compel the reader to a process of selection.

This is also true of the other stylistic pattern to be discerned within the microstructural stratum. Just as with the allusions, there is throughout an abrupt alternation between dialogue, direct and indirect speech, authorial report, first-person narrative, and interior monologue. Although such techniques do impose a certain order on the abundance of allusions, they also invest them with differing importance. An allusion by the author himself certainly has a function for the context different from one that is made in direct speech by one of the characters. Thus extracts from reality and individual events are not contracted merely into allusions, but, through the different patterns of style, emerge in forms that endow them with a varied range of relevance. At the same time, the unconnected allusions and the abrupt alternation of stylistic devices disclose a large number of gaps.

All this gives rise to the stimulating quality of the text. On the one hand, the density of allusions and the continual segmentation of style involve an incessant changing of perspectives, which seem to go out of control whenever the reader tries to pin them down; on the other hand, the gaps resulting from cuts and abbreviations tempt the reader to fill them in. He will try to group things, because this is the only way in which he can recognize situations or understand characters in the novel.

The macrostructure of the chapter lends itself to this need for 'grouping', though in a peculiar way. Heading and 'newspaper column' form the schema that incorporates the allusions and stylistic changes. The heading is an instruction as to what to expect. But the text which follows the caption reveals the composition described above, and so in most cases does not fulfill the expectation raised by the heading. As the newspaper headlines refer to various incidents in the city, the situation of Ireland, and so forth, they would seem to be concerned with everyday events, the reality of which is beyond question. But the column that follows frustrates this expectation, not only by leading commonplace realities off in unforeseeable directions, thus destroying the grouping effect of the headline, but also by fragmenting facts and occurrences in such a way that to comprehend the commonplace becomes a real effort. While the heading appears to gratify our basic need for grouping, this need is predominantly subverted by the text that follows.

In the "Aeolus" chapter, the reader not only learns something about events in Dublin on June 16, 1904 but he also experiences the difficulties inherent in the comprehension of the barest outline of events. It is precisely because the heading suggests a way of grouping from a particular viewpoint that the text itself seems so thoroughly to contradict our familiar notions of perception. The text appears to defy transcription of the circumstances indicated and instead offers the reader nothing but attitudes or possibilities of perception concerning these circumstances. In exploiting these possibilities, the reader is stimulated to a form of activity that B. Ritchie, in another context, has described as follows:

> The solution to this paradox is to find some ground for a distinction between "surprise" and "frustration." Roughly, the distinction can be made in terms of the effects which the two

kinds of experiences have upon us. Frustration blocks or checks activity. It necessitates new orientation for our activity, if we are to escape the *cul de sac*. Consequently, we abandon the frustrating object and return to blind impulsive activity. On the other hand, surprise merely causes a temporary cessation of the exploratory phase of the experience, and a recourse to intense contemplation and scrutiny. In the latter phase the surprising elements are seen in their connection with what has gone before, with the whole drift of the experience, and the enjoyment of these values is then extremely intense ... any aesthetic experience tends to exhibit a continuous interplay between "deductive" and "inductive" operations.[30]

Now it does sometimes occur in this chapter that the expectations aroused by the headings are fulfilled. At such moments, the text seems banal,[31] for when the reader has adjusted himself to the nonfulfillment of his expectations, he will view things differently when they *are* fulfilled. The reason for this is easy to grasp. If the text of the column does not connect up with the heading, the reader must supply the missing links. His participation in the intention of the text is thus enhanced. If the text does fulfill the expectations aroused by the heading, no removing of gaps is required of the reader and he feels the 'let-down' of banality. In this way, the textual pattern in this chapter arouses continual conflicts with the reader's own modes of perception, and, as the author has completely withdrawn from this montage of possibilities, the reader is given no guidance as to how to resolve the conflicts. But it is through these very conflicts, and the confrontation with the array of different possibilities, that the reader of such a text is given the impression that something does happen to him.

It is perhaps not by chance that in this chapter the Homeric parallel has shrunk to the barest recollection, for the basic schema of composition is determined not by the scattering of news to all winds, but by the manner in which this scattered news is received. Joyce makes his theme out of that which did not concern Homer, and this also reveals something of the strategy of literary allusions that Joyce used in *Ulysses*.

A highlight of the experiments in style is the chapter Joyce originally called "Circe"—often designated as "Walpurgis Night." This presents scenes of 'nighttown' Dublin in a series of dialogues in dramatic form. The very use of this form automatically precludes any long stretches of narrative. If one regards the grouping together of events as a basic element of narrative, it would seem as though here the novel is in fact trying to free itself from this basic condition. Even where there is some narration, it is in the form of stage directions, which deprives it of its real narrative character. However, despite its lay-out the chapter can scarcely be called a play at all. The monologues, dialogues, stage directions, exits and entrances it consists of have almost completely lost their dramatic function. The conflicts between the characters end as abruptly as they began, and the cast of characters grows bigger and bigger, for it is not only the characters in the novel that take part in the play—we are also suddenly confronted with Lord Tennyson[32] and Edward VII,[33] the gas-jet whistles,[34] the retriever barks,[35] the voices of all the damned and those of all the blessed ring out,[36] and the end of the world—a two-headed octopus—speaks with a Scottish accent.[37]

The unremitting expansion of the cast is combined with the most extraordinary dialogues. In dramatic dialogue characters generally aim at influencing one another, but here this basic function is carried to extremes. When, at the beginning, Bloom is surrounded by different partners and is confronted with events of the past and present he assumes the form that is being alluded to.[38] Sometimes this tendency is taken to absurd lengths—as in the scene with Bella Cohen, the whore-mistress, when he changes into a woman and creeps timidly under the sofa in order to play a subservient role opposite Bella, who meanwhile has swollen up into a masculine monster.[39] The effect of dramatic dialogue here is so exaggerated that Bloom simply falls into the role assigned to him by his partner. This speedy compliance is not without its problems for the partners either, for Bloom's change of form does not exactly increase their security as regards the process of acting and reacting.

Such scenes show clearly that the dramatic elements are no longer part of any dramatic structure, so that the 'play' rapidly divorces itself from its own 'genre.' While the narrative residue is confined to mere setting of the scene, the dramatic text loses all dramatic teleology. The reader is simply confronted with what is said 'on stage,' and in view of the erosion both of narrative and dramatic forms here, he will feel that the effects of these dialogues get more and more out of control. Consequently, he will be inclined to regard the whole thing as a ridiculous fantasy.

The question is, though, what constitutes the fantasy? While the ramifications of the 'action' become ever more unpredictable, the figure of Bloom becomes ever more dominant. And this figure is shown from a variety of quite astonishing angles. At the very beginning there is a significant, if somewhat indirect allusion to this process, for the stage direction describes Bloom walking through Dublin in the darkness, and looking in convex and concave mirrors which continually change his appearance.[40] This is the theme that is developed throughout the chapter. What Bloom is seems to depend on the perspective from which he is viewed, and his mirror image depends on his environment at the time. It is not surprising then that in the course of the night Bloom becomes Lord Mayor of Dublin[41] and, indeed, the illustrious hero of the whole nation.[42] The beautiful women of Dublin's upper crust go into ecstasies over him[43] and, in the passion of their hero-worship, many commit suicide.[44] However, these same women also take part in a court scene, accusing Bloom of perverse conduct.[45] The question remains open as to whether Bloom is projecting his own feelings onto the accusers, or is trying to rid himself of these feelings by ascribing them to others. In such indeterminate situations, all statements are potential revelations of character. There are innumerable examples of this kind, and if we wanted to list them all, we should virtually have to retell the whole chapter.

The basis of this expansion of Bloom appears to consist of two factors, the one rather more obvious than the other. To deal with the more obvious factor first: in nighttown, everything becomes real for Bloom that is omitted, concealed, or repressed in his daily life. If these aspects of himself are given the same degree of reality as the others, then his life up to now will appear in a somewhat different light. Everyday life, it would seem, has made him into a fragmented character, and only now, in nighttown, can this character once more take on its full potentiality. An obvious case, one might assume, for psychoanalysis. But to preclude any premature analysis, Joyce has already parodied this type of interpretation through the medical student Buck Mulligan, in one of the earlier scenes of the chapter.[46] It seems, then, that the emergence of Bloom's hidden selves is not to be viewed as a symptom of repression, or as a way around the censorship imposed by the superego, but rather as an attempt to realize the potential of a character which in everyday life can never be anything more than partially realized.

This potential becomes richer and richer with the great variety of forms that the hitherto familiar character of Bloom adopts. And, conversely, if one wished to identify the Bloom of everyday life, one would be obliged more and more to pare down this rich virtual character. The everyday Bloom is merely a collection of individual moments in the course of his life—a collection which is infinitely smaller than that of the unlimited possibilities of the Bloom that might be. In the "Circe" chapter, it seems as though each Bloom character is simply a starting-point for a new character, and he himself is present only as the dynamic force producing, linking, and invalidating manifestations of his own potential.

We must now consider how this indeterminate force is translated into all these determinate, if limited forms, and the answer lies in the second, less obvious, factor characterizing the "Circe" chapter. Whatever Bloom reveals of himself is revealed because he is in a particular situation; the forms of his character arise out of changing contexts of life, and so each form is bound to a particular perspective—indeed, this is the only way in which the potential can be realized. With each situation, the character is displayed under specific circumstances, and the faster these change and the more impenetrable the sequence of the individual situations, the more abundant will be the array of possibilities through which the character can reveal itself.

We can now see clearly the function of the extraordinary mode of presentation in this chapter. The drastic reduction of narrative and the abandonment of dramatic coherence intensify the isolation of the individual situations. The disconnectedness virtually makes each one an end in itself, and the reality of the chapter consists in the change from one situation, and hence one manifestation of character, to another. This process is supported by the stage directions—the narrative residue—which relegate the reality of the town of Dublin to a mere theatrical setting. When the obtrusive reality of environment has been cancelled out, the character is inevitably abstracted from all outside restrictions and left free to develop its vast array of possibilities.[47] However, if the unreality of a changing character is to be presented as the reality of this chapter, then it is essential that the reader should constantly be prevented from joining up the patterns of the text. And precisely because there are so many patterns in this text, coupled with the particular expectations which each produces, the omission of connecting links gives rise to a greater degree of reader-provocation than is normal even in this highly provocative book. Here we have dramatic forms with no dramatic intention; we have narrative traces of an author, but he has concealed himself almost completely behind stage directions that serve no stage and head in no direction. The whole chapter seems to drift on unpredictable tides, and if it is to be brought to anchor, then the only weight heavy and steady enough is that of Bloom's potential character. This, however, seems like some sort of fantastic hallucination, for such a reversal of the possible and the factual simply does not correspond to our own experiences, but "... we should never talk about anything if we were limited to talking about those experiences with which we coincide, since speech is already a separation."[48] If one considers the multifarious potential of Bloom as a fantasy, one is already entering into a kind of trap. For such an impression—bordering on a judgment—implies that one knows all about the difference between reality and possibility. Here such differences are extremely blurred—though whether the ultimate effect of this blurring is to perplex or to illuminate must depend on the reactions of the individual reader. What can be said, though, is that an hallucination arising out of pure nonsense would certainly lack any sort of tension, whereas this chapter can scarcely be described as lacking in tension. The high degree of indeterminacy ensures a variety of tensions which, in their turn, will lead the reader to recall to mind—and possibly to see in a different light—all that he had previously learned about Bloom.

This collection of memories is almost certain to be conjured up as a background to the "Circe" chapter. In them the reader will seek the connecting principle denied him, but whatever he may find there, every manifestation of Bloom's character prior to the "Circe" chapter is bound now to seem like the faintest shadow of the vast potential. Who, then, is the real Bloom? Is he what is manifested, or is he the possible? At one point Stephen remarks: "… the fundamental and the dominant are separated by the greatest possible interval."[49] If we take the fundamental as the potential and the dominant as the manifestations we have in a nutshell the 'argument' of "Circe." Bloom, unlike the traditional character in a novel, has no identity but only a "constitutive instability"[50] which enables him to change character as often as he changes situation. The only enduring feature of Bloom is his changeability. Against this background, the conventional assumption that man can be defined in terms of actions, reactions, urges, fantasies, and embodiments of consciousness appears as pure myth.

There remains the question of the Homeric allusion. Harry Levin's observation that the *Odyssey* and *Ulysses* are parallels "that never meet,"[51] applies to this chapter even more than to most others. While Ulysses's friends were turned into swine by Circe, he himself was able to resist the sorcery thanks to the magic plant Moly given to him by Hermes. Ulysses remained himself because he was able to resist Circe's witchcraft. Bloom becomes himself by being transformed into the possibilities of his own character. Transformation means reduction in the *Odyssey*, and expansion in *Ulysses*.

Of a quite different sort is the stylistic experiment in the chapter originally called "Ithaca," which is of particular interest since it deals with the theme of homecoming. This archetypal situation is presented here as an uninterrupted sequence of questions and answers involving the main characters. To all appearances this interrogation is conducted by an anonymous narrator, who more or less asks himself what Bloom and Stephen think, do, feel, intend, communicate, mean etc., and then proceeds, himself, to give answers that are as wide-ranging as they are detailed. But what exactly is the purpose of this inquiry, and why should the narrator be asking all the questions, since he appears to know all the answers anyway?

The effect of the mode of presentation in this chapter is that it seems constantly to place a barrier between the reader and the events of Bloom's nocturnal homecoming that are to be narrated; instead of describing these events, it appears to be continually interrupting them. In this way, the characters in the novel seem to fade into the distance—especially since each question is assigned an answer which is so loaded with precise detail that the reader's comprehension is in danger of being utterly swamped. This tends to divert the reader's attention away from the events and onto the curious nature of this question-and-answer process. For, obviously, the intention of the chapter must lie in this and not in the details of the nocturnal events. But if the mode of presentation sets aside rather than describes the events, and obtrudes on the reader instead of orientating him, then the only justification for this 'going against the grain' must be that it exposes something which generally would be obscured by the mode of presentation. Let us consider an example. When Bloom comes home, he puts some water on the stove because he wants to have a shave. The question-and-answer process now concerns the boiling of the water:

> What concomitant phenomenon took place in the vessel of liquid by the agency of fire?
> The phenomenon of ebullition. Fanned by a constant updraught of ventilation between the kitchen and the chimneyflue, ignition was communicated from the faggots of precombustible fuel to polyhedral masses of bituminous coal, containing in compressed mineral form the foliated fossilised decidua of primeval forests which had in turn derived their vegetative existence from the sun, primal source of heat (radiant), transmitted through omnipresent luminiferous diathermanous ether. Heat (convected), a mode of motion developed by such combustion, was constantly and increasingly conveyed from the source of calorification to the liquid contained in the vessel, being radiated through the uneven unpolished dark surface of the metal iron, in part reflected, in part absorbed, in part transmitted, gradually raising the temperature of the water from normal to boiling point, a rise in temperature expressible as the result of an expenditure of 72 thermal units needed to raise 1 pound of water from 50° to 212° Fahrenheit.[52]

The amount of scientific data—in this chapter a typical feature which becomes even more complicated elsewhere—shows how difficult it is to give the required reason for the phenomenon in question. An impression akin to fantasy is evoked by the chain of cause and effect which, instead of going straight back to the primal cause, seems only to bring out more and more dependent factors. The more precise the description of these factors, the further into the distance recedes the primal cause and the more aware we become of the unexplainability of what is to be explained. As the narrator asks more and more questions, the answers demonstrate not his knowledge so much as the unobtainability of the right answers—and this is emphasized by the very preciseness of what *is* known. Thus the tendency underlying this question-and-answer process is one that aims at showing the degree of indeterminability inherent in all phenomena. It is scarcely surprising then that new questions are constantly thrown up which are meant to limit the amount of indeterminacy, but instead—thanks to their very precision—in fact increase it.

One's immediate reaction to the mass of scientific detail offered in answer to often quite banal questions is bewilderment. And this is so because a simple process is given a precise description. Obviously, then, our normal conception of such processes must be less precise and consequently seems to be straightforward. Why should it be made complicated? Perhaps in order to show the extent to which our knowledge and our decisions are based primarily on pragmatic considerations? However, it is only in this way that we can in fact form conceptions of everyday phenomena. The question-and-answer process makes us aware that the degree of indeterminacy is irreducible, thus indicating that all the semi-consistent conceptions we have of everyday phenomena can only become conceptions because they ignore the unexplainability of reality. They are, in this sense, a fiction.

Now if indeterminacy is only to be removed by means of fiction, the reader finds the ground cut away from beneath his feet whenever he realizes this. The "Ithaca" chapter keeps maneuvering him into a position from which he can escape only by taking up a definite attitude. He might decide that the chain of ironic answers forms a parody of scientific pedantry. But, as Northrop Frye states in another context, the ironic solution is: "the negative pole of the allegorical one. Irony presents a human conflict which ... is unsatisfactory and incomplete unless we see in it a significance beyond itself.... What that significance is, irony does not say: it leaves that question up to the reader or audience."[53] This is the sort of irony we find in the "Ithaca" chapter, which uses its ironic elements to give the reader responsibility for finding his own solution. This, of course, involves interpreting, and in order to ensure that interpretation be kept in its proper perspective, certain warning signals are built into the text. To the question: "What qualifying considerations allayed his [i.e., Bloom's] perturbations?" comes the answer: "The difficulties of interpretation since the significance of any event followed its occurrence as variably as the acoustic report followed the electrical discharge and of counterestimating against an actual loss by failure to interpret the total sum of possible losses proceeding originally from a successful interpretation."[54]

The main problem of interpretation, then, lies in the fact that the meaning of any one event is incalculably variable. The image of the electrical discharge, which disperses its sound waves in all directions, shows that every event, as soon as it happens, sets up a whole spectrum of meanings. If we try to extract one of these meanings and pass it off as *the* meaning of the event, then automatically we are shutting out all the other meanings.

Normally we understand by a successful interpretation one that conveys a specific meaning. But according to the answer given here, an interpretation can only be successful if it takes into account the "possible losses" caused by interpretation—in other words, if it succeeds in returning to the phenomenon interpreted its whole spectrum of possible meanings. And this, as the answer makes clear, is difficult.

Meanings have a heuristic character which, particularly in these scientifically couched answers, bring out the many-sidedness of the phenomena described. In such a description, the phenomena will appear all the richer in meaning if no one meaning dominates. In the "Ithaca" chapter, aspects are not static but seem to be moving, offering an infinitely wider range of perspectives than could be offered if the author were merely to present the reader with his own classified interpretation of the phenomenon. And however confused the reader may feel through this bewildering multiplicity, at least he now has the chance of experiencing for himself something of the essential character of the phenomena. The heightened indeterminacy enables him to view so many different aspects from so many different standpoints, and from the interaction of these aspects and perspectives he himself continually and dynamically formulates the meaning. In this way it is possible for the reader to experience the phenomenon more as itself than as the expression of something else.

Joyce called this chapter "Ithaca." But what sort of homecoming is this? For Ulysses it meant the end of his adventurous journey, with all its attendant dangers and sufferings, and also his reckoning with the suitors; but for Bloom the homecoming passes with innumerable trivial acts and a fantastic, if impotent, condemnation of all Molly's lovers. No one is excepted from this universal anathema; it applies ultimately to marriage as an institution and even to Bloom himself. "What then remains after this holocaust? Only himself with his desires—not as husband or householder but as Leopold Bloom, an Einziger with no Eigentum."[55] Yet again, then, we have in the Homeric allusion a parallel which, if anything, runs in the opposite direction from the original, showing up the individuality of Bloom against the background of what the reader might expect from the archetypal homecoming.

The stylistic experiments of *Ulysses* end with Molly Bloom's much discussed interior monologue, which has the difficult task of bringing to an end an action which essentially cannot be ended. Here the old familiar problem of how a novel is to end appears in its most radical form. The end cannot be presented as a completion, for whose completion should it denote? The conventional rounding-off is clearly impossible here, and so too is its companion piece, the slow fade-out: for after what the experiments have revealed, this would be nothing but a sign of resignation and, in the long run, a meaning grafted on. Joyce had resolved that he would finish the novel with the word "Yes,"[56] and whatever feelings one may have about this intention, the tenor of the whole is one of affirmation. Thus the end had to incorporate the movement of the novel as a whole, enabling the reader to forget that it was the end.

Molly Bloom as the Penelope of *Ulysses*, closes an action that began with Telemachus. It is not only in this external sense that we have a movement doubling back on itself; the interior monologue also shows how a return to memory becomes a new present. The total lack of punctuation suggests a continuum. The ego is united with itself, addressing to itself its own remembered past, and from this world of private reference, the reader is to a large extent excluded. To him, this ego appears less as a continuum than as a kaleidoscopic juggling of fragmentary facets. The framework of the monologue is given by a number of external details. Molly notes that Bloom has come home, has obviously brought someone with him, and finally goes to bed. The alarm clock tells her the time, and in the pale light of early morning she sees the flowers on the wallpaper, which remind her of stars.[57] The external impulses keep losing themselves in the memories they evoke, and these in turn broaden out into events that have not taken place. The present of this nocturnal hour is also overshadowed by a different present, and yet remembered past and existing present are not confronted one with the other; instead, what is remembered actually becomes the present simply because it has been freed from the conditions that originally called it into being. It takes on an existence of its own. But in contrast to its original state, the past now is liberated from all restrictions of time and space, and so situations flow into one another elliptically, regaining the openness of outcome which they had been deprived of long ago in the past.

Here, then, we have the first characteristic of the monologue. Not only does it bring back past life but it also frees it from its past determinacy. Individual situations which had formed links in the chain of the course of life now become open again, once more assuming their inherent richness of potential. The monologue eradicates the teleology of this course of life. It does not convey past and present in the style of an autobiography that is to deliver the meaning of the life concerned, but it shows that the life concerned is like a chain of coincidences if one bears in mind all the possibilities that were inherent in the situations before they became linked together. Once they are released from their specific life-order, situations can be seen through the perspectives of other situations which, through limitations of time and space in 'real' life, had not even the remotest connection. Thus the past remembered suggests completely new combinations, and Molly's own life comes back to her with a surplus of possibilities which can at least give the illusion of a different life-order.

Just like the other stylistic patterns in *Ulysses*, the interior monologue here breaks situations up into fragments and withholds from the reader any principle that might bind them together. In view of this disconnectedness, all events of the past, all future wishes, all lost opportunities are placed on the same level, so that Molly's life, as she recalls it, appears to be in a constant state of transformation. But what is transformed into what? Normally in a novel we are able to define the changes and to hold onto the similarities as our connecting-points, but here there seems only to be perplexity. If the remembered past were brought back as a sort of compensation for frustrated desires, then one could orientate Molly's memories through her particular situation at this particular hour of the night. And if it is a matter of returning to that stage in the past where it was still an unresolved present, then we should have a constant unwinding of retrospective possibilities—like a film being run backward. But neither of these standpoints is clearly discernible in Molly's monologue. She does not seem to be looking back at the past from the standpoint of the present, or to be returning to the past in order to gaze at her situation at five o'clock this morning. As a person, in fact, she seems to disappear behind the richness of her own life. The more indeterminate her character threatens to become, the more dynamic is the impression we have of her life: dynamic, because the reader is confronted with more and more viewpoints to which the individual facets are to be related, or into which they can be transformed. As the monologue does not accentuate any one organizing principle behind all the transformations, these convey an impression of continual expansion—and indeed suggest the inexhaustibility of the past—precisely because there is no point of convergence. The reader finds himself constantly driven by the urge to group things together, to unravel the tangle, but any attempt to do so will tend to reflect his own personal preferences rather than any supposed 'objective' meaning. But perhaps the meaning is the reflection of these preferences.

There remains the question of the Homeric parallel. With the past returning into the present and the present releasing the past from its determinacy there arises the idea of the recurrent cycle. Molly would then be even more than Penelope—she would be Mother Earth herself. But her monologue by no means fulfills the conditions of the mythic cycle. It lacks that essential element—the fact that when things have passed through all the different stages and forms of their realization, they return once more to themselves. It is true that at the end Molly returns to the point where she began—she recalls the first love scene with Bloom—but even the recollected love scenes in this monologue are far more like serial variations than a cyclic return. Molly cannot be reduced to any of her aspects, or even to her love-memories. Nowhere does her whole being come to light, but it is this very emerging of aspects that brings out the driving force which constitutes the inner being. And it is only fitting that the interior monologue should end the novel in a form which sets a life free from all the restrictions of—precisely—its form.

III

The Function of the Experiments in Style

The implication of a novel written in several different styles is that the view expressed by each style is to be taken only as one possible facet of everyday reality. The accumulation of facets has the effect of making these seem like a mere suggestion to the reader as to how he might observe reality. The perspectives provided by the various chapters of the novel abruptly join up, overlap, are segmented, even clash, and through their very density they begin to overtax the reader's vision. The density of the presentational screen, the confusing montage and its interplay of perspectives, the invitation to the reader to look at identical incidents from many conflicting points of view—all this makes it extremely difficult for the reader to find his way. The novel refuses to divulge any way of connecting up this interplay of perspectives, and so the reader is forced to provide his own liaison. This has the inevitable consequence that reading becomes a process of selection, with the reader's own imagination providing the criteria for the selection. For the text of *Ulysses* only offers the conditions that make it possible to conceive of this everyday world—conditions which each reader will exploit in his own way.

What does the achievement of the various modes of presentation consist of? First, one can say that they bring to bear a form of observation which underlies the very structure of perception. For we "have the experience of a world, not understood as a system of relations which wholly determine each event, but as an open totality the synthesis of which is inexhaustible.... From the moment that experience—that is, the opening on to our *de facto* world—is recognized as the beginning of knowledge, there is no longer any way of distinguishing a level of *a priori* truths and one of factual ones, what the world must necessarily be and what it actually is."[58] Through their countless offshoots, the different styles of *Ulysses* preclude any meaning directed toward integration, but they also fall into a pattern of observation that contains within itself the possibility of a continual extension. It is the very abundance of perspectives that conveys the abundance of the world under observation.

The effect of this continual change is dynamic, unbounded as it is by any recognizable teleology. From one chapter to the next the 'horizon' of everyday life is altered and constantly shifted from one area to another through the links which the reader tries to establish between the chapter styles. Each chapter prepares the 'horizon' for the next, and it is the process of reading that provides the continual overlapping and interweaving of the views presented by each of the chapters. The reader is stimulated into filling the 'empty spaces' between the chapters in order to group them into a coherent whole. This process, however, has the following results: The conceptions of everyday life which the reader forms undergo constant modifications in the reading process. Each chapter provides a certain amount of expectation concerning the next chapter. However, the gaps of indeterminacy which open up between the chapters tend to diminish the importance of these expectations as a means of orientating the reader. As the process continues, a 'feedback' effect is bound to develop, arising from the new chapter and reacting back upon the preceding, which under this new and somewhat unexpected impression is subjected to modifications in the reader's mind. The more frequently the reader experiences this effect, the more cautious and the more differentiated will be his expectations, as they arise through his realization of the text. Thus what has just been read modifies what had been read before, so that the reader himself operates the 'fusion of the horizons', with the result that he produces an experience of reality which is real precisely because it happens, without being subjected to any representational function. Reality, then, is a process of realization necessitating the reader's involvement, because only the reader can bring it about. This is why the chapters are not arranged in any sequence of situations that might be complementary to one another; in fact, the unforeseen difference of style rather seems to make each chapter into a turning-point as opposed to a continuation. And as the whole novel consists of such turning-points the process of reading unfolds itself as a continual modification of all previous conceptions, thus inverting the traditional teleological structure of the novel.

IV

The Archetypes

What part do the Homeric allusions play in the overall effect of the work? Do they, or do the archetypes recognizable in *Ulysses*, offer a means of comprehending the novel and ultimately giving it a representative meaning after all? It must be said that the intention underlying the stylistic experiments does not seem to point in that direction. The Homeric allusions vary in density and directness. It is worth noting that they always take on an ironic note when they are clear and direct; Bloom's cigar as Ulysses's spear is a typical example.[59] Such ironic traits draw attention to differences, and however these may be interpreted they are bound to prevent us from equating *Ulysses* with the Homeric parallel. At the same time, the allusions— assuming we take note of them in the first place—draw the archaic world into the everyday life of the novel, though the outline of the ancient story cannot be regarded as encompassing this life.

We might say that the main function of the allusions is to draw attention to the virtual features of the two worlds. At times the Homeric myth is even inverted, with the episodes from the *Odyssey* to be understood as pointers to specific empirical or everyday aspects of life. Everyday appearances are not to be referred back to some underlying meaning; we proceed from the myth and its meaning and see the variety of appearances into which it can be broken up. Things which remain implicit or even totally concealed in the *Odyssey* are revealed in *Ulysses*, and the change of perspective—from Homer to the present, and from the present back to the archaic world—enables both past and present to illuminate one another.

Through the allusions is projected a background that embraces the whole of European literature from Homer to Shakespeare. The reader is provoked into a process of recognition, for recognition, like grouping, is part of his natural disposition and is an elementary activity in reading. As he recognizes the implications of the allusions, he tries to equate them with the events now being set before him, but he finds that they do not actually coincide. There is just enough common ground to make him aware of the differences, and the process of equating and differentiating is one that will be both disturbing and stimulating.

If *Ulysses* does not hark back to the *Odyssey*, and Joyce does not—so to speak—rise out of Homer, then the various transformations which the reader feels constantly forced to experience will not cease with the establishment of a common pattern. As we have already seen, the whole structure and stylistic texture of the novel is geared to such transformations, and a common pattern, of whatever type, would run counter to its basic intentions. The allusions offer a background which, in its own way, remains as fluid as the foreground it sets off, and this very fluidity is the fundamental prerequisite for the effect of the novel.

What of the archetypes themselves? To what extent can they be described as elements of a recurrent myth? The homecoming, the city, and the quest[60]—these are three archetypes which constitute an important structural pattern in the novel and which make *Ulysses* into a sort of glorified epic (the city being a considerably rarer archetypal ingredient of epic literature). In fact, the closest link between *Ulysses* and the *Odyssey* is the homecoming, although Bloom's homecoming does, of course, take place within the city. The quest already shows external differences, insofar as Telemachus searched for his father, while Bloom searches for his son. In the *Odyssey* there is no equivalent to the city as "new Bloomusalem."[61] If we consider the closest link—the homecoming—we will find, just as we did with the direct Homeric allusions, that the similarities serve in fact to point up the differences. For Ulysses the homecoming means the end of his sufferings, whereas for Bloom—the "conscious reactor against the void incertitude,"[62] as he is called in the "Ithaca" chapter—it brings nothing but a heightened sensitivity to the unforeseeable; even more significantly, there is no recognizable parallel anywhere in the novel between characters or archetypal situations. But since the title indicates a connection, we automatically become aware of the differences.

If one looks at Bloom against the background of Ulysses, one is immediately struck by two things: the difference in stature between the humble citizen of Dublin and the Homeric hero, and the many features of Bloom's conduct that either go beyond or fall short of what we know of Ulysses's character. Bearing in mind that Joyce considered Ulysses himself to be the most comprehensive specimen of human conduct,[63] one must also say that Bloom adds a few variants of his own to this 'perfection'—though of course without ever becoming more 'perfect' than Ulysses. Clearly, Bloom lacks most of Ulysses's characteristics, and vice versa, but however far Bloom may fall below the exalted standards of the Homeric hero, the very allusion of the title makes us think of Bloom as a Ulysses, and so offsets those elements of the character which prevailing conventions prevented Homer from dealing with. Human conduct in Homer appears rigidly stylized against that of the everyday Dubliner, while Bloom's conduct (and that of the other characters, too) is as fluid as the other is rigid. And so it would seem that the Homeric parallel is drawn, not to demonstrate the hopeless decline of the modern world compared with its former state, but to communicate the enormous variety of possibilities of human conduct. By evoking and simultaneously deforming archetypal patterns, Joyce succeeds in conveying and throwing into relief the uniqueness of Bloom as a citizen of the modern world. The Homeric archetype provides a starting-point for this individualization of Joyce's Ulysses [i.e., Bloom]. Just as a cartoonist takes an existing face and then distorts its features in order to bring out its uniqueness, so too does Joyce (though obviously in a far less obtrusive manner) take an existing form and manipulate it this way and that in order to convey its singularity. Indeed, it is the very fact that Bloom can be pulled and pushed in this way that sets him apart from the ideality of Ulysses and makes him recognizable as an individual human being, with all the complications and uncertainties thereby involved. The archetype is the general mould; the form Joyce extracts from that mould is the unique character of Bloom.

There is, then, a form of interaction between the Homeric archetype and its modern counterpart. As Joyce evolves constantly changing patterns from the former, so Ulysses's reactions assume a paradigmatic character, and the homecoming, for instance, is transformed into an, 'ideal' homecoming. However, one must bear in mind the fact that the "archetype"[64] does not exist in itself, but must be brought into existence by a realization. It is, so to speak, an empty frame that requires the concrete powers of style and language to provide the picture. The archetype then, can take on as many forms as there are forms of presentation, so that we cannot really say even that the homecoming in the *Odyssey* is the archetype. It is only one rendering among many possible renderings, and, in the light of all the variations apparent in the novel, it becomes retrospectively as restricted as they are. The archetype as such remains a structured blank that bears all potential realizations within itself and provides the basis for all its own subsequent variations.

Clearly, if archetypal situations are potentially subject to so many different presentations, then no one presentation can claim representative significance. For this insight, again we are indebted to the Homeric parallel: by reducing the *Odyssey* homecoming to the level of one idealized realization, *Ulysses* shows all its limitations—and the same applies to the other archetypes of city and quest. Dublin is no heavenly Jerusalem, but as "Bloomusalem"[65] it is the place of exile of one of the unredeemed; the quest is characterized by the uncertainty of what is found, for although Bloom and Stephen finish under one roof, Molly's thoughts, are already on relations with the young 'intellectual,'[66] Bloom's son. In each case, the recurrent archetypal situation lacks the expected archetypal fulfillment—it is left open-ended.

The function of the archetype in relation to the presentational strategy of the novel is, then, to offer a kind of framework. Homecoming, city, and quest are the frames within which the picture of everyday life can be put together. This, of course, does not mean that the composition is determined by the frame. The mode of presentation ensures that the countless literary and historical allusions will not be marshalled into a single cut-and-dried meaning—not for the sake of making the allusions appear meaningless, but purely in order to preserve the infinite potential of their meaning.

V
The Reader's Quest and the Formation of Illusion

If the archetypes provide the action with a frame, the different styles and allusions to literature, both ancient and modern, give the reader more than enough scope to piece together his own picture. David Daiches has observed that: "If Joyce could coin one kaleidoscopic word with an infinite series of meanings, a word saying everything in one instant yet leaving its infinity of meanings reverberating and mingling in the mind, he would have reached his ideal."[67] Certainly this is the direction in which Joyce was striving, and as the limitations of each separate meaning are uncovered, giving rise to new meanings, so the reader is made to feel the overall inaccessibility of the events and characters in question. Any presentation implies selection, and any selection implies omission. Here the omissions lead to new selections in the form of new styles, but as the styles and selections increase, so does the range of implication and omission. The more determinate the presentation, the more 'reality' there is to catch up on, but in his very efforts to catch up, the reader produces in himself the awareness that the world he is trying to comprehend transcends the acts of comprehension of which he is capable.

The composition of *Ulysses* mirrors this impression. Edmund Wilson has summed up both the reader's impression and the structure of the novel as follows: "I doubt whether any human memory is capable, on a first reading, of meeting the demands of 'Ulysses.' And when we reread it, we start in at any point, as if it were indeed something solid like a city which actually existed in space and which could be entered from any direction."[68] The reader is virtually free to choose his own direction, but he will not be able to work his way through every possible perspective, for the number of these is far beyond the capacity of any one man's naturally selective perception. If the novel sometimes gives the impression of unreality, this is not because it presents unreality, but simply because it swamps us with aspects of reality that overburden our limited powers of absorption. We are forced to make our own selections from the perspectives offered and, consequently, in accordance with our own personal disposition, to formulate ideas that have their roots in *some* of the signs and situations confronting us.

This form of reading is predetermined by the novel itself, with its network of superimposed patterns that evoke constantly changing 'pictures' of everyday life. Each reading is a starting-point for the composition of such 'pictures', and indeed the whole process of reading *Ulysses* is a kind of composition. (The same, it is true, can be said of all reading, but in the case of this novel the demands made on the reader's creativity are far greater than normal.) No one picture is representative, and one cannot even say that any one pattern is in itself determinate or determinant, for the different sections of the text only go so far as to offer signs that can be grouped together to form a context. The patterns are, as it were, transitory units which are necessary if everyday life is to be experienced, but are in no way binding as to the nature of the experience.

Each 'picture' composed out of each pattern represents one possible meaning of the text concerned, but the reader will not be content to accept each 'picture' as an end in itself. He will search for a 'complete picture' of everyday life, and this is precisely what the novel withholds from him. The patterns offer him nothing but the conditions for and variations of the presentability of everyday life. There is no overriding tendency, and the mass of details presents itself to the reader to organize in accordance with his own acts of comprehension. This, in turn, demands a heightened degree of participation on the reader's part. The novel thus places itself in the category of "cool media,"[69] as McLuhan called those texts and other media which, through their indeterminacy, allow and even demand a high degree of participation.

Herein lies the main difference between *Ulysses* and the tradition of the novel. Instead of providing an illusory coherence of the reality it presents, this novel offers only a potential presentation, the working out of which has to be done actively by the reader. He is not led into a ready-made world of meaning, but is made to search for this world. Thus reading itself has an archetypal structure which, just like the archetypes in the text, is unable to lead to any defined goal. It is a quest which brings to the surface the possibility of any number of findings. Thus it is possible to discover many different 'pictures' of the everyday world, but they will never converge into a defined picture—and it is this very fact that compels the reader to continue his search. Even though he will never find the object of his search, on his way he will meet with a vast array of possible conceptions, through which the reality of everyday life will come alive in a corresponding number of ways. As these conceptions are not joined together, every picture remains representative of no more than one aspect of reality. The reading process unfolds as a "categorical aspection,"[70] in the sense that the aspects of reality that group together into a 'picture' are continually merging and diverging, so that the reader can experience that reality as he goes along, but being thus entangled in it he can never hope to encompass it all.

The reader, however, will still be continually tempted to try to establish some consistency in all the signs, patterns, fragments, etc. But whenever we establish consistency, "illusion takes over."[71] "Illusion is whatever is fixed or definable, and reality is best understood as its negation: whatever reality is, it's not *that*."[72] The truth of this statement becomes apparent as one reads

Ulysses. At first the inconsistency of the stylistic patterns and structures impels the reader to formulate illusions, because only by joining things together can he comprehend an unfamiliar experience. But even while he is in the process of linking things up, he is bringing into being all the other possibilities of the text that defy integration; and these in turn proceed to overshadow the consistency he had begun to establish, so that in the process of illusion-forming the reader also creates the latent destruction of those very illusions. He will begin to distrust the convenient patterns he has been building and will eventually himself perceive that they are nothing but the instruments he uses to grasp and pare down the mass of detail. Now the very fact that it is he who produces and destroys the illusions makes it impossible for him to stand aside and view 'reality' from a distance—the only reality for him to view is the one he is creating. He is involved in it, in precisely the same way that he gets involved in 'real life' situations. Thus for many Joyce readers, 'interpretation' is a form of refuge-seeking—an effort to reclaim the ground which has been cut from under their feet. Perhaps Bloom's attempts to instruct his wife contain the most succinct summary of Joyce's whole method:

> With what success had he attempted direct instruction? She followed not all, a part of the whole, gave attention with interest, comprehended with surprise, with care repeated, with greater difficulty remembered, forgot with ease, with misgiving remembered, rerepeated with error.
> What system had proved more effective?
> Indirect suggestion implicating self-interest.[73]

NOTES

1. For a detailed discussion of these two interpretations, see "Doing Things in Style," in this volume, pp. 179 ff. For a critical assessment of the Homeric parallel, see also A. Esch, "James Joyce und Homer, Zur Frage der Odyssee-Korrespondenzen im *Ulysses*," in *Lebende Antike* (Symposion für Rudolf Sühnel), ed. H. Meller und H.-J. Zimmermann (Berlin, 1967), pp. 423 ff.

2. Quoted by R. Ellmann, *James Joyce* (Oxford, 1966), p. 535.

3. It is the great merit of R. M. Adams's *Surface and Symbol: The Consistency of James Joyce's Ulysses* (New York, 1962) that he extracted this material from the novel and was able to identify it.

4. See also H. R. Jauss, "Nachahmungsprinzip und Wirklichkeitsbegriff in der Theorie des Romans von Diderot bis Stendhal," in *Nachahmung und Illusion* (Poetik und Hermeneutik, I), ed. H. R. Jauss (Munich, 1964), pp. 161 f. and 241 f.

5. N. Frye, *Anatomy of Criticism: Four Essays* (New York, [5]1967), p. 73.

6. T. S. Eliot, "Ulysses, Order and Myth," in *James Joyce: Two Decades of Criticism*, ed. S. Givens (New York, 1948), p. 201. (The essay originally appeared in 1923.)

7. E. Pound, *Literary Essays*, ed. T. S. Eliot (London, 1960), p. 406. (The essay on *Ulysses* originally appeared in 1922.)

8. "Welt-Alltag"—a term coined by H. Broch, *Dichten und Erkennen* (Zürich, 1955), p. 187, to designate June 16, 1904.

9. J. M. Murry, *The Problem of Style* (London, [9]1960), p. 65.

10. C. Lugowski, *Die Form der Individualität im Roman* (Berlin, 1932), p. 12.

11. Ibid., p. 206.

12. See also S. L. Goldberg, *The Classical Temper: A Study of James Joyce's Ulysses* (London, 1961), p. 288.

13. For details and bibliography see "Doing Things in Style," in this volume, pp. 180 ff.

14. Quoted by Ellmann, *James Joyce*, p. 490.

15. Joyce, *Ulysses* (London: The Bodley Head, 1937), pp. 369 f.

16. Ibid., p. 1.

17. Ibid., pp. 5, 9, 20.

18. These chapter headings are to be found in Joyce's 'note-sheets,' and he used them in grouping together his material. See A. W. Litz, *The Art of James Joyce: Method and Design in Ulysses and Finnegans Wake* (New York, 1964); for an assessment of their importance, see especially ibid., p. 39.

19. See Joyce, *Ulysses*, pp. 7 f.

20. Ibid., pp. 22 f.

21. Ibid.

22. Ibid., p. 22.

23. Ibid., p. 30.

24. Ibid., p. 33.

25. Ibid., p. 34.

26. Stephen is also conscious of this: "You find my words dark. Darkness is in our souls, do you not think? Flutier. Our souls, shamewounded by our sins, cling to us yet more, a woman to her lover clinging, the more the more." Ibid., p. 45.

27. E. Cassirer, *Philosophie der symbolischen Formen* (Darmstadt, [4]1964), III: 185.

28. Joyce, *Ulysses*, p. 45.

29. Ibid., p. 399.

30. B. Ritchie, "The Formal Structure of the Aesthetic Object," in *The Problems of Aesthetics*, ed. E. Vivas and M. Krieger (New York, 1965), pp. 230 f.

31. See Joyce, *Ulysses*, p. 118.

32. Ibid., p. 555.

33. Ibid., pp. 557 and 560.

34. Ibid., pp. 485 and 550.

35. Ibid., p. 567.

36. Ibid., p. 565.

37. Ibid., p. 481.

38. See, for instance, ibid., pp. 423 f., 433 f.

39. Ibid., pp. 500 f.

40. Ibid., p. 414.

41. Ibid., pp. 455 f.

42. Ibid., pp. 460 f.

43. Ibid., pp. 458 f.

44. Ibid., pp. 467 f.

45. Ibid., pp. 443 f.

46. Ibid., pp. 468 f.

47. F. Kermode, *The Sense of an Ending: Studies in the Theory of Fiction* (New York, 1967), p. 141, says with reference to a remark of Sartre's concerning characters in a novel:

"The characters ... ought surely to be 'centres of indeterminacy' and not the slaves of some fake omniscience." In the "Circe" chapter, Bloom's character is revealed most emphatically as a "centre of indeterminacy."

48. M. Merleau-Ponty, *Phenomenology of Perception*, transl. Colin Smith (New York, 1962), p. 337.

49. Joyce, *Ulysses*, p. 479.

50. This is the translation of a term used by Ortega y Gasset to describe the given nature of man. See details in Kermode, *Sense of an Ending*, pp. 140 f., footnote.

51. H. Levin, *James Joyce: A Critical Introduction* (New York, [2]1960), p. 71.

52. Joyce, *Ulysses*, p. 634.

53. N. Frye, "The Road of Excess," in *Myth and Symbol: Critical Approaches and Applications*, ed. B. Slote (Lincoln, [2]1964), p. 14.

54. Joyce, *Ulysses*, p. 637.

55. F. Budgen, *James Joyce and the Making of Ulysses* (Bloomington, 1960), p. 261.

56. See S. Gilbert, *James Joyce's Ulysses* (New York, [7]1960), p. 403, and also a statement of Joyce's quoted by A. W. Litz, *The Art of James Joyce*, p. 46.

57. See Joyce, *Ulysses*, p. 740.

58. Merleau-Ponty, *Phenomenology*, pp. 219 and 221.

59. For such parallels, see R. Ellmann, "The Divine Nobody," in *Twelve Original Essays on Great English Novelists*, ed. Ch. Shapiro (Detroit, 1960), pp. 244 f., esp. 247.

60. See N. Frye, *Anatomy of Criticism*, pp. 118 f. and 141.

61. Joyce, *Ulysses*, p. 461.

62. Ibid., p. 694.

63. See R. Ellmann, *Joyce*, p. 430.

64. N. Frye has a very different conception of the archetype. The most succinct definition I could find in his writings is in the essay "The Archetypes of Literature," which is reprinted in his collection of essays: *Fables of Identity: Studies in Poetic Mythology* (New York, 1963). "The myth is the central informing power that gives archetypal significance to the ritual and archetypal narrative to the oracle. Hence the myth is the archetype, though it might be convenient to say myth only when referring to narrative, and archetype when speaking of significance" (p. 15).

65. See Joyce, *Ulysses*, p. 461.

66. See also Gilbert, *James Joyce's Ulysses*, pp. 386 and 394.

67. D. Daiches, *The Novel and the Modern World* (Chicago, [4]1965), p. 129.

68. E. Wilson, *Axel's Castle: A Study in the Imaginative Literature of 1870–1930* (London: The Fontana Library, 1961), p. 169.

69. See M. McLuhan, *Understanding Media: The Extensions of Man* (New York, [3]1966), pp. 22 f.

70. For the use of this term in describing esthetic objects, see V. C. Aldrich, *Philosophy of Art* (Englewood Cliffs, 1963), pp. 21–24.

71. E. H. Gombrich, *Art and Illusion* (London, [2]1962), p. 278.

72. Frye, *Anatomy of Criticism*, pp. 169 f.

73. Joyce, *Ulysses*, pp. 647 f.

A. WALTON LITZ

Ithaca

If *Ulysses* is a crucial testing ground for theories of the novel, as it seems to have become, then the 'Ithaca' episode must be a *locus classicus* for every critic interested in the traditions of English and European fiction. Here the extremes of Joyce's art, and of fiction in general, are found in radical form: the tension between symbolism and realism, what Arnold Goldman has called the 'myth/fact paradox',[1] gives the episode its essential life. Joyce once told Frank Budgen that 'Ithaca' was his 'favourite episode', the 'ugly duckling of the book',[2] and his frequent references to the episode in his letters reveal a personal and artistic involvement seldom matched in his work on the other chapters. He was acutely aware that 'Ithaca' culminated his risky 'scorched earth' policy of constantly altering the novel's styles and narrative methods, so that 'the progress of the book is in fact like the progress of some sandblast', each successive episode leaving behind it 'a burnt up field'.[3] He also knew that the reader who had mastered the 'initial style' of the earliest episodes, that subtle blending of interior monologue and distanced description derived from *A Portrait of the Artist*, would prefer it 'much as the wanderer did who longed for the rock of Ithaca'.[4]

These defensive remarks were made in mid-1919, when Joyce felt compelled to justify the 'musical' techniques of 'Sirens', and they clearly reflect his anxiety at that moment in the composition of *Ulysses* when the life

---

From *James Joyce's Ulysses: Critical Essays.* © 1974 by The Regents of the University of California.

of the novel began to gravitate from external drama to the internal reality of the various styles and artifices. This clearcut shift in artistic aims midway through Joyce's work on *Ulysses* was somewhat masked by the final revisions, when he recast many of the earlier episodes in forms that satisfied his later sense of the novel's design;[5] but be attached so much importance to this transitional moment in the making of the novel that he once thought of writing an '*Entr'acte*' to celebrate the mid-point in the narrative,[6] and on a chart of the episodes sent to John Quinn in September 1920 the first nine episodes (through 'Scylla and Charybdis') are clearly separated from the last nine (beginning with 'Wandering Rocks').[7] just as the structural centre of *Ulysses* represents a turning point in the motions of Bloom and Stephen, the beginning of their tentative progress toward each other, so it announces a fundamental change in the novel's aesthetic ground-base. From 'Wandering Rocks' and 'Sirens' onward, the 'reality' to be processed into art is both the imitated human action and the rich artistic world already created in the earlier and plainer episodes. Technique tends more and more to become subject matter, and by the time we reach 'Ithaca' the form of the episode is as much the substance as the actual interchanges between Bloom and Stephen.

So both the action and the stylistic development of *Ulysses* reach a climax in 'Ithaca', which Joyce considered 'in reality the end as "Penelope" has no beginning, middle or end'.[8] Although he had a general sense of the novel's ending from the start of his work on it, and could refer easily to the 'Nostos' (the last three episodes) during the process of composition,[9] Joyce evidently had no clear notion of the local form of 'Ithaca' until 1919–20; yet long before any part of the episode reached paper he had unconsciously rehearsed the role 'Ithaca' was to play in a continuing debate on the aims of English and European fiction. It has often been noted that the two lectures Joyce gave at the Università Popolare of Trieste in 1912 established the twin frontiers of his art and looked forward to *Ulysses*.[10] He chose as his subjects Defoe and Blake, treating them as the ultimate masters of painstaking realism and the universal symbolism of spiritual 'correspondences'. But it has not been noted that the tags Joyce chose for his lectures, *verismo* and *idealismo*, were technical terms in a contemporary critical debate on the validity of the 'realistic' novel.[11] What Joyce did in his lectures was to liberate the terms from literary controversy and use them to describe two complementary methods for universalizing experience. One way toward completeness, as the editors of the Blake lecture remark (*CW*, 214), is through the overwhelming accretion of encyclopaedic detail: Robinson Crusoe is an archetypal figure—Joyce speaks of him as such—because we know him, like Bloom, in all the petty but revealing details of ordinary life.

Commenting on Defoe's *The Storm*, Joyce noted that the 'method is simplicity itself'.

> The book opens with an inquiry into the causes of winds, then recapitulates the famous storms in human story, and finally the narrative, like a great snake, begins to crawl slowly through a tangle of letters and reports.... The modern reader does a good deal of groaning before be reaches the conclusion, but in the end the object of the chronicler has been achieved. By dint of repetitions, contradictions, details, figures, noises, the storm has come alive, the ruin is visible.[12]

This is the technique of much of 'Ithaca', an accumulation of details which has no inherent 'aesthetic' limits but relies on the epic impact of overmastering fact. One can see the method in action in the growth of the notorious question-and-answer on the universal significance of water, where the exchange in the basic manuscript

> What in water did Bloom, carrying water, returning to the range, admire?
> Its universality: its equality and constancy to its nature in seeking its own level: its vastness in the ocean of Mercator's projector: its secrecy in springs, exemplified by the well by the hole in the wall at Ashtown gate: its healing virtues: its properties for cleansing, quenching thirst and fire, nourishing plant life: its strength in rigid hydrants: its docility in working millwheels, electric power stations, bleachworks, tanneries, scutchmills: its utility in canals, rivers, if navigable; its fauna and flora: its noxiousness in marshes, pestilential fens, faded flowers, stagnant pools in the waning moon.[13]

finally took this form:

> What in water did Bloom, waterlover, drawer of water, watercarrier returning to the range, admire?
> Its universality: its democratic equality and constancy to its nature in seeking its own level: its vastness in the ocean of Mercator's projection: its unplumbed profundity in the Sundam trench of the Pacific exceeding 8,000 fathoms: the restlessness of its waves and surface particles visiting in turn all points of its seaboard: the independence of its units: the variability of states of

sea: its hydrostatic quiescence in calm: its hydrokinetic turgidity
in neap and spring tides: its subsidence after devastation: its
sterility in the circumpolar icecaps, arctic and antarctic: its
climatic and commercial significance: its preponderance of 3 to 1
over the dry land of the globe: its indisputable hegemony
extending in square leagues over all the region below the
subequatorial tropic of Capricorn: the multisecular stability of its
primeval basin: its luteofulvous bed: its capacity to dissolve and
hold in solution all soluble substances including millions of tons
of the most precious metals: its slow erosions of peninsulas and
downward tending promontories: its alluvial deposits: its weight
and volume and density: its imperturbability in lagoons and
highland tarns: its gradation of colours in the torrid and
temperate and frigid zones: its vehicular ramifications in
continental lakecontained streams and confluent oceanflowing
rivers with their tributaries and transoceanic currents: gulfstream,
north and south equatorial courses: its violence in seaquakes,
waterspouts, artesian wells, eruptions, torrents, eddies, freshets,
spates, groundswells, watersheds, waterpartings, geysers,
cataracts, whirlpools, maelstroms, inundations, deluges,
cloudbursts: its vast circumterrestrial ahorizontal curve: its
secrecy in springs, and latent humidity, revealed by rhabdomantic
or hygrometric instruments and exemplified by the hole in the
wall at Ashtown gate, saturation of air, distillation of dew: the
simplicity of its composition, two constituent parts of hydrogen
with one constituent part of oxygen: its healing virtues: its
buoyancy in the waters of the Dead Sea: its persevering
penetrativeness in runnels, gullies, inadequate dams, leaks on
shipboard: its properties for cleansing, quenching thirst and fire,
nourishing vegetation: its infallibility as paradigm and paragon:
its metamorphoses as vapour, mist, cloud, rain, sleet, snow, hail:
its strength in rigid hydrants: its variety of forms in loughs and
bays and gulfs and bights and guts and lagoons and atolls and
archipelagos and sounds and fjords and minches and tidal
estuaries and arms of sea: its solidity in glaciers, icebergs, icefloes:
its docility in working hydraulic millwheels, turbines, dynamos,
electric power stations, bleachworks, tanneries, scutchmills: its
utility in canals, rivers, if navigable, floating and graving docks: its
potentiality derivable from harnessed tides or watercourses
falling from level to level: its submarine fauna and flora
(anacoustic, photophobe) numerically, if not literally, the

inhabitants of the globe: its ubiquity as constituting 90% of the human body: the noxiousness of its effluvia in lacustrine marshes, pestilential fens, faded flowerwater, stagnant pools in the waning moon. (671.26–672.38)

Here the initial passage was enlarged five-fold as it passed through successive typescripts and proofs, while the subject changed from the normal associations of Bloom's inquisitive mind to a conflation of that mind and the novel's 'epic' aims. Like Defoe's encyclopaedic treatment of the storm, Joyce's catalogue finally convinces 'by dint of repetitions, contradictions, details, figures', until it ultimately becomes the expression of some omniscient mind meditating on the universal virtues of water.

But if the Defoe lecture is filled with Joyce's admiration for a writer who, through accumulated data, can turn fact into myth or archetype, the lecture on Blake reveals his deep affinity with the visionary artist who can divine the universe in a blade of grass, who through symbolic correspondences can make 'each moment shorter than a pulse-beat ... equivalent in its duration to six thousand years' and can fly 'from the infinitely small to the infinitely large, from a drop of blood to the universe of stars' (*CW*, 222). Here the debt to Yeats's interpretations of Blake is obvious, and the theory of the epiphany is not far in the background. Like Whitman, Joyce possessed a talent which was both centripetal and centrifugal, tending toward both the symbolic moment and the scrupulous accumulation of 'fact': and these complementary impulses give 'Ithaca' its form and dynamism.

In speaking of the extremes of Joyce's art, it would be pointless to moderate or ignore their obsessive qualities. Both the symbolism and realism of 'Ithaca' have dimensions which are essentially private and disproportionate. Joyce's famous verification of Bloom's entrance into No. 7 Eccles street is a notorious example of a regard for 'realism' that goes far beyond the normal compact between author and reader:

Is it possible (Joyce wrote to his aunt Josephine) for an ordinary person to climb over the area railings of no 7 Eccles street, either from the path or the steps, lower himself down from the lowest part or the railings till his feet are within 2 feet or 3 of the ground and drop unhurt. I daw it done myself but by a man of rather athletic build. I require this information in detail in order to determine the wording of a paragraph.[14]

In the same way, many of the leading symbols in 'Ithaca' (such as urination) seem to have had more significance for the author than for the reader. Like

Henry James's *The Sacred Fount*, the 'Ithaca' episode relies so heavily on the author's obsessive techniques and themes that they approach self-parody; and although 'Ithaca' is richly comic in its general intent there are times when Joyce, like James, seems unaware of the grotesque effects he is creating. In a sense, 'fact' and the private symbol became substitutes for all those conventional supports of society and art and religion that Joyce had rejected.

These 'obsessive' qualities in 'Ithaca' really lie beyond the reach of conventional criticism, in the realm of psychoanalytic biography or some study of the creative process; they are reminders that most authors need more sanctions and correspondences than they can share with their audience (it is interesting that T. S. Eliot, in his 1956 lecture on 'The Frontiers of Criticism', used J. Livingston Lowes' *Road to Xanadu* and Joyce's *Finnegans Wake* to define the 'frontiers'). But we should not let Joyce's personal obsessions obscure one central fact: that Ulysses is a cross-roads in the history of prose fiction because it both exaggerates and harmonizes certain major tendencies that had marked the novel from its earliest appearances. Emerging in the seventeenth and eighteenth centuries from a convergence of myth (fables, 'Romance', moral tales) and fact (journals, diaries, 'news'), English fiction has always had a paradoxical relation to reality, as the fruitless attempts to separate 'Romance' from 'Novel' testify. If *Ulysses* is to be considered as a novel, rather than an 'anatomy' or some other hybrid form, it must be because the work is true to the fundamental paradox of the genre even while every aspect of the genre is being tested by parody and burlesque.

Perhaps it is a reluctance to accept this essential ambivalence of both the novel-form and *Ulysses* which lies behind the attempts of so many readers to press *Ulysses*—and especially the 'Ithaca' chapter—into some easy equation of 'either/or'. Either Joyce's method is a satire on the naturalistic writer's preoccupation with detail, or it is a humourless exercise in the manner of classic naturalism. Either it is *reductio ad absurdum* of naive nineteenth-century faith in science, or a serious application of scientific theories to human psychology. 'Ithaca' is either a final celebration of Bloom's heroic qualities as Everyman, or a cold revelation of his essential pettiness. Just as the typical reader of *A Portrait of the Artist* finds it difficult to accept the delicate balance of sympathy and irony that marks the novel's close, so the average reader of *Ulysses* seems compelled to indulge in the worst kind of critical bookkeeping, totting up Joyce's ironies and human touches as if some simple formula were really available. But the genius of Joyce and of *Ulysses* lies in the indisputable fact that the form is both epic and ironic, Bloom both heroic and commonplace. The bed of Ulysses is, in its secret construction, known only to Ulysses and Penelope, while the secret of Bloom's bed is a

Dublin joke; but when Bloom dismisses Molly's suitors one by one his reason and equanimity are, as Joyce intended, equal in power to the great bow that only Ulysses could draw. At first Joyce had thought of the slaughter of the suitors as 'un-Ulyssean',[15] a bloody act of violence that could not be translated into modern Dublin or reconciled with Bloom's humanism; but finally he came to see that Bloom's equanimity of mind was in its way a comparable achievement. In his attempt 'to transpose the myth *sub specie temporis nostri*'[16] Joyce realized that the contrasts between the classical world and the modern world would inevitably be ironic on the level of *fact*, leading only to mock-heroic effects where the disparities in setting and action tend to debase the contemporary experience; but he also knew that on the level of symbol, where the fundamentals of human psychology are revealed, Bloom would prove a worthy counterpart to the hero of Homer's epic. Any reading of *Ulysses* that aims at doing justice to Joyce's complex vision must be composed of constant adjustments and accommodations between myth and fact, and it is in 'Ithaca' that these adjustments are most difficult to make.

Joyce began work on 'Ithaca' early in 1921, after completing the drafts of 'Eumaeus', and was still revising the episode on proof in late January 1922, only a few days before the novel's publication ('Penelope' was actually finished before 'Ithaca' so that Valery Larbaud could read it while preparing for his famous séance on 7 December 1921). Thus Joyce could write 'Ithaca' with every detail of the novel's plan and action firmly in mind, and it is not surprising that the episode fits into the general scheme of *Ulysses* with absolute precision. In the first stages of his work on 'Ithaca' Joyce went through the usual process of grouping his raw materials on successive notesheets, listing the themes and motifs and tags of dialogue which were to be transformed into the episode's characteristic styles.[17] As one might expect, the notesheets are filled with the cosmic equivalents (such as '$JC = 3\sqrt{God}$') which Joyce referred to in his well-known letter to Frank Budgen:

> I am writing Ithaca in the form of a mathematical catechism. All events are resolved into their cosmic, physical, psychical etc. equivalents, e.g. Bloom jumping down the area, drawing water from the tap, the micturition in the garden, the cone of incense, lighted candle and statue so that not only will the reader know everything and know it in the baldest coldest way, but Bloom and Stephen thereby become heavenly bodies, wanderers like the stars at which they gaze.[18]

But mixed with these 'cosmic, physical, psychical etc. equivalents' on the notesheets are the terse phrases in Bloom's natural idiom which trigger the cosmic correspondences. For example, an elaborate attempt to relate Stephen and Bloom to Molly in terms of vectors and tangents is prompted by the colloquial 'fly off at a tangent', while a natural phenomenon jotted down in Bloom's staccato speech ('See star by day from bottom of gully') is transformed in the text into pseudo-scientific jargon: 'of the infinite lattiginous scintillating uncondensed milky way, discernible by daylight by an observer placed at the lower end of a cylindrical vertical shaft 5000 ft deep sunk from the surface towards the centre of the earth' (699.22). the notesheets provide overwhelming evidence that the 'dry rock pages of *Ithaca*'[19] are supersaturated with Bloom's humanity, a humanity that is enhanced if anything by the impersonality of the prose. As any viewer of the recent film will remember, 'Ithaca' yielded scenes of far more warmth and feeling than those provided by such 'dramatic' episodes as 'Hades' and 'Nausicaa'. Once again, in the contrast between the apparent coldness of the episode's form and its actual human effects, we are confronted with a paradox to be solved.

It will be best to approach the problems of 'Ithaca' in three stages: (1) an analysis of the catechistical form; (2) a scanning of the episode's scenic progression; and (3) an assessment of the general effect of 'Ithaca' on our experience of the novel. The question-and-answer form is dictated in part by the 'schoolroom' nature of 'Ithaca'; in Joyce's *schema* for the novel the episode is an impersonal counterpart to the personal catechism pursued by Stephen in 'Nestor'.[20] It is customary to think of 'Ithaca' as deriving from the form of the Christian catechism and Joyce's early Jesuit training, but the parallels with the catechistical methods of the nineteenth-century schoolroom are equally convincing. Two recent critics have proposed that the form of 'Ithaca' is directly indebted to Richmal Mangnall's *Historical and Miscellaneous Questions*, a textbook of encyclopaedic knowledge which went through over a hundred editions during the nineteenth century and was still in use in Joyce's day. Stephen refers to the book in *A Portrait* (*AP*, 53), and Robert Graves used it in 1901 at the age of six, although his father thought it out of date.[21] Mangnall's *Questions* is a compendium of undifferentiated 'practical' knowledge, cast in the form of a familiar catechism. Questions that any child might ask are phrased in simple form, while a voice of hectoring authority responds with a surfeit of information and misinformation.

What are comets?
Luminous and opaque bodies, whose motions are in different directions, and the orbits they describe very extensive; they have

long translucent tails of light turned from the sun: the great swiftness of their motion in the neighbourhood of the sun, is the reason they appear to us for such a short time: and the great length of time they are in appearing again is occasioned by the extent and eccentricity of their orbits or paths in the heavens.

How many comets are supposed to belong to our solar system: Twenty-one; but we only know.... [22]

There can be no doubt that Mangnall's *Questions* was a primary source for Joyce's 'mathematico-astronomico-physico-mechanico-geometrico-chemico sublimation of Bloom and Stephen'.[23] To the modern adult reader it is filled with unconscious humour and grotesque distortions, but to the young Joyce it must have shimmered with the poetic magic of unfamiliar names and mysterious words (such as gnomon and simony). In Stephen's daydream of vindication by the rector he associates himself with 'the great men whose names were in Richmal Magnall's [sic] Questions' (*AP*, 53). The form of Mangnall's *Questions* would have been easily assimilated into the authoritarian structure of Jesuit education, and it is clear from Joyce's early Paris notebook (1903) that be found the catechism a congenial vehicle for his own ideas.

Question: Why are not excrements, children, and lice works of art?
Answer: Excrements, children, and lice are human products— human dispositions of sensible matter. The process by which they are produced is natural and nonartistic; their end is not an aesthetic end: therefore they are not works of art. (*CW*, 146)

As Lynch comments later in *A Portrait*, such a question has 'the true scholastic stink' (*AP*, 214), and Joyce himself was certainly aware of the pomposity latent in the form. We may hazard the guess that he chose to cast the most bizarre examples of his aesthetic in catechistical form as a defensive acknowledgment of their potential absurdity. In sum, the catechism must have struck Joyce as a natural and even inevitable form for the climactic episode of Ulysses because it was associated with some of his most profound early experiences, and had proved to be a vehicle for precise intellectual argument which simultaneously allowed scope for exaggeration and self-parody.

The greatest danger inherent in the catcechistical form would seem to be monotony. The effectiveness of the catechism in the classroom depends upon a sameness in form and rhythm which—as Wordsworth said of poetic meter—opens the memory and fixes the mind in a receptive mood. But such an effect, useful as it might be for the pedagogue, would be disastrous for the novelist, and Joyce kept the technique flexible in 'Ithaca' by constant shifts in tone, rhetoric, and quality of subject matter. When we think of the 'style' of 'Ithaca' we usually think of those set pieces where Bloom's thoughts and actions are cast in the self-confident language of Victorian science, but in fact many of the answers are simple and direct:

> What did Bloom see on the range?
> On the right (smaller) hob a blue enamelled saucepan: on the left (larger) hob a black iron kettle.
> What did Bloom do at the range?
> He removed the saucepan to the left hob, rose and carried the iron kettle to the sink in order to tap the current by turning the faucet to let it flow. (670.31)

These plain questions-and-answers are then followed by two elaborate exchanges on Dublin's water supply and the universal qualities of water. The effect is to retard our sense of the action while still rendering it in sharp detail: it is as if we were viewing Bloom and Stephen from a great height, against a vast backdrop of general human action and knowledge, while at the same time standing next to them and observing every local detail. It is this 'parallax' achieved by the macrocosmic–microcosmic point-of-view which gives the episode, like Hardy's *Dynasts*, the grandeur and sweep that Joyce certainly intended.

Arnold Goldman remarks that 'the vein of "Ithaca" has been re-opened in recent French novels. There the entire novel may be in the style of Joyce's chapter, the programmatic intention of the artist being to circumvent the metaphysical antinomy of subject and object by treating everything as an object'.[24] But surely this is just the opposite of Joyce's intention and achievement. Bloom and Stephen do indeed 'become heavenly bodies, wanderers like the stars at which they gaze', but at the same time their subjective lives penetrate every detail of objective description. Alain Robbe-Grillet's famous description of the *nouveau roman* stands at the opposite pole from Joyce's method.

> Instead of this universe of 'signification' (psychological, social, functional), we must try, then, to construct a world both more solid and more immediate. Let it be first of all by their *presence* that objects and gestures establish themselves, and let this presence continue to prevail over whatever explanatory theory

that may try to enclose them in a system of references, whether emotional, sociological, Freudian or metaphysical.

In this future universe of the novel, gestures and objects will be *there* before *something*; and they will still be there afterwards, hard, unalterable, eternally present, mocking their own 'meaning', that meaning which vainly tries to reduce them to the role of precarious tools, of a temporary and shameful fabric woven exclusively—and deliberately—by the superior human truth expressed in it, only to cast out this awkward auxiliary into immediate oblivion and darkness.

Henceforth, on the contrary, objects will gradually lose their instability and their secrets, will renounce their pseudo-mystery, that suspect interiority which Roland Barthes has called 'the romantic heart of things'. No longer will objects be merely the vague reflection of the hero's vague soul, the image of his torments, the shadow of his desires. Or rather, if objects still afford a momentary prop to human passions, they will do so only provisionally, and will accept the tyranny of significations only in appearance—derisively, one might say—the better to show how alien they remain to man.[25]

The relationship between objects and personality in Joyce's writing would seem to be much more complex than in Robbe-Grillet's. While 'Ithaca' does 'resolve' its human figures into their objective counterparts, at the same time the objective universe is suffused with their personalities. Take the following question-and-answer:

By what reflections did he, a conscious reactor against the void incertitude, justify to himself his sentiments?

The preordained frangibility of the hymen, the presupposed intangibility of the thing in itself: the incongruity and disproportion between the selfprolonging tension of the thing proposed to be done and the self abbreviating relaxation of the thing done: the fallaciously inferred debility of the female, the muscularity of the male: the variations of ethical codes: the natural grammatical transition by inversion involving no alteration of sense of an aorist preterite proposition (parsed as masculine subject, monosyllabic onomatopoeic transitive verb with direct feminine object) from the active voice into its correlative aorist preterite proposition (parsed as feminine subject, auxiliary verb and quasimonosyllabic onomatopoeic past

> participle with complementary masculine agent) in the passive
> voice: the continued product of seminators by generation: the
> continual production of semen by distillation: the futility of
> triumph or protest or vindication: the inanity of extolled virtue:
> the lethargy of nescient matter: the apathy of the stars. (734.3)

Here the typical movement from microcosm to macrocosm, from the
'frangibility' of the individual hymen to the 'apathy of the stars', is a reflection
of Bloom's thought as he strives for equanimity by sinking his own anxieties
in the processes of nature. In spite of their pseudo-scientific presentation the
'objects' in this passage are as personal and 'interior' as those in the closing of
'The Dead'. In 'Ithaca' Joyce did not renounce his interest in 'the romantic
heart of things', but simply found new means for expressing it.

   As Joyce's work on 'Ithaca' neared an end in the autumn of 1921 he told
his correspondents that he was putting the episode 'in order'.[26] His methods
of gathering material had been ideally suited to the making of 'Ithaca', each
question-and-answer developing around a phrase or idea and then being
fitted into the general design. Clearly he conceived of 'Ithaca' as a series of
scenes or tableaux, not unlike the narrative divisions in 'Circe', and on the
early typescripts he blocked out these scenes under the titles 'street',
'kitchen', 'garden', 'parlour', 'bedroom'.[27] We may consider the 'narrative'
development of 'Ithaca' under these headings, since each scene builds to a
revealing climax which forwards our understanding of both Bloom and
Stephen.

   The scene in the street (666–669) begins with Bloom and Stephen
moving in parallel but separate courses. The tone is relaxed, the conversation
easy and desultory. Both Stephen and Bloom are 'keyless', the victims of
usurpers, poised between thought and action: 'To enter or not to enter. To
knock or not to knock' (668.18). But whereas Stephen has fallen under the
spell of Hamlet's melancholy and indecision, Bloom—like his Homeric
namesake, or the active Hamlet—devises a 'stratagem', and his acrobatic
entrance into No. 7 Eccles street is described in ponderous language which
simultaneously satirizes the triviality of the event (in its cosmic context)
while emphasizing its importance in the context of Bloom's own life.

> Did he fall?
> By his body's known weight of eleven stone and four pounds
> in avoirdupois measure, as certified by the graduated machine for
> periodical selfweighing in the premises of Francis Froedman,
> pharmaceutical chemist of 19 Frederick street, north, on the last

feast of the Ascension, to wit, the twelfth day of May of the bissextile year one thousand nine hundred and four of the christian era (jewish era five thousand six hundred and sixtyfour, mohammedan era one thousand three hundred and twentytwo), golden number 5, epact 13, solar cycle 9, dominical letters C B, Roman indication 2, Julian period 6617, MXMIV. (668.28)

The entire 'street' scene establishes Bloom as the focus of our interest, and throws the balance of the narrative toward his competence and resourcefulness. In this episode, by contrast with 'Nestor', Stephen will be more learner than teacher.

Events in the 'kitchen' scene (669–697) explore the sympathetic bonds between Stephen and Bloom, as well as their points of difference, culminating in the 'exodus' from kitchen to garden which brings their relationship into focus through a symbolic tableau not unlike that at the end of 'Circe'.

In what order of precedence, with what attendant ceremony was the exodus from the house of bondage to the wilderness of inhabitation effected?

Lighted Candle in Stick borne by
BLOOM.
Diaconal Hat on Ashplant borne by
STEPHEN

With what intonation *secreto* of what commemorative psalm?
The 113th, *modus peregrinus: In exitu Israël de Egypto: domus Jacob de populo barbaro.*
What did each do at the door of egress?
Bloom set the candlestick on the floor. Stephen put the hat on his head.
For what creature was the door of egress a door of ingress?
For a cat.
What spectacle confronted them when they, first the host, then the guest, emerged silently, doubly dark, from obscurity by a passage from the rere of the house into the penumbra of the garden?
The heaventree of stars hung with humid nightblue fruit. (697.33)

Our reading of the symbolic references woven into this scene will determine in large measure our ultimate attitude toward the 'union' of Stephen and Bloom. The echoes from Dante are insistent, and have often been noted.[28] The opening line from the 113th Psalm, 'When Israel went out of Egypt ...' is twice used by Dante as a text to illustrate his fourfold method of allegory (in the *Letter to Can Grande* and the *Convivio*), and it has been suggested that Joyce is covertly instructing us to read 'Ithaca' as a 'polysemous' work, which it certainly is: the literal and the allegorical are never more obvious than in this passage, where each literal detail is packed with ceremonial significance. But an elaborate application of Dante's four 'levels' would seem more problematic, and the tag from the 113th Psalm is best interpreted as a traditional reference to the resurrection which appears at a crucial turning-point in the *Commedia*.

As Dante and Vergil emerge from Hell at the end the *Inferno* they are once more able to see the stars (the word upon which each part of the *Commedia* ends), just as Stephen and Bloom emerge from the house to confront 'The heaventree of stars hung with humid nightblue fruit'. A little later, in the first Canto of the *Purgatorio*, Cato questions: 'Who hath guided you? or who was a lamp unto you issuing forth from the deep night that ever maketh black the infernal vale' (*Purgatorio*, I, 43–45). Similarly, the omniscient voice in 'Ithaca' asks:

> What visible luminous sign attracted Bloom's, who attracted Stephen's gaze?
> In the second storey (rere) of his (Bloom's) house the light of a paraffin oil lamp with oblique shade projected on a screen of roller blind supplied by Frank O'Hara, window blind, curtain pole and revolving shutter manufacturer, 16 Aungier street. (702.17)

In the next Canto of the *Purgatorio* Dante and Vergil encounter the souls about to enter Purgatory, singing the ancient hymn of redemption, '*In exitu Israel de Aegypto*' (*Purgatorio*, II, 46), the same hymn Stephen chants as he and Bloom leave the kitchen.

The symbolic implications of these accumulated references are overwhelming: the meeting of Stephen and Bloom has provided a release from bondage, a release noted through a traditional combination of Hebrew and Christian imagery. The only question is whether we take these implications as a vehicle for irony, an irony based on the disparity between the trivial and allegorical levels, or as a complex statement of psychological potentialities. The critical problem is exactly the same as that produced by the Homeric parallels, and the same solution suggests itself. On the literal level, bounded by the twenty hours of the novel's action, Stephen and Bloom are mock-heroic figures; but on the figurative level they take on heroic and creative possibilities. Having confined himself to a realistic time-scheme which made impossible the actual dramatization of that dynamic growth of personality so characteristic of the conventional novel, Joyce vested this element in his symbolic structures. To paraphrase Santayana, *Ulysses* is mock-heroic in immediacy, but heroic in perspective, and Joyce's delicate balancing of attitudes is nowhere more evident than in this climactic scene. No critical formula of 'either/or' can do it justice. Instead, we must think of Joyce's use of myth in the light of Eliot's 'Tradition and the Individual Talent': a vital interchange between past and present which humanizes the past while it enlarges the present.

As Bloom and Stephen stand in the garden before parting, beneath the lamp of Molly which has been Bloom's guide throughout the day, they urinate together, 'their sides contiguous, their organs of micturition reciprocally rendered invisible by manual circumposition, their gazes, first Bloom's, then Stephen's, elevated to the projected luminous and semi-luminous shadow' (702.35). This is the moment of symbolic union, and the fact that it is richly comic in the manner of Sterne does not detract from its ultimate seriousness. Joyce's identification of micturition with creativity is well known, and although W. Y. Tindall may be overly ingenious in making the identification a major theme in *Chamber Music* (where it is of more interest to the psychoanalyst than the literary critic),[29] the explicit association of urination with creativity in *Finnegans Wake* makes a similar interpretation of this scene in 'Ithaca' more than probable. As Clive Hart his pointed out, the theme of micturition as creation and transubstantiation is established early in *Ulysses* by the Ballad of Joking Jesus (19.8–11),[30] and there can be no doubt that Joyce intended the garden scene in 'Ithaca' to foreshadow a new departure for both Bloom and Stephen. On the literal level they remain divided, each absorbed in his own thoughts; but the 'celestial sign' that they both observe—'a star precipitated ... towards the zodiacal sign of Leo' (703.24)—reminds us that Stephen's daylong pilgrimage has led toward this encounter with the humane and inquisitive Bloom, whose personality supplies the qualities lacking in his own sterile spirit.

When Bloom and Stephen say farewell the literal narrative leaves them separate once again, with their futures adumbrated but not dramatized, and Bloom turns from the chill of 'proximate dawn' to re-enter the house. Having touched the ultimate reaches of symbol and myth, the episode returns to the level of 'objects' and 'things'; and Bloom's exploration of the parlour (705–729) is told in a manner and style that would have delighted Defoe. The catalogues of this section—the furnishings of the room, the contents of the bookshelves, the budget for 16 June 1904—bring the reader back to the irreducible reality of Bloom's life and prepare the way for the next access of myth and symbol at the end of the 'parlour' scene. As Bloom's thoughts drift toward travel and escape (726–727) he is transformed into Everyman and Noman, Elpenor and Ulysses, into a wandering comet whose orbit traces the extremes of his real and potential existences.

> Would the departed never nowhere nohow reappear?
>
> Ever he would wander, selfcompelled, to the extreme limit of his cometary orbit, beyond the fixed stars and variable suns and telescopic planets, astronomical waifs and strays, to the extreme boundary of space, passing from land to land, among peoples, amid events. Somewhere imperceptibly he would hear and somehow reluctantly, suncompelled, obey the summons of recall. Whence, disappearing from the constellation of the Northern Crown he would somehow reappear reborn above delta in the constellation of Cassiopeia and after incalculable eons of peregrination return an estranged avenger, a wreaker of justice on malefactors, a dark crusader, a sleeper awakened, with financial resources (by supposition) surpassing those of Rothschild or of the silver king. (727.35)

We know from both the Library episode (210.7–11) and an earlier section of 'Ithaca' (700.36–701.3) that 4 nova in Cassiopeia (whose form is a capital 'W') announced the birth of William Shakespeare, while 'a star (2nd magnitude) of similar origin but lesser brilliancy' had appeared in the Northern Crown to mark the birth of Leopold Bloom. In this passage Bloom disappears in his own personality only to reappear as his mythic counterpart, a Hamlet or Ulysses freed of anxiety and intent upon his mission of revenge. Such transformations become more and more common as the 'parlour' scene wears to a close, and Bloom gradually takes on all the ritual and ceremonial significances of the day that has passed. In fact, one might say that 'Ithaca' progresses by a rhythmic alternation between mythic or 'epiphanic' moments and longer stretches of 'realism' which validate these moments.

Once in the 'bedroom' (730ff) Bloom stretches out on the bed, which still bears the evidence of Boylan's recent occupancy, and meditates on the 'series originating in and repeated to infinity' (731.22) of Molly's lovers. Robert M. Adams has pointed out the bizarre elements in Bloom's catalogue,[31] but at this stage in the episode the criteria of 'realism' seem curiously irrelevant. 'Ithaca' closes on the highest plane of mythopoetic intensity, as Joyce's intentions—so often stated in the letters—are fully realized. The episode has developed through a measured oscillation between the literal and allegorical levels, until at the end the balance is thrown finally and irrevocably to the side of symbolism. The sequence of Bloom's thought—'Envy, jealousy, abnegation, equanimity' (732.14)—sums up the process, as Molly and Bloom are transformed from individual human beings into types and archetypes. It is possible, of course, to see this process as 'something of an evasion',[32] but only if the life of *Ulysses* is viewed as more surface than symbol. It was Joyce's unique gift that he could turn the substance of ordinary life into something like myth, not only through the use of 'parallels' and allusions but through direct transformation: and the ending of 'Ithaca', like that of 'Anna Livia Plurabelle', would seem to vindicate his method. Most of *Ulysses* can be understood by the same methods one applies to *The Waste Land*, where the manipulation of a continuous parallel between contemporaneity and antiquity 'places' the contemporary action, but the ending of 'Ithaca' consists of metamorphosis rather than juxtaposition. As in the conclusion to 'Circe', the model is the transformation scene of a typical pantomime (perhaps the pantomime of *Sindbad the Sailor*[33]), and we must believe that Molly has merged into her archetype, Gea-Tellus, while Leopold Bloom has become the archetype of all human possibility, 'the manchild in the womb' (737.13). The ironies of the novel still operate on the literal level—Molly is unfulfilled, Bloom unsatisfied—but these are of lesser importance beside the primaeval realities which close the episode. The final questions ('When? Where?') reflect the novel's traditional concerns with time and space, but the answers are a rebuke to such concerns (737.23–29).

> When?
> Going to a dark bed there was a square round Sinbad the
> Sailor roc's auk's egg in the night of the bed of all the auks of the
> rocs of Darkinbad the Brightdayler.
> Where?

In sleep the limits of the rational mind fall away, and Bloom's desire to solve the problem of 'the quadrature of the circle' (699.20, 718.12–13) is satisfied. At the end of 'Ithaca', which is the end of *Ulysses* as novel and fable, Bloom subsides into the mythic world of the giant roc, where light is born out of darkness, and into the womb of infinite possibilities. 'La réponse à la dernière demande est un point', Joyce instructed the printer on his typescript, and that point contains a double meaning. As a full-stop it marks the conclusion of Bloom's day, the terminus of the novel's literal action, but as a spatial object it represents Bloom's total retreat into the womb of time, from which he shall emerge the next day with all the fresh potentialities of Everyman.

Like the Viconian *ricorso*, the final moment of 'Ithaca' is both an end and a beginning.

'Ithaca' provides the capstone of our total experience of *Ulysses*. If the novel ended with this episode our view of the major characters and their motives would remain substantially the same, although our sense of reality would be somewhat different. 'Penelope' is indeed the 'indispensable countersign to Bloom's passport to eternity', as Joyce once called it,[34] since it substantiates the novel's promise of cyclic renewal; but without it we would still have a completed world to savour and interpret. On Joyce's *schema* for the novel, 'Penelope' alone is assigned no specific time; its materials (Bed, Flesh, Earth) are essentially timeless. Although its themes are cunningly orchestrated, the random organization being merely illusion, 'Penelope' does not contribute to the sequence of styles which is one of our chief interests in *Ulysses*. Instead, the novel subsides into an appearance of naturalness, and our final impression is that of a voice, curious, lively, undiscriminating.

'Ithaca', by contrast, has the appearance of extreme artifice, and has often been taken as the final triumph of Joyce the baroque elaborator over Joyce the 'novelist'. But such a view rests on the all-too-common assumption that the 'novelistic' elements in *Ulysses* must be those of the traditional nineteenth-century novel—the revelation of character through setting, plot, and observed consciousness—and that the devices and correspondences that mark the later chapters must be evaluated as either essential or auxiliary to the novelistic effects.[35] Such a view was put forward in my own earlier work, *The Art of James Joyce*, where many of the artifices found in the last chapters are assigned to the play-instinct or to Joyce's personal need for order while gathering his materials. I still believe that the more recondite correspondences in *Ulysses* were more important to Joyce during the process of composition than they can ever be to us during the process of reading and interpreting, but I have long since abandoned the notion—always a reductive one—that the novelistic elements in *Ulysses* can be separated from the *schema* and claimed as the true line of the work's meaning. What Joyce accomplished in writing *Ulysses* was to shatter the form of the well-made novel and expose its multifarious origins (allegory, 'Romance', history, gossip, 'news'), and then to reconstitute these materials in a variety of experimental forms. The result is a work of art which renders the bourgeois world in all its detail and potentiality, uniting fact and myth in a classic portrayal of Everyman as dispossessed hero. In its radical form 'Ithaca' bypasses the familiar conventions of nineteenth-century fiction and shows us another way in which the novelist's passion for omniscience can be achieved without violating our sense of individual and local reality.

NOTES

1. Arnold Goldman, *The Joyce Paradox*, London and Evanston, Ill., 1966, p. 105.

2. Budgen, p. 264.

3. *Letters*, I, 129.

4. Ibid.

5. For discussion of the evolving styles, see Chapter Four of Goldman's *The Joyce Paradox* and Chapter One of my *The Art of James Joyce*, London, 1961. It is interesting to see how the recasting of an earlier episode was often dictated by the form of the later episode then on the stocks. For example, 'Aeolus'—the early episode that underwent the most radical change—was rewritten in 1921 while 'Ithaca' was being drafted, and the inserted newspaper headlines reflect not only the 'history of the language' technique developed in 'Oxen of the Sun' but the chief effect of the question-and-answer method in 'Ithaca', a breaking-down of the narrative into discrete aesthetic units. in a sense, 'Aeolus' slows down the narrative flow of the first half of *Ulysses* and makes the declining pace of the second half less obvious.

6. *Letters*, I, 149.

7. *Letters*, I, 145.

8. *Letters*, I, 172.

9. Litz, *The Art of James Joyce*, pp. 3–5.

10. Harry Levin was the first to discuss the lectures in his *James Joyce: a Critical Introduction*, Norfolk, Conn., 1941, p. 18. The surviving fragment of the Blake lecture is printed in *Critical Writings*, pp. 214–222. For the entire text of the Defoe lecture, see Joseph Prescott, ed., *Daniel Defoe: Buffalo Studies*, I, Buffalo, N.Y., December, 1964.

11. See, for instance, the use of the terms 'verism' and 'idealism' in the criticism of Hamlin Garland, where the continental debate is given a native American context.

12. *Daniel Defoe*, pp. 15–16.

13. Richard E. Madtes, 'Joyce and the Building of Ithaca', *ELH*, XXXI (December 1964), 457–458.

14. *Letters*, I, 175.

15. *Letters*, I, 160.

16. *Letters*, I, 146–147.

17. For information on the episode's composition, see Richard E. Madtes, 'Joyce and the Building of *Ithaca*', pp. 443–459. This article is a summary of Madtes's doctoral dissertation, 'A Textual and Critical Study of the "Ithaca" Episode of James Joyce's *Ulysses*', Columbia University, 1961. The *Ulysses* notesheets in the British Museum have recently been edited by Phillip F. Herring (*Joyce's 'Ulysses' Notesheets in the British Museum*, Charlottesville, Va., 1972). The entries quoted in this paragraph are, following Herring's enumeration, 5.12, 12.87 and 13.110.

18. *Letters*, I, 159–160.

19. *Letters*, I, 173.

20. In the elaborate *schema* which Joyce revealed to Stuart Gilbert, the three episodes of the *Nostos* are mirror images of the three episodes in the *Telemachia*, with the characteristic techniques repeated in opposite form. *Nestor* is described as 'Catechism (personal)', while *Ithaca* is 'Catechism (impersonal)'. This symmetry was not evident to Joyce until he had written the last episodes. In the first known *schema*, sent to Carlo Linati in September 1920, the 'Dawn' (*Telemachia*) and 'Midnight' (*Nostos*) have a less exact relationship: *Nestor* is described as '2-person dialogue / Narration / Soliloquy', while *Ithaca* is 'Dialogue / Pacified style / Fusion'. See the Appendix to Richard Ellmann's *Ulysses on the Liffey* (London and New York, 1972).

21. Robert Graves, *Good-Bye to All That*, London, 1929, p. 38.

22. Richmal Mangnall, *Historical and Miscellaneous Questions*, Fifth American edition from the eighty-fourth London edition, New York, 1869, p. 324.

23. *Letters*, I, 164.

24. Goldman, *The Joyce Paradox*, p. 108.

25. Alain Robbe-Grillet, *For a New Novel: Essays on Fiction*, New York, 1965, pp. 21–22.

26. *Letters*, I, 172, and III, 49.

27. Peter Spielberg, *James Joyce's Manuscripts and Letters at the University of Buffalo*, Buffalo, N.Y., 1962, V.B.15.a. and V.B.15.b.

28. See especially William York Tindall, *A Reader's Guide to James Joyce*, London and New York, 1959, pp. 225–226, Mary T. Reynolds, 'Joyce's Planetary Music: His Debt to Dante', *Sewanee Review*, 76 (Summer 1968), 456–458, and Sultan, pp. 391–392.

29. W. Y. Tindall, ed., *Chamber Music*, New York, 1954.

30. Clive Hart, *Structure and Motif in Finnegans Wake*, London and Evanston, Ill., 1962, pp. 206–207.

31. *Surface and Symbol*, pp. 36–40.

32. Ibid., p. 42.

33. Ibid., pp. 76–82.

34. *Letters*, I, 160.

35. For a discussion of this problem see Peter K. Garrett, *Scene and Symbol from George Eliot to James Joyce*, New Haven, Conn., 1969, pp. 252–271, and Barbara Hardy, 'Form as End and Means in Ulysses', *Orbis Litterarum*, XIX (1964), 194–200.

ROBERT D. NEWMAN

Narrative Transgression and Restoration: Hermetic Messengers in Ulysses

i

Wittgenstein once said that a serious and good philosophic work could
be written that would consist entirely of jokes (without being facetious).
—Norman Malcolm, *Ludwig Wittgenstein: A Memoir*[1]

In *Ulysses* Joyce presents a narrative combatted by its narration. A domestic
novel, written by an exile, modeled on an epic, it roams between literary
forms as Leopold Bloom and Stephen Dedalus meander through the physical
and mental topography of Dublin. As excavators of the text's messages, we
can look at the messenger figures that Joyce adroitly places in *Ulysses* as they
shift perspective and radiate meaning in alternative directions. These
messenger figures function as signposts in the narrative to call attention to
the reader's double motivation to create and to suspect order, thereby
directing us to become meta-readers. In his discussion of hermeneutics as
polarized opposition, Paul Ricoeur explains this position: "According to one
pole, hermeneutics is understood as the manifestation and restoration of a
meaning addressed to me in the manner of a message, a proclamation, or as
is sometimes said, a kerygma; according to the other pole, it is understood as
a demystification, as a reduction of illusion."[2] In *Ulysses*, these contradictory

From *James Joyce Quarterly* 29. © 1992 by The University of Tulsa.

poles converge so that the narrative deconstructs any hierarchical privileging which it also might have advanced. The reader's experience becomes a dialogue with the text, where point of view consistently shifts so that reductive authority is rendered ephemeral. By exposing their own masks, *Ulysses*' messenger figures reveal the narrative masking by which Joyce's parody operates.

In his discussion of reversal and discovery in the *Poetics*, Aristotle uses Oedipus as his example of how discovery (*anagōnrisis*) and reversal (*peripeteia*) combine to arouse pity and fear. He considers the messenger in Sophocles' play the catalyzing agent for reversal and discovery:

> A reversal of fortune is the change of the kind described from one state of things within the play to its opposite, and that too as we say in the probable or necessary sequence of events; as it is for instance in *Oedipus*: here the opposite state of things is produced by the Messenger, who, coming to gladden Oedipus and to remove his fears as to his mother, reveals the secret of his birth.[3]

The various messenger figures in *Ulysses* also signal reversal and discovery; however, Joyce's deliberate accent on the internal structures of the text resists both the climax and the closure found in a work like *Oedipus*. Joyce's poetics enlarges reversal beyond a central narrative turn and renders *Ulysses* polytropic so that multiple reversals occur and some are themselves reversed.[4] Instead of an explicit dramatic insight, discovery occurs implicitly in principal characters as well as in the reader. The tracing, retracing, and expansion of the tributaries of memory in which the characters engage mirror the reader's activity as demonstrated by the blur of penciled notes and crosslistings in most of our copies of *Ulysses*. The numerous synchronicities in Stephen's and Bloom's thoughts and peregrinations enhance the identity between reader and character, inviting the reader to posit symbolic judgments and to project scenarios for the characters. However, reversal and discovery are also conjoined. Reader traps, intentional errors, narrative omissions, and the general relativism encouraged by the text reverse the privileging of any discovery and subvert the authority of any single point of view. The "Circe" episode, for example, violates rational ordering by collecting many of the characters, objects, statements, and events which exist in the narrative memory to that point in the novel and radically rearranging them. In this manner, Ulysses performs as tease, encouraging and checking the reader's impulses for *telos* and identification.

What is constant in the conjunction of reversal and discovery is transformation. Just as the mythological messenger Hermes, or Mercury, foments change in his role as trickster, just as mercury or quicksilver catalyzes alchemical operations, messenger figures in *Ulysses* function as agents of transformation. I wish to consider the messenger's influence on character transformation and to suggest links between this transformation and the messenger's disruptive and restorative effect on narrative direction. The imposition of messengers signals narrative transformation and performs a kind of narrative thievery by robbing authority from the preceding voice and inserting substitute and transitional voices. As navigators of narrative, messengers pilot it in both subversive and restorative directions.

The Homeric analogue which Joyce cleverly knitted into the interstices of *Ulysses* applies when considering the restorative capabilities of the messenger in both Homer's and Joyce's texts. Twice when Odysseus is stranded, in the realms of Calypso and Circe, and the narrative falters, Hermes appears to break the spells that hold him. In doing so, Hermes negates the authority of the captors. Odysseus is able to escape his entrapment; both he and the narrative resume their voyages. In *Ulysses*, Bloom offers Stephen an escape from his psychological entrapment by replacing Buck Mulligan as Stephen's symbolic messenger, a transference over which Bloom's daughter, Milly, presides as cosmic messenger.

By canceling Mulligan's presence from the remainder of the plot, however, Joyce turns the narrative toward another trap. The derisive energy Mulligan embodies frequently intrudes, like a poke in the ribs, to adjust the reader's perspective from its intensive focus on Stephen's brooding and Bloom's troubles. The removal of Mulligan eliminates an identifiable character as a source of these playful disturbances and places mockery exclusively within the purview of a sequence of parodic narrators. Locating ludic power primarily in the tellers rather than allowing it to proliferate to the characters as well exposes authorial authority but tempers the reader's participation in it. Joyce resolves this problem by introducing a character at the beginning of the "Nostos" section who, like a narrator, performs chorically. Like Mulligan, D. B. Murphy, the sailor in the cabman's shelter, is storyteller, trickster, and messenger. Like Mulligan, he possesses the mythological Hermes' power to imitate, to adopt a series of masks. Joyce names Murphy "Ulysses Pseudangelos"—the false messenger—in his schemas for "Eumaeus," and the tattoo the sailor wears that can be manipulated to both smile and frown indicates his duplicity (*U*16.673–89).

When Homer's Odysseus returns to Ithaca to reclaim his authority, his disguise fools the swineherd, Eumaeus, and indicates Odysseus' descent from Hermes. Odysseus' grandfather, Autolycus, was the son of Hermes and was himself a thief and dissembler. In his "Eumaeus" episode, Joyce splits

Odysseus' attributes. As a character, Murphy serves as a foil for Bloom, against whom Bloom asserts his paternal authority. As a Hermes figure, Murphy also serves as an incarnation of the trickster author, whose multiple transformations and disruptions convert readers to the mask of *herm?neus*. Indeed, *Ulysses* teaches its readers what Michel Foucault describes as the author's double function—a person designated by a proper name as well as a mask for the reader: "a projection ... of the operations that we force texts to undergo, the connections that we make, the traits that we establish as pertinent, the continuities that we recognize, or the exclusions that we practice."[5] One of Murphy's masks mirrors the authorial posture that readers learn to wear. Another reveals readers as wanderers in the text, whose efforts to find stasis and closure, like Murphy's (and Bloom's) return home, result in confirmation of their perpetual exile.

The role of the Hermes figure in *Ulysses*, therefore, extends from signifier of character and narrative transformation to signifier of reader response. In the latter case, Hermes is expanded from mythological analogue to philosophical influence as Joyce brings his covert fascination with Hermetic thought to bear on the mask he fashions for his readers. Richard Ellmann's biography details the young Joyce's rejection of the theosophical movement, which involved Yeats and several prominent Irish writers. It also offers numerous instances of Joyce's private indulgence in similar interests. In a letter to Harriet Shaw Weaver regarding these interests, Joyce writes, "I would not pay overmuch attention to these theories, beyond using them for all they are worth, but they have gradually forced themselves on me through circumstances of my own life" (*Letters I* 241). Not only did Joyce's library contain numerous works on mysticism, but his allusions to Hermetic writings and concepts steadily increased with each book he wrote.[6]

Although Joyce once referred to Aristotle as the greatest thinker of all times, he also maintained a lifelong interest in the Renaissance Hermetic philosopher, Giordano Bruno, who zealously attacked the dualism of Aristotle's philosophy.[7] In his insistence on correspondences and mirrored inversions, Joyce employs Hermeticism and its conflict with the fundamental principle of Western metaphysics, Aristotle's law of non-contradiction—"the most certain of all principles ... it is impossible for anyone to believe the same thing to be and not to be."[8] Bruno sees the universe not as a finished product but as an eternally changing unsymmetrical world of process. His opposition to the Thomistic world denies the boundaries of contradiction, embracing instead the Neoplatonic conceit of *concordia oppositorum* realized in an infinitely shifting constellation of relationships between self and other, higher and lower. The satirical attack on the logical categories of Aristotelianism in Bruno's works as well as his use of dialogue form attracted

Joyce's interest as a complement to the didactic absolutes that structured much of his Jesuit education. Bruno's advocacy of natural religion and his pantheistic view of the universe as a living creature pervaded by an immanent divine soul also appealed to Joyce's syncretic impulses.

I wish to argue that the continuous play of transformations within the concordance of *Ulysses* offers a message to read the work Hermetically. I also wish to qualify my thesis by acknowledging that Joyce was no unswerving devotee of Neoplatonic ideals, or of any totalizing principles. Instead, his interest was eclectic and gravitated toward what he could appropriate to undermine authority, including the authority he himself constructed. Hermeticism's emphasis on the simultaneity of opposites obviously appealed to Joyce's attraction to the contradictory. The message to read Hermetically is itself a philosopher's stone, found not at the conclusion of a search, but in the discovery that the search is its own purpose.

ii

we must vaunt no idle dubiosity as to its genuine authorship and holusbolus authoritativeness. (*FW*118.03–04)

The contradictions that the mythological Hermes embodies and resolves certainly appealed to the author who employed the Hermetic *concordia oppositorum* as a thematic design in *Ulysses*. As guide to travelers and god of commerce, Hermes possesses affinities with Bloom's symbolic attributes; and his accoutrements of hat, sandals, and staff link him with Stephen. Hermes is also the god of orators and of thieves, two functions which Michel Serres yokes in his development of the metaphor of the parasite. Serres points out that the parasite takes while giving nothing concrete in exchange, and uses the example of Odysseus eating at Alcinous' table and paying for the banquet with words.[9] In *Ulysses* we witness the notorious parasitism that Ellmann has characterized in Joyce's life transferred to Stephen, whose rhetorical skills bring him offers of drink and employment in "Aeolus" and whose conversation, limited though it appears to be in the early hours of June 17, is sufficient payment for Bloom's hospitality.

In a letter to Frank Budgen, Joyce wrote "Hermes is the god of signposts: i.e. he is, specially for a traveller like Ulysses, the point at which roads parallel merge and roads contrary also" (*Letters I* 147–48). Joyce was referring to Hermes' function as the god of the boundary-stone, the site of demarcation which must be transgressed for economic and cultural exchange to occur. Indeed, Norman O. Brown points out that the name Hermes was derived from the Greek word for "stone-heap," primitive boundary markers placed at entrances to houses and at crossroads.[10] Given two of his other divine duties, god of trade and conductor of travelers, Hermes governs both the signification and the breaching of distinctions. While aiding the preservation of discrete identities, he encourages interactions which will disrupt them. Joyce's stylistic intentions in *Ulysses* follow a similar duplicitous path. As Karen Lawrence argues, Joyce's stylistic conception is "regressive" in making presentations that are subsequently "denied by the rest of the book."[11] What is established is done so to be refuted; borders are created so that they may be traversed.

Hermes' appearance as cosmic messenger in *Ulysses* is initially suggested through an allusion to his golden-winged sandals with which he traverses the sea in Book 5 of the *Odyssey*. It occurs in the context of a conversation between Stephen and Mulligan during which Mulligan expresses his allegiance to mockery. Mulligan's messenger status is underscored by specific links with his mythological counterpart. In "Telemachus" he is referred to as "Mercurial Malachi" (*U*1.518)—"Malachi" is Hebrew for "my messenger"—and, as he plunges into the sea for his morning ablution, "Mercury's hat" is described "quivering in the fresh wind that bore back to them his brief birdsweet cries" (*U*1.601–02). Stephen's mercurial hat and sandals are either handed to him by or borrowed from Mulligan, and Mulligan also comes to control the key to his domicile. When Stephen confronts Mulligan regarding the latter's cavalier dismissal of Stephen's mother's death, Mulligan responds, "It's a beastly thing and nothing else. It simply doesn't matter.... To me it's all a mockery and beastly" (*U*1.206–10). Although his comment does little to prop up Stephen's mood, it demonstrates Mulligan's rejection of Stephen's maudlin obsessions and of his inscriptions of indelible meaning. Like Hermes the trickster, Mulligan shifts roles continuously and beguiles his overly serious companion by endorsing none of them. While Stephen as Telemachus searches for a father, Mulligan derides all authority. As he does with Stephen's Shakespeare theory in "Scylla and Charybdis," Mulligan burlesques solutions and thereby steers the narrative to evade closure and to sustain mystery.

As Mulligan descends from the top of Martello Tower with a partial recitation of "Who Goes with Fergus," a song of comfort in the first version of Yeats's *The Countess Cathleen*, Stephen's interior monologue initially picks up the comforting, positive images from Fergus' song. His associations with the name shift from Fergus mac Roich to Fergus mac Leti, whose gift from the fairies of sandals with which he could walk on or under the water, suggest the link with Hermes:[12] "Woodshadows floated silently by through the morning peace from the stairhead seaward where he gazed. Inshore and farther out the mirror of water whitened, spurned by lightshod hurrying feet" (*U*1.242–44). Stephen's intertextualizing is spurred by images of freedom: Fergus mac Leti receives the sandals as a ransom for freeing the king of the little people; Hermes carries Zeus's instructions to Calypso to free Odysseus, and Fergus' song offers to free Stephen from his obsessive brooding on "love's bitter mystery." However, the reference to the song takes a turn when Stephen recalls singing it while his mother lay dying. His dark memories of her death and his vision of her as a vampiric ghost coincide with the appearance of a morning cloud which covers the sun, until they are interrupted by Mulligan's voice from within the tower. The narrator tells us, "Stephen, still trembling at his soul's cry, heard warm running sunlight and in the air behind him friendly words" (*U*1.282–83). The "warm running sunlight" can again be taken as a reference to Hermes' golden-winged sandals. The friendly words which unwittingly initiated Stephen's lugubrious meditation also conclude it, imposing circularity on this section of the narrative. The appearance of the Hermes reference shifts the narrative voice, creating a fold in the text which becomes one of many such registers of the sources of Stephen's psychological discontent and creative paralysis. The transition back to the narrative proper is again accompanied by a Hermes reference, thereby demonstrating the dual disruptive and restorative functions of the messenger figure.

The synchronicity between Stephen and Bloom is strengthened by narrative parallels. The first Bloom episode, "Calypso," also contains a morning cloud (presumably the same one that passes over Stephen) at about the same distance into the episode that it appears in "Telemachus."[13] Like Stephen, Bloom plunges into a despairing meditation on death and decay at this point in the narrative. Like Stephen's, his depressive soliloquy ends with a Hermes reference: "Quick warm sunlight came running from Berkeley road, swiftly in slim sandals, along the brightening footpath" (*U*4.240–41). Bloom reenters 7 Eccles street, where he will be cuckolded later that day, to discover messages, two letters and a card, on the hallfloor. The letter from Blazes Boylan to Molly will in large part dictate his physical and mental evasions for the rest of the day and inadvertently will result in his meeting Stephen and in the consequent merger of Jewgreek and greekjew (*U*15.2097–98), Blephen/Stoom (*U*17.549–51). The two messages from Milly, a letter to Bloom and a card to Molly, suggest the inequality with which she views her two parents.[14] Molly abruptly acknowledges her daughter's message before demanding that Bloom expedite his preparation of her tea while she tucks Boylan's letter beneath her pillow. Her action, however, does not escape Bloom's notice, and somehow he acquires knowledge of the letter's content, for his dread over their four o'clock appointment recurs throughout the day.

By sharing thoughts and possessing complementary personality traits, Bloom and Stephen are implicitly posed as psychological messengers to each other. An example of this connection occurs in a link between "Aeolus" and "Ithaca." J. J. O'Molloy, speaking of Seymour Bushe's rhetorical prowess in the Childs murder case, pauses dramatically before quoting from Bushe's oration. At this point a vignette appears to form in Stephen's mind: "Messenger took out his matchbox thoughtfully and lit his cigar. I have often thought since on looking back over that strange time that it was that small act, trivial in itself, that striking of that match, that determined the whole aftercourse of both our lives" (U7.762–65). The vignette appears to be picked up again in Bloom's home after the keyless couple enters and Bloom, Stephen's messenger, kneels to kindle the hearth. The lighting of fires is revealed to be a touchstone in Stephen's mind for acts of kindness. He thinks of several such incidents and the narrative ironically posits domestic peace within a household where Molly has just cavorted with her lover (U17.134–47).[15]

However, the "Aeolus" passage, with its mention of "Messenger," is troublesome. It intrudes stylistically and one cannot place it with certainty in Stephen's mind. Don Gifford separates the two sentences, linking "Messenger" with O'Molloy who is about to deliver a message, and with a major figure in Bushe's speech, Moses, who was God's messenger. He identifies the second sentence as a parody of a passage in *David Copperfield* in which David comments on the wedding of Peggoty and Barkis.[16] Robert Spoo argues that the Dickensian parody announces proleptically a more extensive parody of teleology and monocausality which is situated in the problematic status of marriage in the novel. Spoo reminds us that marriage is a common source for teleological metaphors and states, "though the novel jokes about Stephen and Bloom going off to be married by Father Maher [U16.1887–88] and taking nuptial communion together, in reality the later episodes hold off resolution and closure by putting styles and irony between the bride and the bridegroom."[17]

The mention of "Messenger" in "Aeolus" interrupts the narrative flow to create another fold which invites the reader to assign meaning while undercutting that meaning. Teleological order is both promulgated and transgressed, the mystification of narrative links is both enhanced and demystified in a convergence of contrary intentions.

Although never appearing as a physical presence in *Ulysses*, Milly Bloom functions as a messenger figure. For her mother, she serves as a link with the past. Molly takes pride in her daughter's attractiveness and, during the course of her soliloquy, mentions parallels with her own youth. Bloom considers their connection, calling Milly "Marionette," thinking "Molly.

Milly. Same thing watered down," and reflecting on the fact that they often menstruate at the same time (*U*15.540, 6.87, 13.785). But she also functions on a Hermetic level, connecting the cosmic with the earthly and is linked with Hermes in a narrative shift reminiscent of those discussed in "Telemachus" and "Calypso."

The De Quincey parody in "Oxen of the Sun" consists of a parade of constellations which begins as an apocalyptic vision, the zodiacal forms serving as "murderers of the sun" (*U*14.1095). Again the narrative content is transformed from negative to positive with the appearance of a Hermes reference. The harbinger of the daystar, "the bride, ever virgin" is named Millicent and arises "shod in sandals of bright gold" before metamorphosing into "Alpha, a ruby and triangled sign upon the forehead of Taurus" (*U*14.1101, .1103, .1108–09). The pattern of constellations presented in the De Quincey parody replicates Bruno's allegory of cosmic renewal in his *Expulsion of the Triumphant Beast*.[18] Its concluding phrase also signals earthly renewal, for the next section of "Oxen of the Sun," the Walter Savage Landor parody, concludes with Mulligan's pointing out to Stephen Bloom's trance-like staring at the scarlet triangular label on a bottle of Bass's ale. Bloom is himself a Taurus, and the Bass label perhaps reminds him of the red-labeled bottle of poison with which his father committed suicide (cf. *U*6.359). The Macaulay parody informs us that he contemplates transactions which occurred during his boyhood (*U*14.1188–89), and he is so engrossed in his contemplation that he is initially oblivious to Mulligan's request that he pass the ale. The metamorphosis in the sky prefigured by the Hermes reference, signals the potential for a parallel transformation on earth. Bloom's despairing preoccupation with losses of father, son, and wife is modified by his meeting Stephen who becomes a psychological messenger to him. Bloom's wandering acquires a purpose other than evasion, and his mental scheming develops increased breadth and relevance to his personal affairs. When he finally acknowledges Mulligan's request and passes the ale to him, he also acquires the status of Stephen's messenger, a position adumbrated at the conclusion of "Scylla and Charybdis" when he came between Mulligan and Stephen on the library steps. Bloom rids himself of the red-labeled emblem of failed fatherhood and unwittingly usurps the role of the usurper Mulligan by assuming care for Stephen, substituting his human concerns for Mulligan's cynicism as a complementary message for his adopted son.

Mulligan's whistle of call on the first page of the novel is answered by the two strong whistles that pierce the calm of the morning (*U*1.26–27); it is also paralleled by two less professional whistles as Bloom attempts to hail a coachman for Stephen and himself at the beginning of the Nostos section

(*U*16.28–30). Again this correspondence occurs at about the same point in the narrative of the two episodes. Bloom's whistles also answer Simon Dedalus' two shrill whistles at the beginning of the final chapter of *A Portrait* as Stephen prepares to take flight from home (*P*175), further signifying Bloom's substitute paternity. In "Eumaeus" Bloom will unmask another false messenger, one D. B. Murphy, an unmasking that Murphy's status as substitute Mulligan will simultaneously undercut. Mulligan's mockery and abuse initiate Stephen's departure from home; Bloom's angelic ministration offers light to this particular gentile and effects a temporary domestic alternative.

The actual meeting of Stephen and Bloom has long germinated in the reader's expectations due to the series of near-meetings prior to "Oxen of the Sun." However, this climactic encounter achieves no particular dramatic resonance in the protean style that constitutes this episode. Indeed, the narrative presentation linking the development of the English language to embryonic development, itself a demonstration of the limitations of imitative form,[19] obscures the dramatic significance of the first sustained encounter between the novel's two main characters. In the same manner, the narrative voices of "Circe," "Eumaeus," and "Ithaca" distract the reader from Bloom's paternal custody of Stephen. Through their exhibition of perceptual and interpretive constraints, they qualify the very connections they have encouraged the reader to make. In doing so, *Ulysses'* messengers conspire to embrace contradiction.

iii

> The origin lies at the place of inevitable loss, the point where the truth of things corresponded to a truthful discourse, the site of a fleeting articulation that a discourse has obscured and finally lost.
> —Michel Foucault, "Nietzsche, Genealogy, History"[20]

While promulgating his aesthetic theory to Lynch in *A Portrait*, Stephen states, "Aristotle's entire system of philosophy rests upon his book of psychology and that, I think, rests on his statement that the same attribute cannot at the same time and in the same connection belong to and not belong to the same subject" (*P*208). After linking his theory of the process of apprehension to Aquinas, he adds, "when we come to the phenomena of artistic conception, artistic gestation and artistic reproduction I require a new terminology and a new personal experience" (*P*209). The new language and new experience become Joyce's style, an integrated cluster of changing elements that resist reduction to a generative first principle. Witness Joyce's parody of the law of non-contradiction in *Finnegans Wake*:

I cannot now have or nothave a piece of cheeps in your pocket at
the same time and with the same manners as you can now nothalf
or half the cheek apiece I've in mind unless Burrus and Caseous
have not or not have seemaultaneously sysentangled themselves,
selldear to soldthere. (*FW*161.09–13)

In his pretentious dialect the speaker postulates the distinction between
the twins Shem and Shaun, yet the Wake language inherently refutes the
principle of non-contradiction. By substituting the prefix "sys-" which means
"together" for "dis-" as the speaker attempts to say "disentangled
themselves," Joyce paradoxically undercuts Aristotle's principle by
simultaneously promoting and negating it.[21]

In "Scylla and Charybdis" Stephen ponders Aristotle's principle of
identity during his rendition of his Shakespeare theory.[22] While the rumor
of George Russell's gathering a sheaf of younger poets' verses, a sheaf that
would exclude Stephen, is discussed, Stephen looks at his hat and thinks,
"Aristotle's experiment. One or two? Necessity is that in virtue of which it is
impossible that one can be otherwise. Argal, one hat is one hat" (*U*9.297–99).
Unlike Bloom, who typically employs material considerations to escape
unpleasant thoughts or circumstances, Stephen relies on abstract ones.
However, the larger context in which this aside is employed negates the
aside, for Stephen's theory poses Shakespeare as father and son
consubstantial, a sundering which becomes a reconciliation. Although
Stephen later states that he does not believe his own theory, the context is
again one of personal frustration. The theory ultimately offers more
information about Stephen's situation than it does about Shakespeare's.
Stephen's identification with his fictional biography both equates and
separates him from his subject, an equation that offers him insight and a
separation that gives him pause.

Nietzsche, who hammered with the philosophy of perspectivism, states
of Aristotle's law of non-contradiction: "The conceptual ban on
contradiction proceeds from the belief that we are able to form concepts,
that the concept not only designates the essence of a thing but comprehends
it—In fact, logic applies only to fictitious entities that we have created."[13]
Indeed Joyce operates through contradiction, through implicit revisions that
are in a constant state of becoming through self-aware fiction and fictional
self-awareness. As Umberto Eco states, his work is a continuous dialectic
"between Chaos and Cosmos."[24] His references to the law of non-
contradiction and the principle of identity, in *A Portrait*, *Ulysses*, and
Finnegans Wake, occur amid professorial diatribes, by Stephen in the first two
instances and by Shaun in the last. While Joyce, with Aristotle, would attack

Plato's celebration of eternal immutable forms, he would accept Plato as a defender of dialogue, dialogue which is always open to novel turns and which knows no finality. The attraction to Bruno also relates in some measure to Bruno's use of dialogue form. In contrast, Joyce's education via catechism, reflected in "Nestor" and parodied in "Ithaca," ultimately consisted of fixed precepts rather than an ongoing dialogic pursuit. For Joyce, the ontological condition of experience and of language is to be dialogical.[25] The quasi-monologues in which mention of the law of non-contradiction occurs are all undercut, whether by context, subtext, or the language through which they are represented.

As an exile, Joyce's fascination with the idea of return extends beyond geographical locality to metaphysical principle. The Neoplatonic concept of *epistrophe*, the principle of reversion of phenomena back to their archetypes, informs the appeal of Hermeticism to Joyce, for the search for unity is essentially a return. However, Hermetic thought poses no distinction between unity and multiplicity. Instead of the Cartesian *cogito*, where unity is achieved by reducing things to a common denominator, the Hermetic principle of oneness is experienced simultaneously as cosmic unity and plurality. The philosophy of signatures functions through analogy to expand rather than contract. Sympathetic relationships between plants, places, stars, and the human situation oppose the Cartesian logic of hierarchical exclusion through difference.[26] These sympathetic relationships within the primacy of chaos posited by Hermeticism allow for infinite imitation and substitution, a multiplicity of interchanging masks, when subsumed into a literary text. The worlds of *Ulysses* and *Finnegans Wake* consist of correspondences, from the thought fragments that Stephen and Bloom mysteriously share and the elaborate schemas that Joyce constructed linking time, color, and anatomy with episodes of *Ulysses*, to the animistic view of *Finnegans Wake*. Joyce's preference is for the analogical, an attempt to knit together the world. His works grow increasingly encyclopedic, increasingly inclusive, explicitly transgressing the boundaries of identity in "Circe" and in *Finnegans Wake*. As master parodist, he is also supreme imitator, a Hermes himself who exchanges masks in his passage between opposites—a magician, shape-shifter, *pharmakeus*.

iv

a system is like the tail of truth, but truth is like a lizard; it leaves its tail in your fingers and runs away knowing full well that it will grow a new one in a twinkling.
                                        —Ivan Turgenev, *Letter to Tolstoy* 1857[27]

Oscar Wilde once said, "man is least himself when he talks in his own person. Give him a mask, and he will tell the truth."[28] Like the messenger figure in narrative, masks are invariably related to transition and to the transgression of boundaries.[29] In primitive societies their purpose is to establish an equivocal frontier between man and beast by incorporating their differences. By offering the possibility of selective personification, masks have a therapeutic function. They objectify the repressed or unknown and thereby impute ontological status to emotional states. In the tradition of classical theatre and myth, infused with polytheistic preferences, masks as personae testify to the ambiguity and ambivalence central to mutability. Both the Satyr and the Gorgon, which A. David Napier labels the two archetypal mask types,[30] express this ambiguity and ambivalence in their hybridization of human and beast. The very function of the Gorgon is ambivalent. Although it is horrific and deadly, Perseus uses the Gorgon's head to rescue Andromeda and to save his mother from a siege by Polydectes. Indeed Perseus has affinities with Hermes. In addition to the wallet for hiding the Gorgon head and avoiding its lethal stare, he obtains winged sandals and a helmet of invisibility from the nymphs so that he may flee the remaining Gorgons.

In "Circe," an appropriate episode for masking due to its dramatic form and protean character roles,[31] Joyce explicitly mentions masks four times. The initial two instances occur within a theatrical context (*U*15.424, .1690). The third blends mirrored opposites as the Siamese twins, Philip Drunk and Philip Sober, appear masked with Matthew Arnold's face (*U*15.2512–14), foreshadowing the imminent conjunction of the complementary personalities of Stephen and Bloom reflected in the mirror with Shakespeare's face (*U*15.3821–23). The fourth explicit mention of a mask occurs as a stage direction, personifying a transition in time: "(*The night hours, one by one, steal to the last place. Morning, noon and twilight hours retreat before them. They are masked, with daggered hair and bracelets of dull bells. Weary they curchycurchy under veils.*)" (*U*15.4081–84). "Daggered hair" can be seen as a reference to Medusa, particularly in light of the transitional context and as a foreshadowing of the next scene where Stephen confronts his ghoulish mother. The masked noon and twilight hours wearily retreat, their morris dancing signifying change,[32] as the night hours plunge Stephen into his unconscious to therapeutically purge his obsession with his mother.

In "Plato's Pharmacy" Jacques Derrida discusses the Egyptian counterpart of Hermes, Thoth, as a signifier god, a joker capable of infinite substitutions with no fixed identity of his own. As a variable, Thoth/Hermes is capable of taking on the mask of his opposite, thereby opposing himself by taking shape from the very thing he resists and for which he substitutes.[33] Like a mask, the messenger figure translates into its opposite. Joyce's parody is essentially narrative masking. It takes shape from the thing for which it substitutes and conflates differences so that a new order emerges. The connotations of parody are in this sense paradoxical in being both disruptive and restorative.

The term parody is in part derived from "para-ode" in Greek tragedy, meaning the entrance from the side of the stage by the chorus. By offering a social or divine context for the preceding or succeeding actions, the Greek chorus imposes stability on the narrative. In doing so, it demonstrates the restorative function of the messenger figure which complements its transgressive purpose. Rene Girard has written on the sacrificial and restorative functions of the Greek chorus which operates as a collective voice, a voice of moderation and common sense that offers equilibrium in the face of the continual oscillations of the tragic situation. In effect, it dissolves differences to meet the threat of maleficent contagion and to reinforce the domestic status quo.[34] In *Totem and Taboo*, Freud considers how the chorus serves as a sympathetic presence for the tragic hero, warning him of impending disasters and mourning him when he meets his fate.[35] The incarnation of the messenger at the beginning of the Nostos—the return— section of the novel, D. B. Murphy performs chorically.

Murphy is listed in the Gilbert-Gorman and Linati schemas as "Ulysses Pseudangelos"—the false messenger.[36] A sailor from the Rosevean, the threemaster that passed behind Stephen at the conclusion of "Proteus," Murphy returns after a seven-year voyage as mythic storyteller and liar extraordinaire. His return prefigures Bloom's uncomfortable return to 7 Eccles street where, at the conclusion of the episode, the "Ithaca" narrator will simultaneously inflate his peregrinations through Dublin by linking them with the adventures of another mythic sailor—Sinbad—and deflate them with the final dot. As Bloom meditates on the fate of Parnell and Kitty O'Shea and considers the connections with his own marital situation, he thinks, "coming back was the worst thing you ever did because it went without saying you would feel out of place as things always moved with the times" (*U*16.1402–03). His anxiety mirrors that of Stephen, who has returned to Dublin with his pretentions to poetic greatness punctured, and of Molly whose soliloquy recaptures significant events in her life in an attempt to come to terms with the sexual transgression she has performed earlier in the day.

As Ulysses in modern guise, Bloom functions as counterpart to Murphy. The protean face of Murphy's tattoo marks its wearer as an adept at conjuring illusions. Bloom's unveiling of him has been read as the final triumph of this restored hero-patriarch over his Dublin adversaries. As protector of Stephen, Bloom's commonsensical warnings undercut Murphy's recreation of his wanderings. When Bloom asks him about the Rock of Gibraltar, he transforms Murphy from animated storyteller to sulking has-been who confesses to being "tired of all them rocks in the sea" (*U*16.622). Bloom's "Sherlockholmesing" leads him to take the measure of Murphy and to impart a lesson to Stephen: "Our mutual friend's stories are like himself.... Do you think they are genuine? He could spin those yarns for hours on end all night long and lie like old boots" (*U*16.821–23).

Although we see Bloom's victory on one level, we commit a misreading in not also seeing Murphy like Mulligan, as an incarnation of the trickster author and as a mirror for the reader. The master labyrinth weaver also has tired of the fixed rocks of style and form and must fictionize to tell truthfully the tale of narrative memory as the continual exchange of masks. We are also procrustean in our elevation of Bloom in not noting that Bloom's stilted speech and ostentatious commentaries are no more genuine than Murphy's postcard. Bloom's proffering of Molly's photograph as an enticement to Stephen uses visual fiction in an attempt to regain control of his household. In essence, Bloom and Murphy function as counterparts, contained singly in Odysseus.

Like the Man in the Macintosh, Murphy appears as an unsolvable conundrum, a gesture toward the uncertainty principle with which Joyce subtly infuses his work.[37] Murphies and Macintoshes continually create fissures in the narrative flow of *Ulysses* and are endlessly variable in their repetition. They comment on the unfolding plot of Bloom, Stephen, and Molly by intersecting with it and by offering an alternative to the privileging of that plot over another that contains an exposition of the texture and function of narrative. Their messages break the linear flow and cause us to become meta-readers who must reconstruct the text while reminding us of the revisionist tendencies of memory.[38] In our rereadings, we must reexamine our dismissal of Mulligan and Murphy as false messengers and our assured acceptance of Bloom's angelic ministration. In addition to involving us in Joyce's fictions, the messengers in *Ulysses* also cause us to step outside of those fictions.

Return becomes not just a theme in *Ulysses*, but a narrative structure as demonstrated by Joyce's fascination with chiasmus. The principle of return operates on the level of character, narrator, and reader. All read reflexively repeating and reintegrating details and images captured through the paradoxical mask of memory. The genre that emerges is one E. D. Hirsch has termed "intrinsic," manifested not through an ideal model but through the reading process.[39] The impulse to return in the principal characters, the various narrative voices, and the reader stems from the search for unification, the mythic quest for *quinta essentia*, the signatures of the author god in the world of the book. Yet these illuminations are achieved via multiplicity so that re-cognitions are illusory selections from experience, reconstructions infiltrated by mutability.

As Vicki Mahaffey contends, the narrative movement of *Ulysses* splits its readers' minds in two by promising to bring them home while progressively estranging them from what home represents.[40] Inevitably altered by the passage of time, home is rendered fictitious so that one returns to find oneself still in exodus. The destabilizing shifts that narrative masking coerce reveal readers to be exiles, unable to achieve the closure they seek. In addition to attacking readers' sensibilities, however, Joyce's transgressions also liberate them from those sensibilities. As a proto-postmodernist, Joyce invites his readers into the authorial gesture by demonstrating to them their exilic status. Reading, like the quest for home, is displayed as an exercise in approximation rather than attainment, an ongoing dialogue between reader and text that involves selection and change.

When Murphy is unveiled as liar by Bloom, he exits center stage in the "Eumaeus" narrator's rendition of the events in the cabman's shelter. In this manner, Murphy as messenger also functions as scapegoat in the Girardian sense of the term. Girard argues that the original event that led to rite was murder, and that the objective of ritual is to keep violence outside the community. He advances the concept of mimetic rivalry as a universal model for the human psyche, one that logically leads to scapegoating. The surrogate victim, or *pharmakos*, initially functions as the Other and becomes the repository of violent projections and must be killed to restore order to the community. As such the *pharmakos* is like the *pharmakon*, both poison and antidote.[41]

Not only does Murphy offer Bloom the opportunity to prove himself before Stephen by serving as father-protector and wise man at the level of plot, but he also functions to restore narrative order after the violent disruption of "Circe." As scapegoat, Murphy is imbued with Otherness, an Otherness that is actually a projection of the reader's and narrative memory's own anxieties over their own fictionalizing. By sacrificing the messenger whose lies are in actuality reflections of the truth of misreading and narrative revisionism, these anxieties are temporarily allayed and the comfort of a linear plot about characters is ephemerally restored.

D. B. Murphy wears the mask of liar, but it is a monstrous face at which readers resist looking directly afraid of seeing their own reflections. Instead, Joyce's narrative shifts implore his readers to play Perseus, whom Homer calls "preeminent among all men."[42] Because Perseus would perish by gazing directly at the Gorgons, he approaches them by peering into the mirror of Athena's shield and decapitates Medusa. Similarly, Ulysses' messengers permit its readers a deflection through which to approach their anxieties over the fictional nature of their recognitions. In "Eumaeus" Bloom's displacement of Murphy momentarily allows readers to slay these anxieties. However, Joyce remembers that once Medusa's head was severed her children sprang from her neck. Although the scapegoating and choric functions of the messenger figure restore the linear plot by reconciling the Other, the narration must oscillate toward another transgression in order to maintain its dynamism.

By transgressing non-contradiction, Joycean messengers spur us to read Hermetically. We move simultaneously backwards and forwards in the text, associatively replicating experience yet continuously revising those associations as we progress into new experiences. By containing opposites and incorporating the Other, messenger figures unify this multiplicity while providing clues to authorial signatures.

Joyce's narrative masking subsumes the reader into the text as interpreter of *hermēneus*, a diviner of its signatures, yet internal conflicts and implicit parodies render each reading transitory. The boundaries of interpretation are shown to require consistent redefinition and reinterpretation. Perception is showcased as a metonymic and synecdochic act, a combination of memory and forgetting.[43] Joyce forces his readers to make continual choices and changes that may shift with each reading. We move from part to whole, from fetish to allotropic state, in a dynamic discourse where paradigms become contingencies and contingencies paradigms. And in choosing, the reader is permitted to return to the original impulse involved in the creation of the work, to assume the authorial presence, while participating in polytropic enactments of that impulse. Like the satiric underpinnings in Bruno's works, Joyce's synthesis proceeds from and by parody, a gesture toward the limitations and imitations of comprehending based upon a selected order of appearances. As sorters of messages, we engage in infinite permutations and combinations of dialogue with the messengers of meaning in Joyce's text—a process that paradoxically creates unity through disruption and disruption through unity.[44]

NOTES

1. Norman Malcolm, *Ludwig Wittgenstein: A Memoir* (London: Oxford Univ. Press, 1958), p. 29.

2. Paul Ricoeur, *Freud and Philosophy: An Essay on Interpretation*, trans. Denis Savage (New Haven: Yale Univ. Press, 1970), p. 27. Ricoeur's version of hermeneutics goes

beyond that of Gadamer to reject the notion that hermeneutics should restore the past's meaning in its own terms; indeed, he would argue that that meaning should be exposed as a lie of consciousness. William V. Spanos also argues for a destructive poetics, a new hermeneutics which requires a rethinking of Heidegger's existential analytic: "Heidegger's destruction of the Western ontotheological tradition discovers that its metaphysical orientation manifests itself in a coercive 'permanentizing' of being (*Bestandsicherung*), and that this discovery reveals the platonic 'reality' to be appearance, *eidos* (Idea), to be, in fact an *eidolon*, an idol or image." However, Spanos sees the limitations of Heideggerean phenomenology and Derridean deconstruction in their tendency to read literary texts spatially, and contends that temporal reading is best suited to demystification. "Breaking the Circle: Hermeneutics as Disclosure," *boundary 2*, 5 (1977), 421–48.

3. *The Complete Works of Aristotle*, II, ed. Jonathan Barnes (Princeton: Princeton Univ. Press, 1984), *Poetics* 1452a22–26, p. 2324.

4. The seminal discussion of *polytropia* in *Ulysses* is Fritz Senn's "Book of Many Turns," *JJQ*, 10 (Fall 1972), 29–46; rpt. in *Joyce's Dislocutions: Essays on Reading as Translation*, ed. John Paul Riquelme (Baltimore: Johns Hopkins Univ. Press, 1984), pp. 121–37. Brook Thomas develops Senn's discussion in *James Joyce's "Ulysses": A Book of Many Happy Returns* (Baton Rouge: Louisiana State Univ. Press, 1982).

5. Michel Foucault, "What Is an Author?" in *The Foucault Reader*, ed. Paul Rabinow (New York: Pantheon, 1984), p. 110; rpt. from *Textual Strategies: Perspectives in Post-Structuralist Criticism*, ed. and trans. Josué V. Harari (Ithaca: Cornell Univ. Press, 1979). In her excellent book on authority and unauthorized narratives in Joyce's work, Vicki Mahaffey quotes this passage and points out that "Foucault too argues for a reversal of the traditional idea of the author rather than an appreciation of its contradictory nature and potential." *Reauthorizing Joyce* (New York: Cambridge Univ. Press, 1988), p. 25.

6. For analyses of Joyce's complex and paradoxical interest in Hermetic philosophy, see William York Tindall, "James Joyce and the Hermetic Tradition," *Journal of the History of Ideas*, 15 (1954), 23–29; Craig Carver, "James Joyce and the Theory of Magic," *JJQ*, 15 (Spring 1978), 201–14; Barbara DiBernard, *Alchemy and "Finnegans Wake"* (Albany: State Univ. of New York Press, 1980); and Robert D. Newman, "*Transformatio Coniunctionis*: Alchemy in *Ulysses*," in *Joyce's "Ulysses": The Larger Perspective*, ed. Robert D. Newman and Weldon Thornton (Newark: Univ. of Delaware Press, 1984), pp. 168–86.

7. Georges Borach reports Joyce saying in 1917: "In the last two hundred years we haven't had a great thinker. My judgment is bold, since Kant is included. All the great thinkers of recent centuries from Kant to Benedetto Croce have only cultivated the garden. The greatest thinker of all times, in my opinion, is Aristotle. Everything, in his work, is defined with wonderful clarity and simplicity. Later, volumes were written to define the same things." "Conversations with James Joyce," in *Portraits of the Artist in Exile: Recollections of James Joyce by Europeans*, ed. Willard Potts (Seattle: Univ. of Washington Press, 1979), p. 71.
Bruno railed against Aristotle's failure to accept the unity of opposites:

> Aristotle, among others, did not grasp the one, did not grasp being, did not grasp the true, because he never realized how being is one; and though he was free to adopt a significance for being common to both substance and accident, and further to distinguish his categories according to so many genera and species, so many differentiations, he has not avoided being any less ignorant of the truth, through a failure to deepen his cognition of this unity and lack of differentiation in constant nature and being. And, as a thoroughly arid sophist, by his malignant explanations and his frivolous persuasions, he perverts the statements of the ancients and sets himself

against the truth—not so much perhaps through weakness of intellect as through force of jealousy and ambition.

"Concerning the Cause, Principle, and One," in *The Infinite in Giordano Bruno*, ed. Sidney Thomas Greenburg (New York: King's Crown Press, 1950), p. 139. Theoharis Constantine Theoharis quotes this passage and offers excellent readings of Joyce's applications of Aristotle and Bruno in *Joyce's "Ulysses": An Anatomy of the Soul* (Chapel Hill: Univ. of North Carolina Press, 1988), pp. 1–87. See also Richard Ellmann, *Ulysses on the Liffey* (New York: Oxford Univ. Press, 1972), pp. 53–56; Sheldon Brivic, *Joyce the Creator* (Madison: Univ. of Wisconsin Press, 1985), pp. 44–54, and Elliott B. Gose, *The Transformation Process in Joyce's "Ulysses"* (Toronto: Univ. of Toronto Press, 1980), pp. 3–91.

8. *The Complete Works of Aristotle*, II, *Metaphysics* 1005b23, p. 1588.

9. Michel Serres, *Hermes: Literature, Science, Philosophy*, ed. Josué V. Harari and David E. Bell (Baltimore: Johns Hopkins Univ. Press, 1982). p. xxxv.

10. Norman O. Brown, *Hermes the Thief: The Evolution of a Myth* (New York: Vintage, 1969), pp. 33–46.

11. Karen Lawrence, *The Odyssey of Style in "Ulysses"* (Princeton: Princeton Univ. Press, 1981), pp. 204, 206.

12. Standish Hayes O'Grady, "The Death of Fergus mac Leti," in *Silva Gadelica* (London and Edinburgh: Williams and Norgate, 1892), pp. 269–82.

13. In the 1961 Random House text, in "Telemachus" "A cloud began to cover the sun slowly shadowing the bay in deeper green" (*U*9), and in "Calypso" "A cloud began to cover the sun wholly slowly wholly" (*U*61). In the Gabler text, the two appearances of the cloud are a perfect rhetorical match with a "wholly" added to Stephen's vision and taken away from Bloom's, so that for both "A cloud began to cover the sun slowly, wholly" (*U*1.248, 4.218). Jean Kimball points this out in "'Lui, C'est Moi': The Brother Relationship in *Ulysses*," *JJQ*, 25 (Winter 1988), 232. Sheldon Brivic offers a list of synchronicities in *Joyce the Creator*, pp. 145–53.

14. For Molly's reaction to this slight see *U*18.717–18.

15. I previously suggested the connection between the stylistic intrusion in "Aeolus" and the scene in "Ithaca" in "*Transformatio Coniunctionis*: Alchemy in *Ulysses*," pp. 180–81.

16. Don Gifford, *'Ulysses' Annotated* (Berkeley: Univ. of California Press, 1988), p. 146. The passage in *David Copperfield* is "I have often thought, since, what an odd, innocent, out-of-the-way kind of wedding it must have been! We got back into the chaise again soon after dark, and drove cosily back, looking up at the stars and talking about them" (chapter 10).

17. Robert Spoo, "Teleology Monocausality and Marriage in *Ulysses*," *ELH*, 56 (1989), 439–62. Spoo notes another connection between the striking of a match and the marriage motif in "Circe" when Stephen asks Lynch for a cigarette and, immediately prior to lighting it, states "And so Georgina Johnson is dead and married" (*U*15.3619–23).

18. See Michael Seidel, *Epic Geography: James Joyce's "Ulysses"* (Princeton: Princeton Univ. Press, 1976), pp. 55–59, and Robert D. Newman, "Bloom and the Beast: Joyce's Use of Bruno's Astrological Allegory," in *New Alliances in Joyce Studies*, ed. Bonnie Kime Scott (Newark: Univ. of Delaware Press, 1988), pp. 210–16. The actual astronomy of this passage is discussed by Mark E. Littmann and Charles A. Schweighauser, "Astronomical Allusions, Their Meaning and Purpose, in *Ulysses*," *JJQ*, 2 (Summer 1965), 238–46.

19. See Weldon Thornton's discussion of the idolatry of literary form in "Oxen of the Sun," "Voices and Values in *Ulysses*," in *Joyce's "Ulysses": The Larger Perspective*, pp. 244–70.

20. Michel Foucault, "Nietzsche, Genealogy, History," in *Language, Counter-Memory, Practice*, ed. Donald F. Bouchard, trans. Donald Bouchard and Sherry Simon (Ithaca: Cornell Univ. Press, 1977), p. 143.

21. I am indebted to Harry C. Staley for pointing out this *Finnegans Wake* reference to me. His discussion of it occurs in his unpublished manuscript, "No Word is Impossible."

22. Whereas the law of non-contradiction refers to any logical statement, the principle of identity is concerned specifically with substances. See *The Complete Works of Aristotle*, II, *Metaphysics* 1041a7–32, pp. 1643–44.

23. Friedrich Nietzsche, *The Will to Power*, ed. Walter Kaufmann and R. J. Hollingdale (New York: Vintage, 1968), p. 280. See also Michel Foucault's "Theatrum Philosophicum," especially pp. 184–87, in *Language, Counter-Memory, Practice*, pp. 165–96. Foucault states,

> The freeing of difference requires thought without contradiction, without dialectics, without negation; thought that accepts divergence; affirmative thought whose instrument is disjunction; thought of the multiple—of the nomadic and dispersed multiplicity that is not limited or confined by the constraints of similarity; thought that does not conform to a pedagogical model (the fakery of prepared answers), but that attacks insoluble problems—that is, a thought that addresses a multiplicity of exceptional points, which are displaced as we distinguish their conditions and which insist and subsist in the play of repetitions.

For Nietzsche's influence on Joyce see Joseph Valente, "Beyond Truth and Freedom: The New Faith of Joyce and Nietzsche," *JJQ*, 25 (Fall 1987), 87–103.

24. Umberto Eco, *The Aesthetics of Chaosmos: The Middle Ages of James Joyce*, trans. Ellen Esrock (Tulsa: Univ. of Tulsa Monograph Series, 1982), p. 3.

25. See Mikhail Bakhtin's attacks on Romantic and Formalist unification, particularly *Problems of Dostoevsky's Poetics*, ed. and trans. Caryl Emerson (Minneapolis: Univ. of Minnesota Press, 1984) and *The Dialogic Imagination*, ed. Michael Holquist, trans. Caryl Emerson and Michael Holquist (Austin: Univ. of Texas Press, 1981). Bakhtin's emphasis on the carnivalesque promotes the idea that literary works inherently resist the unification advanced by strict hierarchies. For a discussion of the distinctions among dialogics, dialectic, and rhetoric and of the applications of Bakhtin's dialogics to literary criticism see Don H. Bialostosky, "Dialogics as an Art of Discourse in Literary Criticism," *PMLA*, 101 (1986), 788–97. For an application of Bakhtin's idea of the dialogic novel to *Ulysses*, see David Lodge, "Double Discourses: Joyce and Bakhtin," *James Joyce Broadsheet*, 11 (June 1983), 1–2.

26. See, for example, Paracelsus, *Philosophia ad Athenienses* I, 10: "Nature ... is a vast organism in which natural things harmonize and sympathize reciprocally. Such is the macrocosm.... The macrocosm and the microcosm are one. They form one constellation, one influence, one breath, one harmony, one metal, one season, one fruit." For a lucid discussion of the distinctions between the symbolic and scientific perspectives see Gilbert Durand, *"Défiguration philosophique et figure traditionelle de l'homme en Occident,"* *Eranos*, 38 (1969), 45–93.

27. Ivan Turgenev, *Turgenev: Letters*, ed. and trans. David Lowe (Ann Arbor: Ardis, 1983), I, p. 121.

28. *Complete Works of Oscar Wilde*, ed. Vyvyan Holland (London: Collins, 1971), p. 1045.

29. In *Rabelais and His World* (Cambridge: MIT Press, 1968), pp. 39–40, Bakhtin writes:

The mask is connected with the joy of change and reincarnation, with gay relativity and with the merry negation of uniformity and similarity; it rejects conformity to oneself. The mask is related to transition, metamorphoses, the violation of natural boundaries, to mockery and familiar nicknames. It contains the playful element of life; it is based on a peculiar interrelation of reality and image, characteristic of the most ancient rituals and spectacles. Of course it would be impossible to exhaust the intricate multiform symbolism of the mask. Let us point out that such manifestations as parodies, caricatures, grimaces, eccentric postures, and comic gestures are per se derived from the mask. It reveals the essence of the grotesque.

Nietzsche aphoristically states, "Whatever is profound loves masks." *Beyond Good and Evil*, trans. Walter Kaufmann (New York: Vintage, 1966), p. 40.

30. A. David Napier, *Masks, Transformation, Paradox*, (Berkeley: Univ. of California Press, 1986), p. 83.

31. See Cheryl Herr, *Joyce's Anatomy of Culture* (Urbana: Univ. of Illinois Press, 1986) for a discussion of Joyce's appropriation of the Irish popular theatre, particularly pantomime, music hall, and theatrical transvestism, in "Circe."

32. The morris dance is a grotesque dance celebrating the summer and winter solstice. Ankle bells are usually worn by the dancer. A central character in the ritual is the Betty, a hermaphrodite, an appropriate allusion considering Bloom's transformation into the new womanly man in "Circe."

33. Jacques Derrida, "Plato's Pharmacy," *Dissemination*, trans. Barbara Johnson (Chicago: Univ. of Chicago Press, 1981), pp. 61–171.

34. Rene Girard, *Violence and the Sacred*, trans. Patrick Gregory (Baltimore: Johns Hopkins Univ. Press, 1977), p. 202.

35. Sigmund Freud, *Totem and Taboo*, trans. James Strachey (New York: Norton, 1950), p. 156.

36. In the *Poetics*, Aristotle cites a play entitled *Ulysses the False Messenger* as an example of discovery arising from bad reasoning on the part of the audience: "An instance of it is in *Ulysses the False Messenger*: that he stretched the bow and no one else did was invented by the poet and part of the argument, and so too that he said he would recognize the bow which he had not seen; but to suppose from that that he would know it again was bad reasoning." *Complete Works of Aristotle*, II, *Poetics* 1455a12–16, p. 2328. A footnote in the McKeon edition of Aristotle states "authorship unknown" in reference to this play *Introduction to Aristotle*, ed. Richard McKeon (New York: Modern Library, 1947), p. 646n3l.

37. For an elaboration on the uncertainty principle in Joyce's works see Phillip F. Herring, *Joyce's Uncertainty Principle* (Princeton: Princeton Univ. Press, 1987).

38. Jacques Derrida has demonstrated how the text works as a double-bind that anticipates the reader's responses, placing him or her within the text so that the reader becomes a meta-reader, reading *Ulysses* on *Ulysses*. "*Ulysses* gramophone: Hearsay yes in Joyce," in *James Joyce: The Augmented Ninth*, ed. Bernard Benstock (Syracuse: Syracuse Univ. Press, 1988), pp. 27–75.

39. E. D. Hirsch, *Validity in Interpretation* (New Haven: Yale Univ. Press, 1967), pp. 78–89. See also A. Walton Litz's attack on attempts to place *Ulysses* within the genre of the traditional English novel, "The Genre of Ulysses," in *The Theory of the Novel*, ed. John Halperin (New York: Oxford Univ. Press, 1974), p. 109; and Brian G. Caraher's reading of *Ulysses* in terms of intrinsic genre, "A Question of Genre: Generic Experimentation, Self-

Composition, and the Problem of Egoism in *Ulysses*," *ELH*, 54 (1987), 183–214. Hugh Kenner states, "*Ulysses* is the first of the great modern works that in effect create for themselves an ad hoc genre ... and so entail an ad hoc critical tradition." "*Ulysses*," rev. ed. (Baltimore: Johns Hopkins Univ. Press, 1987), p. 3.

40. Mahaffey, *Reauthorizing Joyce*, p. 135. Mahaffey calls *Ulysses* "an imaginative Odyssey, written in the double shadow of Shakespeare, whom Stephen calls a playwright of banishment, and his counterpart suggestively known as '*Homer*.'"

41. In his deconstruction of Plato, "Plato's Pharmacy," Derrida discusses the chain of significations pertaining to the term "*pharmakon*," pp. 95–117. For a reading of Murphy as psychopomp, see Gose, *The Transformation Process in Joyce's "Ulysses,"* pp. 27–28.

42. Homer, *The Iliad*, trans. Richard Lattimore (Chicago: Univ. of Chicago Press, 1951), 14.320, p. 302.

43. For a discussion of the connections between the problematics of perception and representation and those of memory, see Eugenio Donato, "The Ruins of Memory: Archeological Fragments and Textual Artifacts," *MLN*, 93 (1978), 575–96.

44. I am indebted to Richard Costa, Elliot Gose, Phillip Herring, Jean Kimball, Larry Reynolds, Ulrich Schneider, Robert Spoo, Weldon Thornton, and Stephen Yarbrough for their helpful readings and suggestions.

MARYLU HILL

"Amor Matris": *Mother and Self in the Telemachiad Episode of* Ulysses

In the Telemachiad episodes of James Joyce's *Ulysses* we first encounter in microcosm Stephen Dedalus's search for identity—a search which will color the entire narrative. At the heart of it is Stephen's relationship with his mother, both the real mother who nurtured him and is now dead, and an imagined symbolic mother who is a product of Stephen's fearful and anxious consciousness. Stephen desperately needs these two mothers to define him; his selfhood derives simultaneously from the unconditional affirmation which his real mother gave him and from his active struggle against all that the imagined mother stands for—an all-encompassing fertility linked with nature which signals death to Stephen.

What these two mothers have in common is their lack of subjecthood in Stephen's perception—that is, the real mother is forbidden to be anything more than what Stephen wishes her to be, and the imagined mother is nothing more than an object of Stephen's fears. Only by silencing and objectifying the mother can Stephen satisfy his infantile craving for oneness and his adult need for autonomy. This allows Stephen to enter the established paternal order which demands the repression and domination of the mother. But Stephen remains haunted by the memory of his mother's selfhood, represented by her death and the revelation its graphic and grotesque memory forces on him. He is torn between the need for the

From *Twentieth Century Literature* 39, no. 3. © 1993 by Hofstra University.

mother and the desire to imitate the father; however, the nagging reminders of the mother's subjecthood revealed in the Telemachiad continually undercut Stephen's attempts to participate wholly in the paternal order. Consequently, *Ulysses* as a whole illustrates the tension between the law of the father and the selfhood of the mother, and this tension will by the end point toward the potential for a new sense of self.

Stephen's need for his mother is established throughout *A Portrait of the Artist as a Young Man* and continues into *Ulysses*. In *A Portrait* Stephen sees himself as weak and timid in childhood, longing for his mother to protect him from what Suzette Henke calls "the brutal male environment" of school life (84).[1] The affinity between weak child and nurturing mother is echoed in the appearance of Cyril Sargent in the "Nestor" episode of Ulysses, a boy in whom Stephen recognizes his childhood self: "Like him was I, these sloping shoulders, this gracelessness. My childhood bends beside me" (2.168–69). Even Stephen's rebellion at the end of *A Portrait* is not so much to break away from his mother as to test her nurturing powers and push her love to the limits. As Richard Ellmann points out, "when [Stephen] rebels he hastens to let [others] know of his rebellion so that he can measure their response to it" (292). This need for a response indicates that Stephen's conflict goes beyond what Jeanne McKnight refers to as "the infantile conflict between the desire to remain an undifferentiated part of the mother and the developmental wish to be separate and free" (422). His conflict stems from this need for differentiation; however, it centers not so much on his own struggle between nurturance and autonomy as on his perception of his mother, another basic element of differentiation.

In psychoanalytic terms, successful differentiation relies not only on a perception of subjective otherness (simply recognizing physical difference) but also on what Nancy Chodorow calls "the ability to experience and perceive the object/other (the mother) in aspects apart from its sole relation to the ability to gratify the infant's/subject's needs and wants; [it involves] seeing the object as separate from the self and from the self's needs." This process, according to Chodorow, means "according the mother her own selfhood" (7). But because perception of the mother is grounded in pre-Oedipal infantile sensations, this process is

> often resisted and experienced only conflictually and partially. Throughout life, perceptions of the mother fluctuate between perceiving her particularity and selfhood and perceiving her as a narcissistic extension, a not-separate other whose sole reason for existence is to gratify one's own wants and needs. (7–8)

Stephen's struggle is thus between needing his mother as a nurturer wholly subject to his desire and accepting her as an autonomous self with desires of her own. What is particularly threatening to Stephen is his mother's ability to speak for herself, especially since language is his domain both as a writer and as a male. Consequently, the living mother must be silenced and denied the opportunity to speak except as she is filtered through Stephen's censuring consciousness. In the Telemachiad, even the memory of her is consistently silenced, coming to Stephen in a dream with only "mute secret words" (1.272).

But this is nothing new for Stephen; the living mother had been silenced by him in the past just as effectively as he now silences the dead mother. The pattern of mother-silencing goes back to *Stephen Hero* and *A Portrait* in two key episodes. In *Stephen Hero* we are given the only extended conversation between Mrs. Daedalus and Stephen, and even here her words are diffused by Stephen's assumption that his mother knows nothing. Stephen consistently refuses to listen to his mother, preferring instead to rely on his warped interpretation of her words. Accordingly, in the following passage, Mrs. Daedalus's interest in Stephen's scholastic essay and her willingness to listen (which is what he wanted) are immediately denied by Stephen's assumption of mental superiority:

> His mother who had never suspected probably that "beauty" could be anything more than a convention of the drawing room or a natural antecedent to marriage and married life was surprised to see the extraordinary honour which her son conferred upon it. Beauty, to the mind of such a woman, was often a synonym for licentious ways and probably for this reason she was relieved to find that the excesses of this new worship were supervised by a recognized saintly authority. (84)

This passage reveals what Stephen wishes to conceal from himself: his total ignorance of what Mrs. Daedalus really thinks. The "probably"'s indicate both ignorance and, more important, a desire to remain ignorant of her thoughts.

The conversation on theater which follows the above passage continues in the same vein. Mrs. Daedalus shows herself to be a woman of some literary awareness though her married life has prevented much active participation in it: "I don't speak about it but I'm not so indifferent" (85). Indeed, Stephen's own sensitivity and creative impulses seem clearly inherited from his mother since, as the narrator tells us, "a similar taste [for literature] was not discoverable" in the father (87). Stephen, however, quickly becomes uncomfortable with the revelation of his mother's interest. He first denies outright its possibility: "But since you married neither of you so much as bought a single book!" (85). Next he maneuvers the conversation back to himself and his father, who he says does not understand him. When Mrs. Daedalus reasserts her interest, Stephen swiftly contradicts her and assures her of her ignorance, effectively silencing her: "You evidently weren't listening to what I said or else you didn't understand what I said" (86). Even when she reads the books he has suggested and tries to talk to him about them, he rebuffs her attempts:

> But the play which she preferred to all others was *The Wild Duck*. Of it she spoke readily and on her own initiative: it had moved her deeply. Stephen, to escape a charge of hot-headedness and partisanship, did not encourage her to an open record of her feelings. (86)

Through the contrast between Mrs. Daedalus's words and Stephen's subsequent interpretations of them we can glimpse briefly the real Mrs. Daedalus, as can Stephen though he works to deny it. Significantly, when *Stephen Hero* was revised into *A Portrait*, the above conversation disappears entirely, leaving a text in which the mother is more efficiently silenced. Here the only real conversation between mother and son is reduced to a diary entry presented entirely from Stephen's point of view, although we can still get a sense of Mrs. Dedalus's true voice:

> Began with a discussion with my mother. Subject: B.V.M. Handicapped by my sex and youth. To escape held up relations between Jesus and Papa against those between Mary and her son. Said religion was not a lying-in hospital. Mother indulgent. Said I have a queer mind and have read too much. (*P* 248)

It is clear that the mother is winning the argument and also clear that she cares about Stephen, both in her "indulgence" and by giving him money at the end of the discussion. But her selfhood as far as Stephen is concerned is almost totally repressed; we see her as a representative of traditional religion rather than as May Dedalus. In *A Portrait* she is consistently objectified as Ireland and religion, becoming that which Stephen rebels against, even as she is forced by his manipulations to be also the all-giving mother. *A Portrait* solidifies her character as both the silent affirmer and the object of Stephen's rebellion.

While his mother is alive, Stephen has mastered all the tricks by which he can deny her selfhood, and thus keep her safely within reach for both comforting and denying. But with her death all this changes. The fact of it causes Stephen's crisis of identity by forcing him to recognize her selfhood insofar as her death is contrary to his desire. He is left mirrorless and objectless, with the added dimensions of guilt for having figuratively killed her with his demands for unconditional love and acceptance, and fear that the ghoulmother will now revenge herself on him.[2]

This crisis forces Stephen to recreate the mother image through language and memory. By reducing her to an object wholly perceived by his consciousness he attempts to deny any selfhood she once had, particularly that which asserted itself through her death. The riddle he poses to his class in "Nestor" and which recurs later in "Circe" indicates the power of language to control her image as the "fox" determines whether she enters or leaves heaven:

> 'Tis time for this poor soul / To go to heaven. (2.106–07)
> 'Tis time for her poor soul / To get out of heaven. (15.3580–81)

This pattern is strikingly reminiscent of Freud's anecdote of the child playing "fort/da" (gone/there) with his toys, a game which helps "the child ... control his anxiety at the mother's absence. The game and shouted words replace the mother's physical presence by a symbolic structure" (Freud 8–11). Language thus continues to be for Stephen a method by which he can control the mother and make her subject to his desires. Even though she is physically dead, Stephen can call her back to act as a mirror for further rebellion. It also becomes the means by which he can punish her for the selfhood that excludes him; she is trapped within his metaphors and images, constantly victimized by his characterizations of her as a "ghoul."

At the same time, however, Stephen still clearly fears the mother's selfhood, and this fear dominates his perception of her. Throughout the Telemachiad she is linked in Stephen's mind with death, revenge, nature/the sea, and creativity/fertility—all things which, despite Stephen's efforts to deny them, are characterized by their autonomy. Yet, paradoxically, their autonomy is limited by Stephen's narcissistic assumption that each of them is actively seeking to engulf him or otherwise threaten him. As far as he is concerned, none of them possesses meaning except insofar as it relates to him, just as he refuses to admit his mother has any reality except in relation to him. Daniel Ferrer describes this as the "paranoid position":

> The subject, whose Self is scarcely integrated at all, is constantly being overwhelmed by his anxiety, by his fear of the persecuting

"bad object," by his own aggressive impulses, and is incapable of
conceiving a "complete" object with which he could identify.
(139)

Thus each of Stephen's symbols for the mother takes on terrifying aspects.

The most obvious of these symbols is the mother personified as Death.
In her three major appearances, Mrs. Dedalus is portrayed as a rotting corpse
(significantly not a ghost or spirit) who later on in "Circe" will threaten
Stephen with the grave: "all must go through it" (15.4182–83). The
autonomy of this figure is made all the more powerful because it represents
the vengeful mother who is out to punish her son for his denial of her: "Her
glazing eyes, staring out of death, to shake and bend my soul. On me alone....
Her eyes on me to strike me down" (1.273–74, 276). By envisioning his
mother as a "ghoul" (1.278), he can blame her for threatening his identity
and attempting to engulf him, thus again using her as a means to define
himself. The fact that she returns to persecute him also diminishes her
autonomy by making her, even in death, wholly concerned with him.

Other symbols demonstrate the same mixture of a threatening
autonomy that is yet centered on Stephen. The sea, which Mulligan
eulogizes as "our great sweet mother" (1.80), becomes for Stephen first a
reminder of Mrs. Dedalus's deathbed: "a dull green mass of liquid" likened
to "the green sluggish bile which she had torn up from her rotting liver"
(1.108–09). In "Proteus" the sea is further linked with death through the
recurring image of the drowned man. The ocean is portrayed as a powerful
and deadly force: "His human eyes scream to me out of horror of his death,
I ... with him together drown" (3.328–29). It is also described as the killer of
the father and a castrater of men: "Full fathom five thy father lies.... A quiver
of minnows, fat of a spongy tidbit, flash through the slits of his buttoned
trouserfly" (3.470, 476–77). The sea/mother represents a powerful "other"
who longs to engulf the self. Again, the mother is seen only in relationship
to the male child who is fearful of being sucked in.

The theme of creativity and fertility reveals a similar pattern. Here
again the mother is seen as frighteningly omniscient. She is a representative
of Eve, "standing from everlasting to everlasting" (3.43–44). She is the first
source of identity; her stamp on the child is that of the navel which marks
him as hers forever. The concept of "*amor matris*," or mother love, displays
the power of the mother's fertility. She serves as the ultimate protector and
nurturer: "But for her the race of the world would have trampled him
underfoot, a squashed boneless snail. She had loved his weak watery blood
drained from her own" (2.140–43). Yet her power, like the ghoulmother and
the sea, becomes something sinister and threatening. The womb imagery,

which proliferates throughout the Telemachiad, is indicative of this. Jeanne McKnight notes that the womb is represented as a tempting darkness in which all identity is lost (423). Allied with the sea imagery it becomes the "allwombing tomb" (3.402) in which Lycidas, the drowned man, and the father all lie. Christine van Boheemen comments on the interwoven nature of death and life in the sea/womb imagery: "For Stephen, his mother, and the sea with which she is associated by symbolic identification, stands for both the idea of nature as complex inexhaustible life and the threat of individual extinction through engulfment" (182).

The imagery used for Cyril Sargent's mother (and by extension Mrs. Dedalus) also indicates sinister overtones by suggesting that she is somehow responsible for the child's weakness and dullness: "with her weak blood and wheysour milk she had fed him" (2.166). The child feeds off the mother and is poisoned by her; she is to blame for unmanning him and making him a "knock-kneed mother's darling" (2.315). As noted before, the mother is defined only in relation to the child even as the child is defined by her: "*Amor matris*: subjective and objective genitive" (2.165–66). Through such a definition, Stephen traps the mother within her own biology; her position in bed is the means by which her cycle of existence is recorded: "bridebed, childbed, bed of death, ghostcandled" (3.396). Stephen hopes to deny any possibility of selfhood for Mrs. Dedalus outside the limiting roles of wife and mother.

Throughout the Telemachiad, Stephen uses these images of his mother to maintain his sense of identity in the wake of her demise. They provide the impetus to rebellion and denial, and only by simultaneously sustaining them within his consciousness and actively denying their power can Stephen bolster his sense of identity. Accordingly, his denials of these images are constantly countered by returns to them; like the fox, he buries his grandmother only to dig her up again:[3] "His hindpaws then scattered the sand, then his forepaws dabbled and delved. Something he buried there, his grandmother" (3.359–60). He pleads with his ghoulmother to "let me be and let me live" (1.279), yet he will not let her be. He concocts riddles about her, imagines his parents coupling, and returns to her deathbed over and over. It is clear that he is not yet ready to live without her, and, what is more, he assumes that she is not able to be without him, even in death-hence her haunting activities.

The sea imagery also demonstrates the denial-and-return pattern. Stephen avoids the water, aware that he is "not a strong swimmer" (3.324), yet the sea draws him. In his imagination he experiences drowning with the drowned man, and, despite his fear of the sea, he finds in it (and his mother) a muse for some poetry—the only thing he writes in all of *Ulysses*. His ambivalent attitude toward mother love is likewise mirrored in these denials and returns. Though he suggests that mother love is something poisonous, it is clear that he longs for it. On the beach in "Proteus" (again near the water) he yearns for a love that is at once maternal and erotic with its emphasis on soothing and comforting hands and eyes: "Touch me. Soft eyes. Soft soft soft hand. I am lonely here. O, touch me soon, now. What is that word known to all men? I am quiet here alone. Sad too. Touch, touch me" (3.434–46).

Stephen's search for a father figure with whom to identify also falls into the cycle of denial of and return to the mother. Parentage is posed as a mixture of two elements, flesh and spirit, symbolized in Mulligan's "Ballad of Joking Jesus": "my mother's a jew, my father's a bird" (1.585). The juxtaposition of flesh and spirit is repeated with references to the Annunciation, to Leda and the swan, and to the obvious connection with Daedalus, the winged man and fabulous artificer. In this context, flesh/mother indicates the grosser realities of sexuality, death, and other things of a non-intellectual nature, while spirit/father points to the supposedly superior values of intellect, art, beauty, and language (Henke 84). More important, turning from flesh to spirit indicates initiation into what Lacanian psychology refers to as the "Name-of-the-Father," the order of language. Julia Kristeva and Josette Feral point out that this initiation depends on the repression or denial of the mother in order to identify with the father or symbolic order (Kristeva 136; Feral 10).[4] Dianne Hunter describes this initiation:

> Our sense of ourselves as separate beings, as "subjects," is bound up with our entry into the order of language, in which speech becomes a substitute for bodily connection.... When we accede to the world where communication in words allows both separation and intimacy, we are relinquishing the immediacy of semiotic and corporeal rapport with our nurturer from whom we recognize our separation.   (98–99)

Stephen clearly participates in the symbolic order of language and the paternal order with his subjugation of the mother by language, both by silencing her and by re-defining her within his own language constructs. But his identification with the father is also a means by which he can return to the mother. This Oedipal impulse appears in Stephen's thoughts on consubstantiality and, more significantly, his thoughts on parentage: "By them, the man with my voice and my eyes and a ghostwoman with ashes on her breath" (3.45–47). His identification with the father, limited though it is to shadowy eyes, voice, and wings, reveals his desire to possess the mother as the father does, as well as to be loved by her as her child. Through this father/son combination of identity, the son's need for the mother (and thus his concession to her power) is counterbalanced by the father's dominance over the mother. Identification with the father and his power allows the son the means by which he can control the mother within his mind, whereas otherwise she would control him. In this context the mother is effectively repressed even while desired. She is again denied selfhood as she becomes the object of both son and father.

In attempting to establish his father's identity Stephen unwittingly turns up one key to the mother's selfhood—the key that undercuts dramatically the name-of-the-father and re-establishes the autonomy of the mother. It can be found within Stephen's own theory of Hamlet and Shakespeare, specifically within the cuckoldry theme his theory develops. The cuckolding of Hamlet's father by Gertrude, hinted at in the Telemachiad and discussed at length in "Scylla and Charybdis," serves to remind Stephen of the mother's selfhood expressed in the symbolic possibility of adultery, which effectively denies both husband and child the identity they seek in her. As Jane Gallop notes,

> The Name-of-the-Father is the fact of the attribution of paternity by law, by language. Paternity cannot be perceived, proven, known with certainty; it must be instituted by judgment of the mother's word.... Any suspicion of the mother's infidelity betrays the Name-of-the-Father as the arbitrary imposition it is.... Infidelity then is a feminist practice of undermining the Name-of-the-Father. (47, 48)

Stephen's fixation on Gertrude's adultery makes it clear that he is aware of the mother's selfhood, even as he struggles to recreate her without selfhood. What he does not realize, and will recognize only partially and incompletely by the end of *Ulysses*, is that only by according the mother her selfhood can he break out of his narcissistic vision of self to find a new identity unreliant on the mother for total definition and affirmation. The ghoulwoman can be exorcised only when Stephen grants his mother's autonomy and recognizes that it is he who is feeding on her, not she on him. In the Telemachiad the solution (insofar as there can be a solution for Stephen) is provided, although it will not be entirely recognized until the end of "Circe."

There are three significant moments in the Telemachiad which reveal a different picture of both Mrs. Dedalus and Stephen. The first is Stephen's recollection of singing to his mother on her deathbed. The song he sings is a poem by William Butler Yeats entitled "Who Goes with Fergus." Fergus was an ancient Irish king, and the song concerns his renunciation of the world and his decision to go to the woods to ponder philosophy. It is a melancholy song, suggesting that total renunciation is not possible, and we are thus condemned always to ponder "love's bitter mystery." What is significant is Mrs. Dedalus's reaction—not to her son, but to the poem, to language and literature:

> Her door was open: she wanted to hear my music. Silent with awe and pity I went to her bedside. She was crying in her wretched bed. For those words, Stephen: love's bitter mystery. (1.250–53)

This short passage indicates the one time Stephen sees her not as mother but as a person, wretched perhaps, and ill, but still able to cry over a line of poetry. She proves herself capable of being moved by language and poetry just as he is. It is also the only place in the narrative where we hear Mrs. Dedalus speak clearly, without being filtered through her son's fears and anger. It reveals an entirely different woman from the ghoulish corpse-chewer that Stephen's imagination has created. For a moment Stephen is able to see her apart from himself; he approaches her with "awe and pity," clearly amazed at what he sees. The passage continues with Stephen seeing her with new eyes; he ponders her secrets and memories, all those moments that did not include him but defined her as a person in her own right. The mementos in her drawer and unexplained memories prove her possession of a life and reality beyond that which Stephen usually concedes her. Stephen sees her, not merely as mother, but as a person drinking water, roasting an apple for herself, washing clothes, and killing lice. The power of this newly independent woman is, however, too much for Stephen, and he returns to the ghoulwoman who is again forbidden to speak for herself: "her breath bent over him with mute secret words" (1.271–72). But the words of the poem haunt him throughout the rest of the narrative.

Connected with this repressed realization of the mother's selfhood is the poem Stephen writes on the beach in "Proteus." It is the only time he is stirred to creativity in the narrative, despite his view of himself as the bard, and, significantly, it deals with his mother:

> He comes, pale vampire, through storm his eyes, his bat sails bloodying the sea, mouth to her mouth's kiss.... His lips lipped and mouthed fleshless lips of air: mouth to her mood Oomb, all wombing tomb. (3.397–98, 401–02)

It recalls the mother-love theme in "Nestor," where the child drains blood from the mother, but the vampire is now identified more clearly. With the imagery of eyes and wings the vampire is the ghostly father, but, more important, through Stephen's theory of consubstantiality, the vampire is also the son. The ambiguity of the line "His lips lipped and mouthed fleshless lips of air" points first to an identification with the father in the poem then also to Stephen himself, enacting the poem on the beach with lips of air. The image of the vampire sucking the woman/mother dry points to an important realization for Stephen; it is not the mother who engulfs him but he who engulfs and kills her. By placing himself in the role of vampire, Stephen subconsciously admits that he is the threat to her selfhood and not the other way around.

The final significant image is that of another predator—the black panther. Haines's raving at night about shooting a black panther causes Stephen to fear for his life; he identifies himself with the panther not only because he is dressed in mourning but because he also senses his predatory nature, especially toward his mother. The panther image becomes allied with that of the vampire, as both stalk the mother to feed upon her.

Stephen's other animal counterparts also illustrate this predatory nature. His appearance as the fox places him at the mother's grave, digging with sharp claws:

> A poor soul gone to heaven: and on the heath beneath winking stars a fox, red reek of rapine in his fur, with merciless bright eyes scraped in the dirt, listened, scraped up the earth, listened, scraped and scraped. (2.147–50)

The association with the sacred bird or the winged god (with its double connotation of Mary's conception by the Holy Spirit and Leda's conception/rape by the swan) puts him in the role of an attacker or rapist as the quotation in French illustrates: "*Qui vous a mis dans cette fichue position? C'est le pigeon, Joseph*" (3.162–62). Finally, in "Proteus," the associations of panther, fox, bird, and also dog are tied together:

> He rooted in the sand, dabbling, delving and stopped to listen to the air, scraped up the sand again with a fury of his claws, soon ceasing, a pard, a panther, got in spouse-breach, vulturing the dead. (3.361–64)

In this construct the mother is clearly not all-powerful but instead is only human—a victim attacked by sons and fathers, and subsequently bled dry.

Despite the mythological imagery woven about her, the reality of her life in Dublin with a drunken husband and rebellious son makes Mrs. Dedalus a victim, stripped of autonomy and freedom. Her tears at the line "love's bitter mystery" take on a special poignancy in view of all the bitter loves of her life.

These elements foreshadow the end of the "Circe" episode, after Stephen has confronted and smashed the ghoulwoman of his imagination. With that defiant gesture toward the image/object he had created, he reverts at the close of the episode to a metaphorical womb of drunkenness—a state which is dearly closer to the subconscious than to the waking mind. In token of this, he shifts into a fetal position, "doubling himself together" and curling his body (15.4934, 4944). As he moves back into this womb, awaiting some sort of rebirth, he mumbles "Black panther. Vampire ... Who ... drive ... Fergus now / And pierce ... wood's woven shade ...?" (4930, 4932–33).

The placement of these three elements suggests that Stephen is finally aware that his identity up to this point was that of the panther or vampire, gaining meaning and figurative life from the imaginatively objectified mother. He is reminded once more that her reaction to the poem indicated her selfhood, especially since the line of poetry remains in his memory even after he has killed the ghoulmother. The real mother, the woman who existed as a person before she was a mother, has been reasserted in his awareness. Through the remembered line of poetry and the recognition of himself as panther and vampire, Stephen's relationship with her, both as it was and as it should have been, is revealed to him at last, if only for an instant. Bloom's comment as Stephen lies asleep becomes particularly apropos as he thinks "face reminds me of his poor mother" (15.4949). With that comment, it is clear that the conflict within Stephen about his mother has been resolved, at least for the moment. No longer is he the insubstantial voice and eyes of the father; instead, he is like the mother. He does not become her—there is no consubstantiality here. Rather, similarity can be recognized without a loss of identity to either subject; the ability to admit similarity while yet maintaining difference is a hallmark of successful differentiation. As Nancy Chodorow comments,

> One can be separate from and similar to someone at the same time.... One can recognize another's subjectivity and humanity as one recognizes one's own, seeing the commonality of both as active subjects. (8)

Stephen's recognition of himself as panther/vampire reveals to him the victimization of the mother caused by the father's and the son's selfish disregard. Joyce's comments to Nora regarding his own mother's death reveal an awareness of this:

My mother was slowly killed, I think, by my father's ill-treatment, by years of trouble, and by my cynical frankness of conduct. When I looked on her face as she lay in her coffin—a face grey and wasted with cancer—I understood that I was looking on the face of a victim and I cursed the system which had made her a victim.   (Ellmann 169)

The recognition that the mother had an identity in her own right accordingly places Stephen on the road toward an identity which, while admitting similarity to both mother and father, does not wholly rely on either for its verity. In proof of this, when Stephen awakes he encounters the father figure of Bloom but does not undergo any sort of mystical merger with him. Nor is there the same need now for Stephen to establish paternity, to "prove by algebra" the name of his father. After conversation, comparisons, and some dissent, Stephen parts from Bloom, rejecting Bloom's offer to put him up.

But despite the fact that Stephen seems to have reached a resolution to his internal conflict by the end of "Circe," he does not build upon it in the sight of the reader; more important, he does not *choose* to build upon it. Though the mother's selfhood is revealed, it seems that Stephen deliberately chooses to ignore it, indicating a fundamental inability to consciously mature beyond his infantile desires. His great moment of revelation occurs in a drunken stupor; once sober, he returns to his narcissistic ways. Accordingly he can comment in "Eumaeus" that Ireland, associated throughout *A Portrait* and *Ulysses* with women and particularly mothers, "must be important because it belongs to me" (16.1164–65). But the subconscious revelation of the mother as autonomous self continues to assert itself and eat away at him; he still hears the funeral hymn as he wanders away from Bloom's house.

For Stephen, *Ulysses* ends with the same conflict with which it began—the dominating character of the paternal order and the figure of the mother which constantly haunts and subverts it. Nor is this conflict completely resolved for anyone else in *Ulysses*; Bloom and Molly, for example, are only ambiguously and uncertainly reconciled. But *Ulysses* does end with the extraordinary if controversial voicing of Molly's selfhood which can be seen as an attempt to un-silence the woman at last. However, it is clear that *Ulysses* was not intended to provide all the answers. By placing Stephen, and later Bloom, in an uneasy balance between the conventions of patriarchy and the subtle reality of woman as self, *Ulysses* refuses to trivialize itself by reducing these conflicts to a simple answer. Rather, it unsettles our opinions regarding the conventions which have grown out of these conflicts.

Notes

1. Henke gives a detailed discussion of young Stephen's relationship with his mother.

2. Daniel Ferrer discusses Stephen's need for both internal and external mothers. As long as the mother is alive, Stephen can compare her with "the mother he has interiorized" in order to reassure himself that his sadism has not really wounded her. With her death he is left with only the interiorized mother, and, since this mother is the one he has wounded, he rightfully fears its vengeance. For, as Ferrer points out, "the dead mother returns, but returns as a dead mother. There can be no question of healing her wounds" (139).

3. Bonnie Kime Scott discusses the image of the fox "as a significant identification for Stephen as he works furtively, perhaps from guilt, to bury his failure with his mother, now seen as a victim of figurative rape." She goes on to note the denial-and-return pattern: "Stephen tries to bury his past and move on, but he also keeps scraping back over it" (28).

4. Kristeva comments, "Language as symbolic function constitutes itself at the cost of repressing instinctual drive and continuous relation to the mother" (136). Feral notes similarly that "the Name-of-the-Father, in order to establish itself, needs the repression of the mother. It needs this otherness in order to reassure itself about its unity and identity, but is unwittingly affected by this otherness that is working within it" (10). Kristeva, however, goes on to discuss the difference between language as symbolic function and poetic language, stating that "the unsettled and questionable subject of poetic language (for whom the word is never uniquely sign) maintains itself at the cost of reactivating this repressed instinctual, maternal element" (136). This distinction is useful in understanding Stephen Dedalus's ambiguous attitude toward his mother. The poet/artist side of his nature must be reconciled with the mother to create, as on the beach in "Proteus"; yet the philosophical and theological side—the father's tongue—struggles to contain and repress the mother, and by extension the creative self.

Works Cited

Boheemen, Christine van. *The Novel as Family Romance*. Ithaca: Cornell UP, 1987.

Chodorow, Nancy. "Gender, Relation, and Difference in Psychoanalytic Perspective." *The Future of Difference: The Scholar and the Feminist*. Ed. Hester Eisenstein and Alice Jardine. Boston: Hall, 1980. 3–19.

Ellmann, Richard. *James Joyce*. London: Oxford UP, 1982.

Feral, Josette. "Antigone or The Irony of the Tribe." Trans. Alice Jardine and Tom Gora. *Diacritics* 8 (1978): 2–14.

Ferrer, Daniel. "Circe, Regret and Regression." *Post-Structuralist Joyce*. Ed. Derek Attridge and Daniel Ferrer. Cambridge: Cambridge UP, 1984. 127–44.

Freud, Sigmund. *Beyond the Pleasure Principle*. Trans. James Strachey. New York: Norton, 1961.

Gallop, Jane. *The Daughter's Seduction: Feminism and Psychoanalysis*. Ithaca: Cornell UP, 1982.

Henke, Suzette. "Stephen Dedalus and Women: A Portrait of the Artist as a Young Misogynist." *Women in Joyce*. Ed. Suzette Henke and Elaine Unkeless. Urbana: U of Illinois P, 1982. 82–107.

Hunter, Dianne. "Hysteria, Psychoanalysis and Feminism: The Case of Anna O." *The M(other) Tongue*. Ed. Shirley Nelson Garner, Claire Kahane, and Madelon Sprengnether. Ithaca: Cornell UP, 1985. 89–115.

Joyce, James. *A Portrait of the Artist as a Young Man*. Ed. Chester G. Anderson. New York: Viking, 1968. (*P*)

————. *Stephen Hero*. Ed. John J. Slocum and Herbert Cahoon. Norfolk, Conn.: New Directions, 1963. (*SH*)

————. *Ulysses*. The Corrected Text. Ed. Hans Walter Gabler. New York: Vintage, 1986. (*U*)

Kristeva, Julia. *Desire in Language*. New York: Columbia UP, 1980.

McKnight, Jeanne. "Unlocking the Word-Hoard: Madness, Identity and Creativity in James Joyce." *James Joyce Quarterly* 14 (1977): 420–35.

Scott, Bonnie Kime, *James Joyce*. Atlantic Highlands, NJ.: Humanities, 1987.

NICHOLAS A. MILLER

Beyond Recognition: Reading the Unconscious in the "Ithaca" Episode of Ulysses

In a deservedly notorious footnote to *Civilization and Its Discontents*, Freud unveiled his extraordinary account of the fluid origins of human cultured civilization:

> It is as though primal man had the habit, when he came in contact with fire, of satisfying an infantile desire connected with it, by putting it out with a stream of his urine. The legends that we possess leave no doubt about the originally phallic view taken of tongues of flame as they shoot upward. Putting out fire by micturating—a theme to which modern giants, Gulliver in Lilliput and Rabelais' Gargantua, still hark back—was therefore a kind of sexual act with a male, an enjoyment of sexual potency in a homosexual competition. The first person to renounce this desire and spare the fire was able to carry it off with him and subdue it to his own use. By damping down the fire of his own sexual excitation, he had tamed the natural force of fire. This great cultural conquest was thus the reward for his renunciation of instinct. Further, it is as though woman had been appointed guardian of the fire which was held captive on the domestic hearth, because her anatomy made it impossible for her to yield

From *James Joyce Quarterly* 30. © 1993 by The University of Tulsa.

to the temptation of this desire. It is remarkable, too, how regularly analytic experience testifies to the connection between ambition, fire, and urethral erotism.[1]

The explicit figuring of human sexual desire as a biological flow of waste in this passage reveals an important contradiction at work within Freud's familiar theory of cultural production. The renunciation of instinct in order to produce a useful and valuable object of culture requires, in this case, the stopping of urinary flow, itself a material production of the body. In Freud's paradoxical economy of cultural conquest, then, the "reward" of production is only obtained by literally ceasing to produce.

If the association of micturition with cultural production, and specifically with writing, emerges with some regularity in Joyce's works, it is in *Ulysses*'s penultimate episode that the terms of this association seem to have a particularly Freudian resonance. Superficially the homosocial mixing of waters in Bloom's garden offers a near symbolic equivalent to Freud's primal scene of acculturation: it is as though Bloom were a Gulliver and Stephen a Gargantua, two giants who commemorate their mythic origin as cultural men as they gaze upward to the *sanctum sanctorum* of domesticity itself, the bedroom, where Molly ("woman") guards the fire of civilization. In their competition—Bloom's stream is "longer, less irruent," Stephen's "higher, more sibilant" (*U*17.1193, 1197)—a repressed eroticism emerges, a homosocial dynamic now rendered impotent as the homey glow of culture, here represented by the lamp, continues to burn in the bedroom above.

Yet, beyond supplying a narrative and metaphoric structure with which to decode the appearance of urinary waste at "Ithaca"'s dramatic climax, Freud's footnote reveals the repressive methodology by which that decoding takes place. For readers of "Ithaca," as for Freud's "primal man," the acquisition of culture is adequate recompense for having renounced, or at least subdued, a flow of material excess. "Ithaca," and by extension *Ulysses*, emerges as a cultural document, a coherent and exemplary work of art, only when its various excesses have been damped down by specific acts of interpretation. This interpretive damping down appears most obviously in the well-known historical renunciation of Joyce's many offenses against "modern drainage and modern decorum" by a critical practice invested in the cultural value of his texts.[2] In this connection, it seems sufficient to note that in the critical containment of urinary symbolism in "Ithaca," the garden scene has been both denigrated for its "grotesque effects" and celebrated as the locus of Bloom and Stephen's long-awaited mystical union.[3] However Joyce's "cloacal obsession" is made safe for art, the evidence of the text would seem to suggest that the differences between the exercise of literary genius on the one hand and the contemptible indulgence of juvenile humor on the other are indeed vanishingly small:

Were they indefinitely inactive?

At Stephen's suggestion, at Bloom's instigation both, first Stephen, then Bloom, in penumbra urinated, their sides contiguous, their organs of micturition reciprocally rendered invisible by manual circumposition, their gazes, first Bloom's, then Stephen's, elevated to the projected luminous and semiluminous shadow. (*U*17.1185–90)

But the scholarly effort to contain "Ithaca"'s fluid excess extends well beyond the decoding of the episode's less elegant symbols. In view of the episode's textual largess, it seems ironic that "Ithaca" has come to be recognized as the novel's episode of answers, the home for narrative meaning in which Joyce's myriad "enigmas and puzzles" are finally anchored and resolved. "Like the final chapter of a Victorian novel," wrote Hugh Kenner, "'Ithaca' abounds in detailed revelations that refocus what we had thought we knew and substantiate what we only guessed."[4] The episode, this argument runs, represents a kind of homecoming, not only for the world-weary Bloom/Odysseus, but for the text-weary reader longing for the familiar and recognizable domicile of textual meaning.[5] Indeed, within certain strains of *Ulysses* criticism, it has become something of a tradition to acknowledge "Ithaca," and not "Penelope," as the novel's proper conclusion.[6]

Yet the episode itself holds little solace for the reader craving a homecoming to narrative closure. On the contrary, to such a reader, facing the voluminous and unrelenting force of the episode's textual abundance, "Ithaca" resembles less a rock of narrative solidity than a gushing textual cataract. Bloom's famous encomium to water (*U*17.183–228) is only the most obvious example of this diluvian textuality. Hardly the stuff of Victorian dénouement, the episode's protracted catalogues and detailed descriptions seem to expand outward exponentially, effectively subordinating the efficiency of answers to a value of prolixity and superabundance. Moreover, through its parodic mimicry of scientific discourse, the text disavows the efficacy of its own language in supplying answers to the questions of the novel. The opacity of arcane or specialized language words like "luteofulvous," "rhabdomantic," "minches," "scutchmills," and "lacustrine"—thoroughly deflates any lingering hopes for the clarity and resolution which it is traditionally an answer's chief function to supply.

If in reading "Ithaca" we seem to return "home," if the episode resolves and clarifies much of our confusion, if it appears familiar and recognizable, it is because in reading the text, we find ourselves, like Bloom before the door of number 7 Eccles Street, in a peculiar position of keyless competence (*U*17.1019). As in Bloom's case, keylessness denies us immediate access to our "home," but interpretive competence—at once receptive of the text as a decodable object and intrusive upon it—effectively assures our entry by stratagem.

The critical effort to stay the episode's unwieldy effluence has produced a number of such stratagems by focusing on the formal properties of the episode and their resemblance to various historical analogues. Of these the Jesuit catechism employed in Joyce's own early schooling is only the most frequently cited formal paradigm; scholars have explored others as diverse as Socratic dialogue, legal inquiry and modern advertising ("What is home without Plumtree's Potted Meat?").[7] Presuming the discrete identity of the catechistical form *per se*, comparisons of this sort subject the text of "Ithaca" to a specific economy of signification based on that identity; that is, in each of these paradigms, the play of questions and answers functions as a means to the efficient production of meaning, a project for which the text of "Ithaca," as we have seen, shows little concern. "Ithaca"'s "answers" thus emerge only within specific selective economies of interpretation and virtually always at the cost of a great wastage of other information. Without the stabilizing claims of criticism, the text continues to flow and to overflow the constraints of such recognition.

A critical act of renunciation or repression thus structures a meaningful text, which we encounter not as a productive flow of material excess, but as a Maynooth catechism, a deposition or advertisement, or even as "Ithaca," *Ulysses*'s episode of answers. What is literally read, once the text is subdued to a specific cultural use or value, is not the text, but an image of the text. Textual representation is itself not a mode of expression at all, but a sort of template which structures and organizes a home for meaning within the text. Once interpretive analysis has begun such a comparison, the closed door before which we stand keyless yawns wide, and we are drawn instantly into the familiar confines of textual meaning.

Jean-Michel Rabaté has argued that in *Dubliners*, a textual silence functions precisely within the text's ability to speak and to signify so that "a maximum of legibility, of transparence, is coupled with the insinuation of a perversion at work within the signifiers of the text."[8] In "Ithaca," it is not silence, but an equally non-signifying textual excess that works within the literary to pervert the business of signification. A literal machine for the production of textual excess, "Ithaca" produces a language which is never wholly recuperable for or by containing structures of literary signification.

It is precisely this movement of the text beyond recognition, this perversion at work within the unrecuperable flow of textual excess, that points toward the functioning, within signification, of the textual unconscious. The use of this term does not denote the existence of an essential representation, signified though unread, within the text; neither does it name a mystical or unseen source of textual meaning. We have seen that meaning is, on the contrary, the result of repressing textuality. A productive movement rather than a stable entity, the textual unconscious has nothing whatever to do with representation, textual or otherwise; it cares nothing for the passionate signifier and knows no need of expressing itself. It comes into being, rather, as a process of production, as Gilles Deleuze and Félix Guattari have remarked, at "the moment when language is no longer defined by what it says, even less by what makes it a signifying thing, but by what causes it to move, to flow, and to explode-desire."9

Deleuze and Guattari's definition of the textual unconscious as the productive, physical working of desire in the text implies the possibility of an engagement with textual excess through reading that does not resort to strategies of containment in order to produce a home for meaning within the text. While such stratagems infuse the text with "the false pretenses of residence" (341), and thus suspend the whole of its functioning from a recognition of its meaning, Deleuze and Guattari insist that reading is fundamentally an engagement of productive textuality without a stable textual image: "For reading a text is never a scholarly exercise in search of what is signified, still less a highly textual exercise in search of a signifier. Rather it is a productive use of the literary machine, a montage of desiring-machines, a schizoid exercise that extracts from the text its revolutionary force" (106).

This "literary machine" is not an image that structures textual meaning, but a movement or action at work within textuality; it is, literally, the work of the text. To read "Ithaca" as a literary machine in this sense is therefore to engage its textuality as a production rather than as an expression. What is produced by this textual production is a physical, rather than representational, flow of textuality that forges connections and disconnections continually. These connections and disconnections in turn produce textual quantities that are residual rather than residential; that is, characters and events emerge and function in the literary machine not as symbols and meanings, but as temporary entities alongside the machinic movement of textual production.

In traversing the literary machine, desiring-production produces textual quantities as temporary, residual effects—the Bloom-effect, the Stephen-effect—that continually exceed and elude the stable subjectivities and symbolic identities that align themselves within the repressive template of textual representation. Bloom, for instance, is not simply represented in the text of "Ithaca" as a discrete identity, a stable character who moves with heroic integrity through a narrative of homecoming. To be sure, the text of "Ithaca" produces this character "Bloom," within its ironic reuse of Odysseus's narrative of arrival. But the machinic text engages this consistency of character only as a latency within the satisfaction of its primary aim, the production of excessive textuality. Its narrative reuse becomes a linguistic ruse, a textual game of excess that is continually played out within and in spite of its own ability to represent. Thus, reading the machinic unconscious does not offer a corrective to repressive economies of interpretation so much as it reveals a perversion of stability which is already at work within such economies.

Bloom appears variously in the text of "Ithaca" as "waterlover," "watercarrier," "jew," "Papli," "Old Ollebo, M.P.," and so on (U17.183, 530, 1792, 409). Interpretive reading regards this series as textuality's submission to representation; a collection of textual quantities becomes, for the purposes of narrative signification, a sequence of names that adequately represent the stable identity of a character. When the young Leopold submits a bit of doggerel to the weekly newspaper, the *Shamrock*, he asks that its editors find room not only for the publication of his verses, but for the representation therein of his name (U17.392–401). Similarly, interpretation condescends to find room for a discrete identity in a series of textual verses or versions of a character, and so places at the end of the list the name that structures its meaning, the heroic *"yours truly, L. Bloom"* (U17.401).

Yet within the movement of the machinic text, the name "Bloom" functions, along with all of the other names, as a quantity of textual flow. A textual quantity that acts rather than expresses, this "Bloom" connects periodically with other flows to produce provisional entities, the legible, temporary residues that crop up here and there in the machinic text. It is in this sense that Bloom has travelled *with* and not *as* a number of identities: Sinbad the Sailor, Tinbad the Tailor, Jinbad the Jailer, and so on. A unitary Bloomian identity does not move through the text donning a sequence of costumes that, gathered in a list at the episode's end, will constitute a multiple representation, the final meaning of "Bloom." Within the residual productions of the machinic text, meanings are certainly legible to a practice of reading that stops the material flow of text at a given point of representation. As textual flows, however, the myriad Failers and Railers and Phthailers of the machinic text comprise an assemblage of residual quantities, a confluence of partial flows of textuality with which a productive text, a machinic Bloom, both rests and has travelled, flows and stops flowing.

A machinic reading of Bloom and Stephen's shared act of micturition similarly reveals the productive functioning of the textual unconscious within and in spite of interpretive strategies of symbolic decoding. The "meaning" of fluid waste does not occur within its narration as an event in a garden scene; indeed, Bloom's and Stephen's urination itself cannot be localized as a discrete moment of representation within the textual process. While conventional notation pinpoints the event at "episode 17, lines 1186–90," the material flow of liquid actually begins over one thousand lines before, as the same water which Bloom and Stephen are eventually to "make" begins its journey from "Roundwood reservoir in county Wicklow" (*U*17.164), flowing through various pipes and aqueducts to emerge in the kitchen at number 7 Eccles Street, thence to be collected in a kettle, boiled, added to cocoa and cream, and drunk by Bloom and Stephen. Finally it is carried out into the garden within their bodies—literally "bodies of water"[10]—where the two, their eyes on the fire of Molly's lamp, at last urinate.

In the expansive textuality of the literary machine, urination is thus available as an isolated symbolic act only to a reading that stops its textual flow at certain points and not at others. As a partial flow of textuality micturition forges continual connections with other textual flows, producing the residual quantities river, lake, ice, steam, and so on. Moreover, this machinic system of connections and disconnections produces a number of fluid competitions in addition to that in which Bloom and Stephen engage in the garden. On the global scale, for instance, water enjoys a "preponderance of 3 to 1 over the dry land of the globe" (*U*17.193). More locally Bloom and Stephen consume "Epps's massproduct" in a similar proportion, the host taking "three sips to his opponent's one" (*U*17.369, 380). In a literal sense, then, the machinic text does not express micturition as a single representational event or symbol, but produces it repeatedly as a micturition-effect, a fluid machine which traverses the landscape of the text, while various other mechanisms engage its liquid flow: pipes channel it, faucets cut it off, kettles give it shape. At any given point, its temporal and spatial locations emerge not as representations of its discrete meanings, but as temporary residual productions of the machinic text.

In reading the textual unconscious, we continue to cross thresholds, not to enter homes of meaning, but to traverse other residual productions of unconscious flow. "Ithaca"'s formal structure is the site not only of literary representation, but of literature's functioning. Without the filter of a representational template, an image of the text, the "catechism" of "Ithaca" is nothing but a functional splitting of textuality. This split produces a duplicity which is nonetheless not that of a text that simply questions in order to answer, a text that both knows and doesn't know. The episode's duplicity emerges, rather, in its productive division between the functioning of its textuality and the expressions of its text. Like the fluid trajectory which Bloom produces in the garden, "in the incomplete form of the bifurcated penultimate alphabetical letter" (*U*17.1193–94), *Ulysses*'s penultimate letter embodies a double stream of material excess, the formal expression of which as question and answer is incomplete because it cannot possibly recuperate fully the myriad productions of its own machinic exchange. It is in this sense that "Ithaca"'s textuality is machinic: it is incessantly productive, rather than adequately representational; its textual movement does not structure an edifice of answers, but produces an unrepentant prodigality that does not come home.

A striking example of this machinic engagement of textual flow occurs near the close of "Ithaca," as Leopold Bloom, world-weary traveler, newly returned home, rejects the possibility of departing anew in favor of a warm bed:

> What advantages were possessed by an occupied, as distinct from an unoccupied bed?
>
> The removal of nocturnal solitude, the superior quality of human (mature female) to inhuman (hotwaterjar) calefaction, the stimulation of matutinal contact, the economy of mangling done on the premises in the case of trousers accurately folded and placed lengthwise between the spring mattress (striped) and the woollen mattress (biscuit section). (*U*17.2035–41)

Depending on how one channels or "represses" textual flow, the word "mangling" in this passage releases different, and opposed, meanings: one refers to violent laceration or beating beyond recognition, while the other indicates the pressing of material to remove (or create) wrinkles. Taken in either sense, an "economy of mangling" approximates the violent transformation that takes place when a traditional reading structures and encloses a text. Such a reading not only disfigures or "mangles" the text, it also *figures* that text, lends it the specificity of a referential value, without which it would not be recognizable. Just as the machinic mangle produces pressed garments, so critical reading renders the text presentable, removes unsightly inconsistencies, and places significant wrinkles where they "ought" to be. In the process of publication, a text is "pressed" in just this way: set in type, neatly creased, bound, and made presentable for dissemination. In being read it is "repressed" repeatedly or mangled over and over so as to produce various, temporary meanings.

But the function of the mangle also changes our apprehension of the bed and suggests that it is not simply present in the text as a fixed or known identity. On the contrary it is explicitly characterized as a machine that performs a number of functions, only one of which is the production of sleep and rest. It is not in its objective singularity that this bed-machine becomes productive, moreover, but in the indiscrete assemblages that it forms with other textual machines: its periodic flow—producing connections with Bloom-machines, Molly-machines, and Boylan-machines. Thus, Bloom's homecoming as the symbolic conquering hero is in another sense the arrival of a removable, spare part which, once connected to the machinic bed, enhances its capabilities and efficiency. Within this machinic assemblage, the bed produces not only restful sleep, but companionship ("[t]he removal of nocturnal solitude"), warmth ("human ... calefaction") and arousal—sexual or otherwise ("the stimulation of matutinal contact"). This machinic potential of the bed is only heightened by the reference to its functioning as a clothes-press, a sartorial suiter connecting with the flow of the machinic suitors. An incidental residuum of textual flow, the bed maintains a tenuous hold on its identity as a discrete object, at any moment slipping into the new identity "mangle" as the flow of the textual unconscious moves on.

Approaching the literary machine of "Ithaca," keyless competence cuts into the flow of the textual unconscious to produce a stratagem for engagement. As interpretive reading reaches into the depths of a back pocket (key-producing machine), the flow is broken by a malfunction, and at the same instant we enter the discursive machinery of memory, where we learn, through abstract analysis, that the machine we need is plugged in elsewhere, that our "other pants" are, so to speak, currently being (re)pressed in the bed/mangle-machine where we left them. This is the position of interpretation as it turns to a stratagem of comparison, a representational image in terms of which the text becomes familiar.

While in this sense critical analysis enables the reader to "come home" to "Ithaca," to enter, understand, and recognize the text, it is precisely the illusion of being "inside" that blinds us to the fact that we never were locked out in the first place, that there was never anything to be locked out of, that the whole bloody business—key stratagem, and our selves included—is a giant machine that goes on accreting and dissolving, cutting and flowing.

If reading the textual unconscious in "Ithaca" produces a kind of answer, it is not one that adequates itself to the demands of representational understanding. In asking "What does it mean?" interpretive competence recognizes the text as a kind of ready-made, decodable, symbolic structure, a home in which answers reside. In a similar way theory asking "How does it work?" locates its answers within a recognition of textuality as its own justification or explanation. The question that is answered by the textual unconscious, unconcerned with the structuring of textual meaning and yet eminently literary is "Where?" "Ithaca"'s answer, the •, is both a significant and a non-signifying textual surface, not a picture of the unconscious, not its symbolic representation, but, as Deleuze and Guattari put it, "a writing which is strangely polyvocal, flush with the real" (87). It is a desiring-machine among desiring-machines, a smooth-surfaced body that, in emerging precisely *there* where it is, without organs and without organization, engages the fluid "Where?" of the textual unconscious and produces thereby an answer: "[t]here where there is desire" (283).

NOTES

1. Sigmund Freud, *Civilization and Its Discontents*, trans. and ed. James Strachey (New York: Norton, 1961), pp. 42–43, n. 4.

2. See in particular H. G. Wells's review of *A Portrait*, reprinted in James Joyce, *A Portrait of the Artist as a Young Man*, ed. Chester G. Anderson, Viking Critical Library (New York: Penguin, 1968), p. 330.

3. See for example A. Walton Litz's essay, "Ithaca," in *James Joyce's "Ulysses": Critical Essays*, ed. Clive Hart and David Hayman (Berkeley: Univ. of California Press, 1974), especially pp. 390, 401.

4. Hugh Kenner, *Ulysses*, rev. ed. (Baltimore: Johns Hopkins Univ. Press, 1987), p. 141.

5. See Marilyn French, *The Book as World: James Joyce's "Ulysses"* (Cambridge: Harvard Univ. Press, 1976), pp. 3–5. But cf. Vicki Mahaffey's treatment of the text-as-voyage metaphor as "a paradox that forces us to experience the stress as well as the release of understanding." Vicki Mahaffey, *Reauthorizing Joyce* (Cambridge: Cambridge Univ. Press, 1988), p. 134.

6. A certain degree of support for this view is lent by Joyce's assertion, in a letter to Harriet Shaw Weaver (7 October, 1921), that "Ithaca" "is in reality the end as Penelope has no beginning, middle or end." See *Letters I* 172. See also Litz, p. 386, and French, p. 240.

7. Richard E. Madtes, The "'Ithaca' Chapter of Joyce's 'Ulysses'" (Ann Arbor: UMI Research Press, 1983), p. 67.

8. Jean-Michel Rabaté, "Silence in *Dubliners*," in *James Joyce: New Perspectives*, ed. Colin MacCabe (Bloomington: Indiana Univ. Press, 1982), p. 58.

9. Gilles Deleuze and Félix Guattari, *Anti-Oedipus: Capitalism and Schizophrenia*, trans. Robert Hurley, Mark Seem, and Helen R. Lane (Minneapolis: Univ. of Minnesota Press, 1983), p. 133. Further references will be cited parenthetically in the text.

10. Water is praised in "Ithaca" for, among other things, its "ubiquity as constituting 90% of the human body" (*U*17.226–27).

WELDON THORNTON

Authorial Omniscience and Cultural Psyche: The Antimodernism of Joyce's Ulysses

In *A Portrait of the Artist as a Young Man*, and more fully in *Ulysses*, Joyce developed a distinctive mode of omniscient authorial perspective that can best be understood as simulating a cultural psyche. *Ulysses* especially is characterized by a pervasive cultural psyche that forms the "psychic medium" sustaining the characters and events of the novel. While a number of the novel's critics have acknowledged such an entity, this dimension of the book has never been taken as seriously as it deserves.[1] Critics have for the most part failed to recognize the distinctiveness of Joyce's authorial perspective and have obscured its most important implications by attributing to it total authorial effacement and value-neutrality, or "objectivity."

Any claim for a collective mentality in *Ulysses* is usually grounded in the ideas shared among the individual characters, especially Stephen and Bloom, which are apparently inexplicable without reference to a communal mind such as W. B. Yeats describes in his well-known 1901 essay "Magic."[2] While I concur in this reading of the psychological evidence, my argument is based on considerations of narrative technique, of the "point of view" through which the novel is presented: I believe the distinctive form of omniscient narration Joyce uses in *Ulysses* can best be understood as simulating the cultural psyche. The evocation of such an entity by the psychological texture and point of view of *Ulysses* runs counter to prevailing modernist ideas, and

From *Bucknell Review: Irishness and (Post)Modernism* 38, no. 1. © 1994 by Associated University Presses, Inc.

in this regard the novel is "antimodernist." While I cannot here fully demonstrate these claims, I hope to make my main thrust clear, and elicit response from those who find the argument worth pursuing.

Modernism as Involving an Erosion of Social Psyche

In my forthcoming book *The Antimodernism of Joyce's Portrait of the Artist*, I develop the idea that modernism involves an erosion of the collective psyche. Under the influence of Descartes's distinction between *res extensa* (matter) and *res cogitans* (mind), which itself grew out of Galileo's earlier distinction between primary and secondary qualities, the modernist mind has come to believe that "psyche" exists only within individual persons—i.e., that a mind can be sustained only by a brain, though how even that can be we do not understand. While the Galilean and Cartesian dichotomies have been extensively discussed, we do not yet fully appreciate the effects they have had on our worldview and on our image of our selves, especially in regard to our attitude toward the ontological status of human consciousness and of the psychic aspects of reality generally. Let us attend briefly to the distinction between primary and secondary qualities that has been so influential in Western thought for the past several centuries. Though usually associated with John Locke, this distinction was clearly articulated by Galileo. It was appropriate that he do so, because the distinction was fostered by the precise observation and quantification enabled by instruments such as the telescope. As it became possible to study phenomena more precisely, Galileo wished to distinguish between those qualities "in the objects themselves" (such as mass and extension) and those engendered by the observer's response (such as taste, color, odor). The former, Galileo called primary qualities, the latter, secondary qualities, and of these Galileo said, "I think that tastes, odors, colors, and so forth are no more than mere names so far as pertains to the subject wherein they reside, and that they have their habitation only in the sensorium. Thus, if the living creature were removed, all these qualities would be removed and annihilated."[3] Galileo goes on to say "I do not believe that for exciting in us tastes, odors, and sounds there are required in external bodies anything but sizes, shapes, numbers, and slow or fast movements; and I think that if ears, tongues, and noses were taken away, shapes and numbers and motions would remain but not odors or tastes or sounds. These are, I believe, nothing but names, apart from the living animal" (311). From this distinction, it was an easy step to Descartes's proclamation of two distinct modes of reality, mind and matter, thus creating the still intransigent "mind/brain problem."

The modernist perspective engendered by these ideas of Galileo and

Descartes not only denies any psychic dimension to physical nature, it denies as well that there can be any social or collective psyche, on the grounds that such a psyche has no physical substrate in which to exist, other than the minds (i.e., brains) of individual persons. As a result of this reductionistic thinking, the cultural psyche that had traditionally been taken for granted was during the nineteenth century called into question and found by proto-modernist thinkers to be an unsustainable, unnecessary hypothesis.

Let me briefly illustrate this erosion of the received idea of a cultural psyche. In his essay "The Critic as Innovator: A Paracritical Strip in X Frames," Ihab Hassan proposes a juxtaposition illustrating an important shift of perspective during the nineteenth century. He suggests how several contemporary attitudes are foreshadowed by Oscar Wilde's essays, and says: "Matthew Arnold, we recall, enjoined critics 'to see the object as in itself it really is.' This precept soon began to shift toward a more subjective focus in the criticism of Ruskin and Pater. But it remained for Oscar Wilde to stand Arnold on his head, and scandalously suggest that the aim of the critic is to see the object as it really is not."[4]

Between these dicta of Arnold and of Wilde, there exists a major watershed of Western thought in regard to the reality status of psyche. In enjoining the critic to see the object "as in itself it really is," Arnold is presuming an object that (in spite of Galileo) *inherently* involves qualities, forms, colors, not one that consists simply of matter in motion and endowed with qualities by an observing mind. He is calling on the critic to avoid any personal idiosyncrasy that might distort his perspective and keep him from doing justice to what is undeniably a qualitative, public object. Arnold's adjuration, that is, presumes a public object with its "secondary qualities" and its object quality very much intact, sustained by the medium of the cultural consciousness. For Wilde, on the contrary, there was a terrible presumptuousness and irony in Arnold's behest, since Wilde—having implicitly bought into Galileo's denigration of secondary qualities and the idea of inert matter it implies—presumed that for someone to describe the object per se would necessarily strip from it all of the qualitative accoutrements given it by the subjectivity of the observer. To describe an entity as it really is, "objectively," without the enhancements of color and texture provided by someone's personal subjectivity, would require us to talk only of matter in motion, of mass and extension, which—according to Galileo and to Newtonian physics—is all that the object in itself really involves. And having implicitly accepted the Newtonian metaphysic, Wilde insisted that the critic must describe this paltry, objective entity as it really is *not*—i.e., he must describe it as it appears "subjectively," to some individual person.[5]

While the modernist mind was becoming fixated upon this schizophrenic division between mind and matter, subject and object, Joyce was searching for ways to dramatize the speciousness of these presumed dichotomies and to illustrate the various confusions and contradictions that modernist thinking had fallen into, especially in regard to our understanding of the self and of the reality-status of "psyche." One of Joyce's fundamental aims in *Portrait* is to show that while Stephen is very much under their influence, such modernist dichotomies involve a distorted, insufficient view of psyche and of reality; this is a large part of what I mean by referring to Joyce's novel as "antimodernist."

It may be that Joyce's Irishness had some influence on his antimodernism. Irish writers such as Yeats and Synge and Joyce—all of whom I consider antimodernist in their challenges to the fragmentary and atomistic assumptions of much modernist writing—were facilitated in finding their antimodernist perspective by their access to a tradition of thought, a fundamental orientation toward reality, different from the so-called empiricism and the shallow rationalism that came to be privileged in European thought from the time of Galileo and Bacon and Descartes.[6]

One way Joyce reveals the distortion and insufficiency of the modernist severance of mind and matter is through development of narrative techniques involving the inextricability of such presumed dichotomies. These techniques involve a narrative perspective that must be called "omniscient," not simply because it persistently tells us "information" the characters cannot know, but because it involves qualitative and evaluative terms not attributable to any character in the novel, nor to any tangible "persona." In defiance of modernist separations and dichotomies, Joyce's narrative voice inextricably blends "inner" and "outer" and persistently involves qualitative and evaluative elements best understood as invoking a collective psyche.

Modernist Disdain of Omniscient Point of View

The distinctiveness of Joyce's narrative method becomes clearer in light of certain critical claims about narrative technique, especially in regard to omniscient point of view. In my book on the antimodernism of *A Portrait* I document two reiterated assumptions about point of view in modern fiction. The first is that the author eschews the omniscient point of view that was such a staple of fiction writing for virtually all earlier novelists; the second is that this purported disdain of omniscience reflects the death of God, the assumption being that such a point of view simulates an omniscient God, whose death in the late nineteenth century most thinkers acknowledge. For example, Morton P. Levitt speaks of "the Modernists' endeavor to develop narrative techniques which place man in his true setting—principally their development of a point of view that removes the omniscient-omnipotent Victorian God at the center of the narrative and replaces him with limited, representative man."[7]

But this claim that modern fiction disdains omniscient point of view is a misapprehension, stemming apparently from the critics' simplistic identification of omniscient point of view with such explicit, suprafigural statements of information and values as we find in the novels of Fielding or Eliot or Hardy. Perhaps modern novels do not often resort to a voice so overtly omniscient as that of many traditional novels, and certainly recent fiction contains many carefully crafted first-person narratives that presumably finesse omniscience.[8] But while relatively few twentieth-century novels *appear* so traditionally omniscient as *Tom Jones* or *Vanity Fair*, most are nonetheless omniscient in very meaningful ways.

It is not clear why present-day critics are reluctant to acknowledge the omniscient perspective within much modern fiction. Perhaps their reluctance reflects contemporary biases against "authority" generally; perhaps they presume an "omniscient" perspective is outmoded in fiction as well as in religion and metaphysics. Or this misunderstanding may result from an equivocation on "omniscient" point of view. That is, if we consider traditional fiction, we may presume the hallmarks of omniscient point of view to be a more or less tangible authorial persona and explicit nonfigural valuational statements, which can suggest that any narrative lacking such a persona or explicit statements is not "omniscient." Another possible source of confusion is that an omniscient author can present his or her perspective through a third-person syntax, so that a narrative cast in the third person is often in effect omniscient. That Joyce's *Portrait* is narrated in the third person should not cloud the fact that its authorial voice is, in meaningful ways, omniscient. Whatever the reasons, many critics are reluctant to impute to modern novels anything approaching omniscience.[9]

While overt evaluative judgments or the tangible presence of an authorial persona may be the most salient signs of omniscience, they are by no means essential to it. Any authorial perspective has a good claim to omniscience if it has the following characteristics: if it involves ubiquity— i.e., moves instantaneously among locales or characters; if it provides information or exposition that does not come through the characters; if it tells us the thoughts of various characters, and presents their psyches in more depth than they could; and (most important) if it involves value judgments and qualitative descriptions that do not stem from any character. A novel involving these traits is omniscient, even if it lacks the homilies or the distinct persona we associate with traditional omniscient fiction. *Ulysses* possesses every one of these traits.

Moreover, a species of authorial "omniscience" manifests itself in certain fundamental ways in virtually all works of fiction. This point should not need to be made, but in a milieu where critics can talk seriously about novels as "self-generating," we may have to restate the obvious.[10] The author's "omniscience" manifests itself in the very creation of characters and events comprising the novel, in the ordering of those events, in authorial choices as to the relative prominence given to various events and the perspective from which they are presented. Even in such experiments with authorial authority as Flann O'Brien's *At Swim-Two-Birds*, where we are offered three separate openings, or Fowles's *French Lieutenant's Woman*, where we have a choice of endings, the underlying fiction is generated by O'Brien and Fowles, and the "options" exist only within parameters they have created.

Given human ingenuity, it is predictable that there should be works of fiction—not all of them modernist—that assiduously, if playfully, explore the limits of authorial control. These include characters who seem to become self-generating (O'Brien's *At Swim-Two-Birds*), or hiatuses to be filled in by the reader (as in *Tristram Shandy*, volume 6, chapter 38). To put such experiments in perspective we need simply ask ourselves where they would be if their authors had not lived to write those novels. Critics may talk airily about "self-generating texts," but had Joyce died as young as Keats, all the readers in the world could not have brought *Ulysses* into being.

Let us turn to the question of what the omniscient perspective in Joyce's fiction represents or simulates. Modernist critics have presumed that traditional omniscient point of view represents an omniscient deity, and that the disavowal of omniscient perspective in modernist fiction reflects skepticism in regard to any such deity. But even in traditional fiction where the tangibility of the persona invites us to imagine some supracharacter or deity, the authorial presence—which manifests itself far more pervasively than simply through authorial voice—to some extent simulates the social psyche that serves in every culture as the invisible, intangible medium within which the individual psyches and cultural values have their being. The very idea of such a cultural/psychic medium is hard to grasp, both because it is so inherently *implicit* and "erased" a feature of our individual experience, and because so many features of the current climate of opinion militate against it. The reductionistic, materialist bias of modernist thought makes it difficult to understand how even an individual mind and brain can co-exist, much less to take seriously the existence of any supraindividual psychic entity.

The modernist view of authorial presence comes close to the ideal of effacement and objectivity presumably espoused by Stephen Dedalus in *A Portrait of the Artist*, according to which "the artist, like the God of the creation, remains within or behind or beyond or above his handiwork, invisible, refined out of existence, indifferent, paring his fingernails."[11] While this statement has come to epitomize modernist "refinement of the author out of existence," it does not accurately represent Joyce's own practice, or even Stephen's full statement on the matter. Sheldon Brivic points out that Stephen's phrase doesn't preclude the author's going *into* his work. He says "the doctrine of authorial absence has led us to see Stephen in *A Portrait* as saying that an author disappears *from* his work rather than *into* it. But Stephen says, 'The personality of the artist passes into the narration itself ...' and in the dramatic form, that personality 'fills every person with such vital force that he or she assumes a proper and intangible esthetic life.'"[12] It is noteworthy that Stephen here is describing a mode of authorial presence in the *dramatic* form, where the author is of course most effaced, and yet even within that form the authorial "personality" is said to subsist within every character of the work. This sounds very much like the idea of a supraindividual psyche.

A voice simulating a collective psychic milieu can be detected even as early as *Dubliners*. Consider the opening paragraph of "Two Gallants": "The grey warm evening of August had descended upon the city and a mild warm air, a memory of summer, circulated in the streets. The streets, shuttered for the repose of Sunday, swarmed with a gaily coloured crowd. Like illumined pearls the lamps shone from the summits of their tall poles upon the living texture below which, changing shape and hue unceasingly, sent up into the warm grey evening air an unchanging unceasing murmur."[13] The ambience seems almost tangible, and the "atmosphere" being evoked is cultural/psychic as well as physical, as Joyce's explicit reference to the "living texture" pointedly suggests. The passage brings to mind Virginia Woolf's famous metaphor of a "semi-transparent envelope surrounding us from the beginning of consciousness to the end."[14] But the "atmosphere" here in "Two Gallants" is too palpable, the narrative voice too tangible, the language too figurative, to simulate so implicit a thing as the cultural milieu.

A Portrait contains many passages involving a blend of affective, qualitative, and evaluative elements and of the perspective of the narrator and the character. Consider the following paragraph in which some sentences seem sheer exposition, and others hover indeterminately between ordinary narrative and figural presentation, each of them leading us progressively deeper into Stephen's psyche:

The wide playgrounds were swarming with boys. All were shouting and the prefects urged them on with strong cries. The evening air was pale and chilly and after every charge and thud of the footballers the greasy leather orb flew like a heavy bird through the grey light. He kept on, the fringe of his line, out of sight of his prefect, out of the reach of the rude feet, feigning to run now and then. He felt his body small and weak amid the throng of players and his eyes were weak and watery. Rody Kickham was not like that: he would be captain of the third line all the fellows said. (8)[15]

The first sentence presents exposition or "ordinary narration" with virtually no coloring of affect, its mature language contrasting with the childlike tenor of the preceding section; in most novels, this sentence would be sheer exposition. The second sentence, still expository and in a mature syntax and vocabulary, does involve affective terms—*urged, strong*—but these do not seem to stem from Stephen's individual psyche. The third, still apparently expository, still syntactically mature and not yet invoking any individual consciousness, does involve specific sensations (*pale, chilly*) and even a distinctive image of the ball as a bird—though we do not yet obviously have a personal consciousness for these sensations to reflect. The fourth sentence, beginning "He," invokes a personal psyche, but the sentence (still mature) seems expository and the perspective exterior to Stephen—though "feigning" involves a distinctive intent on the boy's part. The fifth sentence, beginning "He felt," specifically invokes the boys sensations and feelings, and the syntax is simpler, but it does not very fully simulate the feel of the boy's psyche. Only in the sixth sentence do we move "into" the boy's psyche, with the syntax and diction distinctively reflecting his perspective—though even here the presentation is third person and past tense. The following paragraph picks up where this last sentence has arrived, consisting of simple diction and syntax and conveying the boys perspective very fully.[16]

The Distinctive Narrative Perspective of *Ulysses*

Certain features of the narrative voice of Joyce's *Ulysses* suggest a collective psyche as the most appropriate way to understand this voice. The novel is presented from an "omniscient" perspective involving a persistent authorial presence or voice that cannot be identified with any one of the characters. But while this voice manifests itself in a variety of ways, including evoking qualitative and evaluative modes of experience, it does nothing to project itself as a "persona," or to attract attention to itself. In contrast to most omniscient fiction, where we have a voice sufficiently distinct to suggest personification, in *Ulysses* the narrative "presence" exists more implicitly, not as a tangible persona, but as a context or milieu sustaining the personal responses and judgments of the characters. This involves quite different implications as to what is represented or simulated by this presence.

Through this distinctive narrative perspective Joyce skillfully subverts the Cartesian distinctions undergirding the modernist worldview, including those of inner and outer and private and public, blending these categories so subtly that we cannot maintain the distinction. He does this for example by presenting within the same sentence elements that are authorial and that are distinctively those of the character, and by the use of qualitative and evaluative terms that we cannot attribute to one or the other. Another technique contributing to this inextricable blending is Joyce's abjuring quotation marks in favor of the introductory dash to indicate dialogue, with its inevitable blurring of the line between characters' statements and authorial context. The episodes in *Ulysses* best illustrating these distinctive qualities of Joyce's narrative voice involve a "third-person" (actually omniscient) presentation of characters moving about in the public world, thus including sensations, perceptions, public persons and events, as well as some degree of interior monologue or "stream of consciousness," rather than those that have an "Arranger" whose presence is announced by some striking mode of presentation (e.g., headlines in "Aeolus," question and answer in "Ithaca") or by some mode of organization and presentation ("Wandering Rocks"), or by some anomalous style ("Sirens," "Oxen of the Sun").[17]

There are four relevant aspects of the distinctive mode of narrative presentation in *Ulysses*.

The Existence of a Narrative Voice Distinct from that of the Characters and Having Omniscient Traits

In most episodes of the novel, the presentation is third person and past tense, and so we do undeniably have a voice that cannot be identified with Stephen or Bloom. Moreover, this voice can align itself with different characters and can provide various kinds of information: "Buck Mulligan attacked the hollow beneath his underlip"[18]; "Talbot slid his closed book into his satchel" (2.90); "Stephen closed his eyes to hear his boots crush crackling wrack and shells" (3.10); "The cat walked stiffly round a leg of the table with tail on high" (4.15); "An incoming train clanked heavily above his head, coach after coach" (5.313); "Ned Lambert glanced back" (6.692). Even in those episodes devoted almost entirely to Stephen or Bloom, the authorial perspective does not remain confined to them; for a brief portion of "Telemachus" we are with

Mulligan rather than Stephen (1.1–10), and in "Hades," viewed almost entirely through the eyes of Bloom, we are for a time in the presence of other characters who are talking about Bloom (6.526ff. and 6.690ff.).

Furthermore, the text of these episodes involves expository and descriptive phrases that do not originate with the characters or reflect their perspective, some of them revealing information about the characters—even their thoughts—others simply providing information about the physical setting or milieu. The opening paragraph of "Calypso" provides us with "private" information about Mr. Leopold Bloom's distinctive tastes for the inner organs of beasts and fowls, and especially for grilled mutton kidneys. The second paragraph, still presented in third person and past tense, tells us what is going on in his mind: "Kidneys were in his mind as he moved about the kitchen" (4.6). And during the coach ride in "Hades," we depart from Bloom's perspective when we are told "Mr. Power gazed at the passing houses with rueful apprehension" (6.310). Such constructions demonstrate that there is a voice other than that of the characters, and that the kind and range of information that this voice provides is consistent with "omniscience."

The Presence of Qualitative and Evaluative Terms
in the Narrative Voice

According to the modernist critical view, if a novel involves an "effaced" authorial perspective that cannot be identified with any individual character, this voice should confine itself to descriptive information. For it not to do so—for this un-personified voice to indulge in evaluative terms—would suggest the antimodernist idea of some discarnate "psyche" capable of exercising judgments or evaluations.[19]

Before illustrating such evaluative and qualitative elements in the authorial voice of *Ulysses*, I wish to focus more sharply a relevant point. For the modernist line of argument to have any validity, any consistency, it should apply not simply to evaluative terms, but to all *qualitative* terms as well. That is, if we accept the modernist idea that the world apart from an individual observer consists only of matter in motion, then we should acknowledge, as Galileo insisted, that qualities such as warm or cold or smooth or rough exist only in the sensorium of the observer, and thus have no more "objective" existence than do moral judgments or evaluations. To be metaphysically consistent, then, any authorial perspective not identifiable with that of an individual character should eschew qualitative terms as well as evaluative judgments.

In fact the authorial voice in *Ulysses* does *not* eschew evaluative or qualitative terms, for the novel contains many instances of both not attributable to any character. That is, the narrative voice in *Ulysses* is "omniscient" in the significant sense that it does persistently deal in such qualitative and evaluative judgments. In "Lotus-Eaters," we are told of Bloom, "While his eyes still read blandly he took off his hat quietly inhaling his hairoil and sent his right hand with slow grace over his brow and hair" (5.20). Several words in this sentence clearly involve a qualitative, evaluative account, but do not stem from the mind of Bloom: *blandly, quietly, with slow grace*. We may be tempted by the unobtrusive appropriateness of these terms, or by their arising so directly from Bloom's acts, to see them as Bloom's own, or perhaps to call them an "objective" account, but they are not. While Bloom is of course *experiencing* these acts, he is not using, even implicitly, these words to describe the acts; the specified words stem rather from the authorial voice. Similarly, in "Hades," as the cortege proceeds down Brunswick Street, we are told "They went past the bleak pulpit of saint Mark's" (6.183); here *bleak* certainly involves a qualitative, evaluative response, but it is not justifiable to attribute this to any individual in the carriage, especially in light of the opening *They*.

The Omniscient Voice Blends Indistinguishably with the Personal Voices of the Characters and with Their Qualitative Responses, Conscious and Unconscious

Joyce often makes it impossible for even the most astute reader of *Ulysses* to distinguish the psyche of the character from that of the narrative voice. That is, the text contains qualitative and evaluative terms that we cannot assign with certainty either to character or to authorial voice, suggesting that our so-called personal or individual evaluations shade off imperceptibly into the circumambient psychic milieu—as we saw above in the passage from *A Portrait of the Artist*.

Consider for example the obviously authorial sentence from "Proteus," "He turned northeast and crossed the firmer sand towards the Pigeonhouse" (3.159–60). This appears to be a sheerly authorial, expository sentence, of the sort that in another modern novel would be unremarkable, but upon examination we find that it has subtle, inextricable relationships with Stephen's mental processes. The word "northeast" seems purely authorial, for Stephen would hardly think it to himself. (I shall return shortly to its implicit cultural content.) The words "firmer sand" are interesting, since they involve a qualitative judgment Stephen presumably does not articulate, and are thus similar to the qualitative terms looked at above that arise from the authorial voice, yet this phrase reflects Stephen's own kinesthetic experience. That is, the firmness of the sand is *experienced* by Stephen, but *stated* by the narrative voice, thus involving an inextricable blending of the two. Interesting also is the authorial orientation "towards the Pigeonhouse," without any indication that Stephen perceives or even looks at that structure. Yet if we pursue Stephen's thoughts into succeeding sentences, we find that they involve the "pigeon" that impregnated Mary—clear evidence that he did on some level of his psyche apprehend the Pigeonhouse, whether he named it to himself or not, again showing how inextricably blended the authorial voice and that of the character have become.[20]

Having shown the subtle relationship between "public" and "private" in this sentence, I want to go back to the authorial term *northeast*, for while it is not overtly qualitative, it is nonetheless "acculturated," and thus not utterly "objective." That is, in its easy resort to compass points to establish the character's orientation, the term implicitly conveys a frame of reference distinctive to our culture. The authorial voice in another culture might convey orientation by saying "toward the rising (or setting) sun," or "toward the great mountain," or "into the evening wind," rather than invoke something so abstract as the compass points. I have already suggested that modernist critics betray a lack of metaphysical rigor if they do not proscribe qualitative as well as evaluative terms from "disembodied" (i.e., nonfigural) narration; now I suggest that many "descriptive" terms implicitly smuggle in cultural predispositions and values and that critics who speak so easily of "objective" description have not reflected on how culturally charged much of that "objective" description is.

It is clear that this sentence (as many others in this episode) involves an authorial voice referring to Stephen in the third person and the past tense, and is thus quite distinct from the character, and that this voice provides suprafigural information and exposition—functions that we associate with omniscient narration. Second, this voice involves qualitative judgments that are not articulated by Stephen ("firmer"). Third, it is virtually impossible to separate Stephen's psyche from that of the authorial voice, as shown both by the term "firmer" and by the subsequent effect within Stephen's thoughts of the authorial invocation of the Pigeonhouse.

The Omniscient Voice Remains Implicit, Never Assuming the Tangibility of a "Persona"

We are all familiar with what Hugh Kenner has dubbed the "Uncle Charles principle" in Joyce's fiction, according to which the narrative voice so wonderfully approximates the perspective of a character that the expository or descriptive words themselves take on the coloring of that individual's personality.[21] Though by no means unique to Joyce, his characteristic use of this tactic deserves thinking about more carefully, lest we gloss over some of its important implications. We should recognize that while the presentation in such instances seems to approach a first-person perspective, it remains firmly third-person, so that the words that are being spoken cannot be attributed to the character himself, but necessarily proceed from some narrator, as was stressed in the first mode of narrative discussed above. Furthermore, it is noteworthy that various degrees of distance can exist between the individual character and the narrative voice so that the authorial presentation is more or less strongly colored with the personality of the character, implying something similar to a gravitational or magnetic field that becomes stronger as we approach the source. While this narrator may asymptotically approach effacement into the personality of a given character, the third-person authorial voice nonetheless remains distinguishable, and this voice does subsequently withdraw from that character's sphere of influence and gravitate toward that of another character, altering its quality in the process.

It is important, however, that in *Ulysses* this chameleonic voice never assumes a tangible persona, much less a distinctive character; if it were to do so, the implication would arise that all of the authorial qualitative and evaluational terms reflect the psyche of that persona-character. The distinctiveness of Joyce's authorial mode lies in the pains he takes to keep his authorial voice present but beneath our notice. In virtually every other writer, while the authorial voice may for a time merge itself with that of a character, it does at some point emerge with such distinctiveness as to attract attention to itself, if not as a persona, at least as a voice with a characterizable stance and tone. This is true not simply of traditional omniscient novels, but modern ones as well. Conrad's *Nostromo*, for example, contains many statements so clearly omniscient and, overtly judgmental as to evoke some authorial persona, but this voice never emerges as a character in the novel, in spite of certain anomalous first-person statements (e.g., the first paragraph of part 1, chapter 8). Consider for example the following statement about Decoud: "He imagined himself Parisian to the tips of his fingers. But far from being that, he was in danger of remaining a sort of nondescript dilettante all his life. He had pushed the habit of universal raillery to a point where it blinded him to the genuine impulses of his own nature" (part 2, chapter 3, paragraph 6). Such statements are omniscient (i.e., not those of any character), but their overtness renders them qualitatively different from Joyce's authorial statements in *Ulysses*, causing us to look for some "persona" to ground them in, as Joyce's do not.

The tangibility of the persona-character can of course vary greatly, from the full-blown character of Nick Carraway in *The Great Gatsby*; to the "I" who speaks in the first paragraph of James's *The Ambassadors* (and who is of course quite distinct from Strether); to the distinctive voice that occasionally (and inconsistently) speaks as a villager in Trollope's *The Warden*; to the voice that certainly has a distinct, characteristic tenor but never emerges as a character in Austen's *Pride and Prejudice*; to the intermittent, sometimes almost impalpable, authorial voice in Woolf's Mrs. Dalloway.

In contrast to all of these, Joyce's authorial presence in the early episodes of *Ulysses* never assumes sufficient tangibility to suggest a character, or even a persona; we are not in the slightest invited to speculate about its "personal" qualities, much less to hypostatize it as a Victorian deity. This is not to say that the authorial voice in *Ulysses* is "objective," but neither is it utterly undetectable or uncharacterizable. I cannot, however, agree with Kenner's vaguely worded claim that the style of "Telemachus" involves "Edwardian novelese"[22]; anyone tempted to take that claim seriously should simply read a few paragraphs of Galsworthy's *The Man of Property* (1906), or H. G. Wells's *Tono-Bungay* (1909), or Arnold Bennett's *The Old Wives' Tale* (1908). What does characterize this voice is selectivity, economy, and precision, so that our attention is directed at the objects or events of the novel, not to the mode of expression. When we do take note of the presentation, it is to admire its deftness.

The distinctive Joycean voice so subtly blends "objective" description with qualitative evaluation, and so subtly blends the interior or personal perspective of the character with that of the narrating voice, that we cannot discriminate them. As a result, this voice simulates a continuum that spans several categories that the modernist mentality would presume to be separate and virtually incompatible: objective/subjective, quantitative/qualitative, descriptive/evaluative, public/private, individual/cultural. Furthermore, this voice, in contrast to the more traditional omniscient voice, remains implicit, attracting attention to itself only minimally and never in such a way as to invite our projection of it as a persona.

In *Ulysses*, then, there is an omniscient authorial perspective involving qualities and evaluations, but this perspective never emerges into personhood, existing rather as an indistinguishable continuum with the personal psyches of the characters, conscious and unconscious. The most feasible and satisfying way to regard this authorial presence is as a simulation of the collective psyche that is the medium of all "individual" thoughts, feelings, judgments. One of the main purposes of Joyce's distinctive mode of authorial presence is to evoke this broader psychic ambience, so that we must acknowledge the presence not simply of the psyches of his individual characters, but of the psychic medium sustaining the characters.

Not every form of omniscient point of view suggests or simulates a collective psyche: some modes, especially those overtly judgmental or involving a characterizable persona, evoke too tangible a sense of persona to suggest anything so implicit as a cultural milieu. Joyce's simulation of the collective psyche depends upon his achieving just the right balance between authorial presence and authorial effacement. In the care he takes to maintain the precise balance and the distinctive mode of omniscience necessary to simulate this medium, Joyce shows himself at odds with the totally "objective" mode of authorial presence presumed to characterize modernist literature and reveals a profoundly "antimodern" view of psyche.

NOTES

1. Robert M. Adams, speaking of the way that characters' thoughts and personalities seem to interpenetrate, says that "when other people's words turn up in Bloom's monologues, or his in theirs, it isn't a 'dropping out of character' but a deliberate dropping of character into some other continuum." See "Hades," in *James Joyce's Ulysses: Critical Essays*, ed. Clive Hart and David Hayman (Berkeley: University of California Press, 1974), 110. Baruch Hochman says that *Ulysses* dramatizes "the slipperiness not only of individual consciousness, but of communal consciousness as well." In *The Test of Character: From the Victorian Novel to the Modern* (Rutherford, N.J.: Fairleigh Dickinson University Press, 1983), 199; but he seems to see the communal consciousness at work in the obtrusive voices of the later episodes, whereas I find it better evoked in the "effaced" narrative voice of the early episodes. Tim Cribb, in "James Joyce: The Unconscious and the Cognitive Epiphany," in *Modernism and the European Unconscious*, ed. Peter Collier and Judy Davies (New York: St. Martin's Press, 1990), speaks of the epiphanies as involving "a symptomology of the social unconscious" (65), and of *Ulysses* he says, "The unconscious now is united with the conscious mind, and both with the world and the body, through a constantly interacting dynamics that makes any systematic separation between the elements impossible" (73); he goes on to claim that in *Ulysses* the unconscious is presented as involving every dimension of experience and of language. Sheldon Brivic discusses the idea of the "Author" in *Ulysses* in ways that sound very much like a collective mind in his *The Veil of Signs: Joyce, Lacan, and Perception* (Urbana: University of Illinois Press, 1991), especially in chapter 2, "The Author as Other." Later, in his discussion of "Stephen and Bloom at Gaze," Brivic says, "The lines that Stephen and Bloom share throughout the novel and the predictions in which they are involved, like the mythological and structural references that pop up in people's minds ... serve to make it clear that the individuals are part of a larger mental continuum" (107). Cheryl Herr finds what she calls the "cultural unconscious" in *Ulysses* (though no cultural consciousness), but her use of the term has very different sources and implications than my own. See her "Art and Life, Nature and Culture, *Ulysses*," in *Joyce's* Ulysses: *The Larger Perspective*, ed. Robert D. Newman and Weldon Thornton (London: Associated University Presses, 1987), especially 33–36.

2. Sheldon Brivic speculates on the many elements common to the minds of Stephen and Bloom in *Joyce between Freud and Jung* (Port Washington, N.Y.: Kennikat Press, 1980), 170–73. Perhaps most inexplicable is the presence in Bloom's thought in the "Sirens" episode of ideas and phrases from Stephen's reflections in "Scylla and Charybdis" about

Gerard's rosery in Fetter Lane (*Ulysses* 9.651 and *Ulysses* 11.907). This is especially problematic because of how smoothly the elements from Stephen's thought blend with those from Bloom's; as Brivic says, "Rather than being interpolated, these lines ... fit into Bloom's thoughtstream" (171). In his 1901 essay "Magic," Yeats expresses his view of the social or collective psyche under three doctrines: "(1) That the borders of our mind are ever shifting, and that many minds can flow into one another, as it were, and create or reveal a single mind, a single energy. (2) That the borders of our memory are as shifting, and that our memories are a part of one great memory, the memory of Nature herself. (3) That this great mind and great memory can be evoked by symbols." In *Essays and Introductions* (New York: Collier Books, 1968), 28; Joyce's Trieste library contained the 1905 edition of this book. Craig Carver agrees that Joyce knew this essay and explores Joyce's broader interest in the idea of a universal memory in his "James Joyce and the Theory of Magic," *James Joyce Quarterly* 15 (Spring 1978): 201–14.

   3. From Galileo's "The Assayer," in *The Controversy of the Comets of 1618* (Philadelphia: University of Pennsylvania Press, 1960), 309; subsequent page references will be cited parenthetically in the text.

   4. This is in Hassan's *The Postmodern Turn: Essays in Postmodern Theory and Culture* (Columbus: Ohio State University Press, 1987), 124. Hassan goes on to quote from Wilde's "The Critic as Artist." As Isobel Murray points out, the original title of Wilde's essay, "The True Function and Value of Criticism," "suggests that Wilde is setting out to answer Arnold's 'The Function of Criticism at the Present Time,'" and Murray goes on to refer specifically to Arnold's statement about seeing the "object as in itself it really is." In *Oscar Wilde*, ed. Isobel Murray (Oxford: Oxford University Press, 1989), 589.

   5. I carry these ideas out more fully in the first chapter of *The Antimodernism of Joyce's Portrait of the Artist*. It is clarifying (if disturbing) to see what "the object as in itself it really is" looks like from a rigorously naturalistic perspective: note how much Paul Churchland's account of reality in *Matter and Consciousness: A Contemporary Introduction to the Philosophy of Mind* (Cambridge: M.I.T. Press, 1984) owes to Galileo's primary quality/secondary quality distinction: "But the argument [from introspection] is deeply suspect, in that it assumes that our faculty of inner observation or introspection reveals things as they really are in their innermost nature. This assumption is suspect because we already know that our other forms of observation—sight, hearing, touch, and so on—do no such thing. The red surface of an apple does not *look* like a matrix of molecules reflecting photons at certain critical wavelengths, but that is what it is. The sound of a flute does not *sound* like a sinusoidal compression wave train in the atmosphere, but that is what it is. The warmth of the summer air does not *feel* like the mean kinetic energy of millions of tiny molecules, but that is what it is. If one's pains and hopes and beliefs do not introspectively seem like electrochemical states in a neural network, that may be only because our faculty of introspection, like our other senses, is not sufficiently penetrating to reveal such hidden details" (15).

   6. See my "Between Circle and Straight Line: A Pragmatic View of W. B. Yeats and the Occult," *Studies in the Literary Imagination* 14 (Spring 1981): 61–75; chapter 2 of my forthcoming book on Joyce's *Portrait*; and chapter 2 of my *J. M. Synge and the Western Mind* (Gerrards Cross: Colin Smythe, 1979).

   7. Morton P. Levitt, *Modernist Survivors: The Contemporary Novel in England the United States, France, and Latin America* (Columbus: Ohio State University Press, 1987), 20. See also the section of Michael Levenson's *A Genealogy of Modernism: A Study in English Literary Doctrine, 1908–1922* (Cambridge: Cambridge University Press, 1984) entitled "The modernist narrator on the Victorian sailing ship" (1–10), where he discusses "the use of the narrator as part of the subjectivist perspective" (3) in Conrad's *The Nigger of the Narcissus*. In the course of the discussion Levenson criticizes George Eliot's mode of presentation in *Middlemarch*, saying, "The narrator is not another character, but a

disembodied presence, moving freely over the dramatic scene, and granted prerogatives not allowed to mere mortals. Without becoming implicated in the recorded scene, the narrator becomes an assimilating, amalgamating force who makes transparent the opacities between individuals, who lets moral evaluation mingle freely with description, who sees hidden thoughts quite as clearly as natural landscapes, who hears distinctly the faintest whispers of introspection" (8). Turning to Conrad, he says: "The rejection of omniscience was a complicated matter" (8). I comment on both of these critics' claims in the first chapter of *The Antimodernism of Joyce's Portrait*.

8. Such first-person works include Conrad's *Heart of Darkness*, Anderson's "I Want to Know Why," Hemingway's "My Old Man," and Fitzgerald's *The Great Gatsby*. Even these works, however, implicitly involve information and values that enable our evaluation of the I-narrator.

9. For instance, Richard Brown's *James Joyce* (New York: St. Martin's Press, 1992) contains a chart describing the point of view of the various episodes in *Ulysses*, no one of which is described as omniscient: virtually every episode except "Circe" (described as "Drama") is characterized as "3rd person" and/or "inner monologue" (66). Brown explains that "Joyce's 'third-person' narrative is never merely conventional" (67), but gives no hint of its omniscience.

10. On the strange idea that Joyce's fictions write themselves, or are written by Stephen Dedalus, see the sources cited in my "Voices and Values in *Ulysses*," in *Joyce's Ulysses: The Larger Perspective*, 244–70, especially footnotes 1 and 4. One example is Shari Benstock's "Who Killed Cock Robin? The Sources of Free Indirect Style in *Ulysses*," where she says: "The technical devices that collectively become the means for rendering plot and establishing tone and point of view are generated from subject matter and context rather than imposed from above (or behind) by an authorial presence hovering close to the narrative product," and of "Aeolus," "These headlines arise in the text of *Ulysses* as they do in most newspapers, from the context of the day's news." In *Style* 14 (Summer 1980): 261, 271.

11. James Joyce, *A Portrait of the Artist as a Young Man* (New York: Viking Press, 1964), 215; subsequent page references will be cited parenthetically in the text. Stephen's phrase adapts ideas Flaubert expressed in his letters: see, for example, the letters reprinted in *The Workshop of Daedalus: James Joyce and the Raw Materials for A Portrait of the Artist as a Young Man*, ed. Robert Scholes and Richard M. Kain (Evanston, Ill.: Northwestern University Press, 1965), 247–48.

12. Sheldon Brivic, "Joyce's Consubstantiality," in *James Joyce: The Centennial Symposium*, ed. Morris Beja et al. (Urbana: University of Illinois Press, 1986), 149.

13. James Joyce, *Dubliners*, ed. Robert Scholes and A. Walton Litz (New York: Viking Press, 1969), 49.

14. Woolf's statement in "Modern Fiction" deserves quoting, both because what she calls for sounds like some circumambient collective psyche, and because she recognizes this quality in Joyce's work: "Life is not a series of gig lamps symmetrically arranged; but a luminous halo, a semi-transparent envelope surrounding us from the beginning of consciousness to the end. Is it not the task of the novelist to convey this varying, this unknown and uncircumscribed spirit, whatever aberration or complexity it may display, with as little mixture of the alien and external as possible? ... It is, at any rate, in some such fashion as this that we seek to define the quality which distinguishes the work of several young writers, among whom Mr. James Joyce is the most notable, from that of their predecessors." In "Modern Fiction," *The Common Reader* (New York: Harcourt Brace, 1925), 154. Three sentences later Woolf refers specifically to "*Ulysses*, now appearing in the *Little Review*"; by April 1919, the date of writing of this essay, the first eight episodes of *Ulysses* had appeared.

15. R. B. Kershner has made a similar point about this paragraph—"the sentences become smoothly and increasingly interior"—but he regards this as an acute instance of the "difficulty in ascertaining the epistemological status of the book's narration." In *Joyce, Bakhtin, and Popular Literature: Chronicles of Disorder* (Chapel Hill: University of North Carolina Press, 1989), 160. I see this paragraph as an integral part of Joyce's showing the inextricability of "inner" and "outer," of individual character and authorial voice.

16. Dorrit Cohn makes a similar point about the confession scene in *Portrait*, saying "note how ... the text weaves in and out of Stephen' s mind without perceptible transitions, fusing outer with inner reality, gestures with thought, facts with reflections." In *Transparent Minds: Narrative Modes for Presenting Consciousness in Fiction* (Princeton: Princeton University Press, 1978), 103. I discuss other ways Joyce's presentation in *Portrait* merges these post-Cartesian categories in a chapter of *The Antimodernism of Joyce's Portrait* entitled "The Verbal Simulation of Stephen's Psyche."

17. The authorial presence most clearly exemplifies a collective psyche in the first six episodes, most of "Aeolus," all of "Lestrygonians," parts of "Wandering Rocks," and parts of "Cyclops" and "Nausicaa." My approach to those episodes where another narrative voice intervenes is presented in my "Voices and Values in *Ulysses*," as well as in my forthcoming book on *Portrait*. The term "Arranger" was coined by David Hayman in his *Ulysses: The Mechanics of Meaning*, rev. ed. (Madison: University of Wisconsin Press, 1982).

18. James Joyce, *Ulysses*, ed. Hans Walter Gabler (New York: Random House, 1986), I.115; subsequent quotations are from this edition and will be cited by episode and line number in the text.

19. This is essentially Levenson's claim about Conrad's *Nigger of the Narcissus*, that Conrad "clings fastidiously to externals" until he has a first-person narrator to serve as an evaluator of the scene (*A Genealogy of Modernism*, 5).

20. Interesting in this regard is James Michels's "The Role of Language in Consciousness: A Structuralist Look at 'Proteus' in *Ulysses*," *Language and Style* 15 (Winter 1982): 23–32. Michels sets out to argue that language and thought are coterminous, but his analysis of certain passages in "Proteus" is so subtle that it demonstrates levels and modes of consciousness in Stephen beneath those carried by words, involving perceptions, images, and even an "ironic mode" (30).

21. Developed in chapter 2 of Hugh Kenner's *Joyce's Voices* (Berkeley: University of California Press, 1978).

22. Ibid., 69.

JOSÉ LANTERS

Old Worlds, New Worlds, Alternative Worlds: Ulysses, Metamorphoses *13, and the* Death of the Beloved Son

It was perhaps W. B. Stanford who first attracted our attention to the fact that Joyce, for the portrayal of his modern-day Odysseus, *Ulysses*, used not only Homer's *Odyssey* but drew on Homeric scholarship, as well as on much of the post-Homeric development of the Ulysses myth, including depictions of the Ulysses figure by Virgil, Ovid, Dante, Shakespeare, Racine, and many others.[1] According to Stanford, the evidence shows that Joyce took great trouble "to master not merely Homer's version but the whole literary tradition of Ulysses's exploits."[2] Other Joycean commentators since Stanford have reminded us that in discussing details of the Homeric story, it is important to ask "which Homer [Joyce] had in mind, which *Odyssey*, which Odysseus."[3] Moreover, Joyce's approach to his borrowed material is never straightforward. As Richard Ellmann points out, "the Homeric adventures and heroes become pliant under Joyce's hand. He tried to make his book thick with all the hidden possibilities of his material."[4]

Joyce's trans-Homeric approach to the Ulysses figure is evident in the description of the essential characteristics of the Ithacan hero that he gave to two of his friends, Frank Budgen and Georges Borach, in which he emphasized details of events preceding the Trojan War not found in Homer. Budgen records that Joyce regarded Odysseus as a literary example of the complete man and that he listed his attributes as follows:

From *James Joyce Quarterly* 36, no. 3. © 1999 by The University of Tulsa.

"He was subjected to many trials, but with wisdom and courage came through them all. Don't forget that he was a war dodger who tried to evade military service by simulating madness. He might never have taken up arms and gone to Troy, but the Greek recruiting sergeant was too clever for him and, while he was ploughing the sands, placed young Telemachus in front of his plough. But once at the war the conscientious objector became a jusqu'auboutist."[5]

Borach remembers a very similar conversation in which Joyce told him the following:

"Now *al mezzo del' camin* I find the subject of Odysseus the most human in world literature. Odysseus didn't want to go off to Troy; he knew that the official reason for the war, the dissemination of the culture of Hellas, was only a pretext for the Greek merchants, who were seeking new markets. When the recruiting officers arrived, he happened to be plowing. He pretended to be mad. Thereupon they placed his little two-year-old son in the furrow. In front of the child he halts the plow. Observe the beauty of the motifs: the only man in Hellas who is against the war, and the father."[6]

The full anecdote referred to in these conversations is provided by Robert Graves:

Now, Odysseus had been warned by an oracle: "If you go to Troy, you will not return until the twentieth year, and then alone and destitute." He therefore feigned madness, and Agamemnon, Menelaus, and Palamedes found him wearing a peasant's felt cap shaped like a half-egg, ploughing with an ass and an ox yoked together, and flinging salt over his shoulder as he went. When he pretended not to recognize his distinguished guests, Palamedes snatched the infant Telemachus from Penelope's arms and set him on the ground before the advancing team. Odysseus hastily reined them in to avoid killing his only son and, his sanity having thus been established, was obliged to join the expedition.[7]

Stanford points out that the ploughing incident, which will be the focus of my discussion, should probably be regarded as evidence of Odysseus's dedication to his family but that it is invariably used by Odysseus's detractors in the later tradition to suggest his unheroic nature. Possibly for this reason, the incident is not referred to by Homer at all; as Stanford puts it, "The fact that Homer does reveal, very casually, Odysseus's reluctance to join the Greek host against Troy [24:118–19] perhaps indicates that he knew the legend but deliberately gave no details of it, for the sake of Odysseus's prestige as a hero" (*Theme* 83). Homer is generally silent about pre-war events, so too much significance should not be attached to his reticence on this point. How Joyce first became acquainted with the legend is a matter of speculation: versions of the story can be found in Wilhelm Heinrich Roscher's *Ausführliches Lexikon der griechischen und römischen Mythologie*,[8] which Joyce knew and used, and another reference to the episode, probably the most accessible one in a classical source, is provided by Ovid in *Metamorphoses*, book 13, a work with which Joyce certainly was familiar.[9] Aspects of this latter text deserve closer scrutiny.

In book 13 of the *Metamorphoses*, Ajax and Ulysses verbally contend with each other for possession of the armor of Achilles. Ajax, characterized by Ovid as "a quick-tempered fellow" (285), addresses the assembly first and tries to convince the chieftains of Ulysses' inferiority by insisting on his cowardice:

> "Or am I to be refused the arms because I came forward to the war before he did, and needed no informer to compel me to fight? Will you prefer a man who was the last to take up arms, who evaded military service, by pretending to be mad, till another, shrewder than himself but less aware of his own interests, revealed his cowardly trick? It was Palamedes, son of Nauplius, who dragged Ulysses to the war he had avoided. Is he, then, to carry off these magnificent weapons, because he was reluctant to carry any? Am I to be dishonoured and deprived of my kinsman's possessions, because I offered myself to danger from the start?" (286)

Ajax then expresses a retrospective wish: "'I only wish that that madness of his had been real, or that it had been accepted as such! If only this scoundrel had never accompanied us against the Phrygian citadels, with his criminal suggestions!'" (286). This leads us to a tantalizing question: *what if* Ulysses's madness had been real or had been accepted as such? *What if* Ulysses had never gone to Troy? Ajax suggests that some events would have had a very different outcome; for example, "[w]ithout him, we should never have been guilty of abandoning Philoctetes" (286). But how does Joyce's *Ulysses* incorporate these hypothetical possibilities?

In the *Metamorphoses*, Ovid is fond of introducing hypothetical or speculative statements that show his awareness of how things might have been different in an alternative universe. In book 8, for example, Nisus's daughter exclaims, "I am sorry that Minos is my enemy, when I love him so: but if there had been no war, I should never have known him" (180). In that same book, we are told how Nestor had a brush with death while hunting the Calydonian boar: "Nestor of Pylos, too, might well have perished before the time of the Trojan war, had he not used his spear as a vaulting pole, and leaped into the branches of a nearby tree" (189). In *Ulysses*, the question of hypothetical and unrealized possibilities is an even more pervasive one. On several occasions, Stephen Dedalus contemplates the ousted possibilities of history—"things that were not: what Caesar would have lived to do had he believed the soothsayer: what might have been: possibilities of the possible as possible" (*U* 9.348–50)—and asks himself, "But can those have been possible seeing that they never were? Or was that only possible which came to pass?" (*U* 2.51–52). The implicit answer is that in literature, if not in history, the actual and the possible can coincide. For while history allows for only one possibility to be actualized, literature, with its use of metaphor and its complex relationship between surface and symbol, allows the writer to include several possibilities, even if these contradict each other. In *Lycidas*, for example, the poem that Stephen reads with his pupils in "Nestor," Milton can mourn the drowning death of his friend while at the same time reminding himself that "*Lycidas, your sorrow, is not dead*" (*U* 2.65). Joyce's method is similarly inclusive: when confronted with a choice between two possible (even paradoxical) options, Joyce invariably chooses to include both.

While Leopold Bloom, on the book's "historical" level of 16 June 1904, is consciously aware of the "irreparability of the past" and the "imprevidibility of the future" (*U* 17.975, 980), on a hypothetical or a metaphorical level *Ulysses* manages to include many discarded possibilities and alternative routes of history. In the "Ithaca" episode, for example, hypothetical questions and answers abound, including speculations about the past—"What future careers had been possible for Bloom in the past?" (*U* 17.787); the present—"For what personal purpose could Bloom have applied the water?" (*U* 17.275), and "If he had smiled why would he have smiled?" (*U* 17.2126); and the future—"Might he become a gentleman farmer of field produce and live stock?" (*U* 17.1603), and "What would be his civic functions and social status among the county families and landed gentry?" (*U* 17.1606–07). Of greater significance for the present argument are instances where Joyce deliberately opts for the road not taken by previous writers on the same subject. For example, Fritz Senn has noted that in the "Circe" episode Joyce uses as his starting point a subjunctive passage in Horace suggesting what *might* have happened to Ulysses *if* "'he had drunk with the others, foolish and greedy, with cupidity.'" [10] Senn points out that "Horace specifies a probability, a turn that might have been taken, an alternative," and that "Joyce's longest chapter suggests the alternative that Homer's and Horace's exemplars prudently avoided" (41).

In this context, Ajax's hypothetical and belated wish about Ulysses's madness in Ovid's *Metamorphoses* takes on a special significance and has profound implications for the plot of *Ulysses*. For if Ulysses really had been mad or had carried his pretended madness to its logical extreme, he would not have stopped the plough in front of Telemachus but would (unintentionally or deliberately) have sacrificed his only son to avoid taking up arms; if his madness had been accepted as real, Ulysses would not have left home for the Trojan war, and epic history would have taken a very different turn. I would argue that, while *Ulysses* is, on the surface, clearly modeled on the events of the *Odyssey*, this plot is superimposed upon the alternative plot sketched by Ajax in Ovid's *Metamorphoses*, which might help explain why Leopold Bloom's biological son, Rudy, dies in infancy, why madness is a pervasive theme in Ulysses, why Bloom's wanderings are confined to his hometown, and why the emphasis in *Ulysses* has shifted away from Odysseus's heroic prowess towards Bloom's antiheroic pacifism.

The inclusion in *Ulysses* of the alternative outcome of the story of Odysseus's madness, wishfully hinted at by Ajax, correlates with the fact that

> Joyce's version of the epic story is a pacifist version. He developed an aspect of the Greek epic which Homer had emphasized less exclusively, namely, that Ulysses was the only good *mind* among the Greek warriors. The brawny men, Achilles and Ajax and the rest, relied on their physical strength, while Ulysses was brighter, a man never at a loss. But of course Homer represents Ulysses as a good warrior, too. Joyce makes his modern Ulysses a man who is not physically a fighter, but whose mind is unsubduable. The victories of Bloom are mental, in spite of the pervasive physicality of Joyce's book. This kind of victory is not Homeric, though Homer gestures towards it; it is compatible with Christianity, but it is not Christian either, for Bloom is a member of a secular world. Homer's Ulysses has been made less athletic, but he retains the primary qualities of prudence, intelligence, sensitivity, and good will. Consequently Joyce, as might be expected, found the murder of the suitors at the end of the Odyssey to be too bloody as well as too grand. (*JJII* 360–61).

Bloom, then, as Budgen notes, "believes in non-violent methods of realising his aims" (149). But such an abhorrence of violence is not incompatible with the notion of sacrifice, especially when the alternative is worse and less justifiable violence on a larger scale. God Himself, after all, sacrificed His Son for the good of mankind. A pacifist Ulysses, true to Bloomian principles of nonviolence, might have had to sacrifice personal happiness (his family) for the greater public benefit of resisting an unjust war. Budgen suggests a similar motive behind Bloom's humanitarianism, which has him "making good on the large field of society what he has lost in the family bedroom, thus turning private woe into a source of public weal" (164).

Child sacrifice was by no means unknown to the ancient Greeks. In the Greek tradition, Odysseus may not have killed Telemachus, but, according to some accounts, it was he who hurled Hector's infant son Astyanax from the battlements of Troy.[11] The notion of sacrificing a child also made perfect sense to him when, according to Ovid, he persuaded Agamemnon to sacrifice his daughter Iphigenia—for reasons of war, however, rather than peace; in book 12 of Ovid's *Metamorphoses*, this sacrifice is described in relatively neutral terms: "So the claim of the common good prevailed over private affection, and the duty of a king conquered a father's feelings" (269). In book 13, Ovid makes Ulysses say:

> "It was I who, by my words, persuaded the soft-hearted parent to consider the good of the state. It was a difficult case I had, I admit—may Atrides forgive me for the admission!—with the judge biased against me. However the people's good, his brother's cause, and the chief command that was vested in him, induced Agamemnon to consider the killing of his daughter justified by the glory it would bring." (290)

It was Ulysses, moreover, who "was sent to the girl's mother, who had to be, not encouraged, but cunningly tricked into agreement" (290). The death of Iphigenia was directly responsible for the souring of the relationship between Agamemnon and his wife Clytemnestra; the latter took a lover in her husband's absence. In the *Odyssey*, the marriage of Agamemnon and Clytemnestra is constantly held up as a negative example, the mirror-image of the happy relationship between Odysseus and Penelope. Joyce's *Ulysses*, consistently transforming the binary either/or scenarios of epic into ironic both/and situations, suggests that Bloom is, in a way, both Ulysses *and* Agamemnon, just as Molly is both Penelope *and* Clytemnestra. The dead child functions as a bridging device between their contrasting narratives.

Surprisingly, perhaps, the death of Rudy Bloom has been largely glossed over or ignored by commentators on *Ulysses*. Ellmann merely suggests that the miscarriage suffered by Nora Joyce in 1908 during the third month of her third pregnancy "helped to make Bloom's chief sorrow, in *Ulysses*, the death just after birth of his son Rudy" (*JJII* 269). *Ulysses* remains vague about the cause of Rudy's death, but it is evident that the event was a crucial factor in the deterioration of the Blooms' sexual relationship and that Leopold Bloom feels he is somehow to blame for his son's demise. Bloom's sense of guilt may in part be a reflection of Joyce's own feeling that "for everything that turned out bad for his beloved daughter and son, he was the cause through all the abnormality that his genius possessed. That thought crucified him."[12] At the same time, it may also have a potential Ulyssean parallel. This parallel is not apparent to the characters themselves: Bloom, of course, is not aware that he is acting out the part of Ulysses; his explanation of Rudy's death, "If it's healthy it's from the mother. If not from the man" (*U* 6.329), reflects the ancient Jewish belief "that the health of a child is a reflection on the virility of the male."[13] As Stanford points out, Bloom "is shaped from inside, as it were, by his Jewish heredity; from outside by the Homeric parallelism" (*Theme* 221). This is complicated by the fact that the Homeric parallels are not always straightforward Homer, as Stanford himself was the first to point out. A closer study of ancient Jewish belief with regard to the only beloved son actually lends credence to the inclusion in *Ulysses* of the notion of child sacrifice. Jon D. Levenson's book, *The Death and Resurrection of the Beloved Son*, discusses the notion of child sacrifice in relation to the Hebrew Bible.[14] He argues that "child sacrifice was at one time part of the official cultus of YHWH" and that the first-born son was "the most precious offering" a father could make to God (11). The sacrifice of the only beloved son ties the Homeric myth (in its alternative, hypothetical form) to aspects of Judaism and to the founding principles of Christianity.

On the historical surface level of Bloomsday 1904, the notion of sacrificing his child for the sake of a greater cause does not, of course, occur to Bloom; in fact, Bloom is a model of compassion, and "Ithaca" states specifically that he is "reluctant to shed human blood even when the end justified the means" (*U* 17.293–94). The suggestion of the child murder/sacrifice (for the distinction between them is mainly a matter of faith) is therefore incorporated in *Ulysses* almost entirely on a secondary, abstract level and merely hinted at in connection with the death of Bloom's son. For example, "Oxen of the Sun" suggests various causes of infant mortality, including "the atrocious crime of infanticide" (*U* 14.1261); given this context, the subsequent question, "why a child of normally healthy parents and seemingly a healthy child and properly looked after succumbs unaccountably in early childhood (though other children of the same marriage do not)" (*U* 14.1274–76), a question of some relevance to the Blooms, takes on an intriguingly suggestive quality. Bloom himself, musing about the cruel games that people play with their children, appears to infer a semiconscious desire on the part of the parent to kill the infant: "'Throwing them up in the air to catch them. I'll murder you. Is it only half fun?'" (*U* 13.1191–92).

A more direct connection between infanticide or child sacrifice and the death of Rudy Bloom can be constructed from a suggestive sequence of allusions in the "Hades" episode. On his way to the cemetery, a child's funeral cortege puts Bloom in mind of his son's death and his own related feelings of guilt: "A dwarf's face, mauve and wrinkled like little Rudy's was.... If it's healthy it's from the mother. If not from the man" (*U* 6.326–29). A reminder of how Bloom's father died immediately follows this contemplation: Mr. Power remarks that suicide is the greatest disgrace to have in the family and that the man who does it is a coward, leading Bloom to observe, "They have no mercy on that here or infanticide" (*U* 6.345–46). The mental shift from father to child is not surprising, given that the roles of fathers and sons are fluidly interchangeable in *Ulysses*. In Bloom's mind, murder, suicide, and madness are closely related: in "Ithaca," he worries about "[t]he committal of homicide or suicide during sleep by an aberration of the light of reason" (*U* 17.1766–67). If suicide can be forgiven on the grounds of "[t]emporary insanity" (*U* 6.339), as Martin Cunningham charitably suggests, can the same excuse be used for a man who commits homicide or infanticide—a temporarily insane Odysseus, say?

Other suggestive connections are created in "Hades" by means of homonyms and word-association. Shortly after passing the house where, according to Mr. Power, "Childs was murdered" by his brother (*U* 6.469), Bloom wonders, "Where is that child's funeral disappeared to?" (*U* 6.506). The Childs murder thus comes to represent—historically—the notion of fratricide (to provide an additional connection between Ulysses and the plot of *Hamlet*[15]) and—metaphorically and homonymically—the notion of infanticide. It is important to note that Levenson makes a poignant connection between Biblical stories about the sacrificial death of the beloved son and stories about sons murdered by their brothers, as Abel was by Cain, arguing that there is an "intimate association ... between Abel's status as the preferred son and his violent death" (77). The Childs case makes Bloom think, "Murder. The murderer's image in the eye of the murdered" (*U* 6.478); earlier he had imagined Rudy alive, with "[m]e in his eyes," and blamed himself for his death: "From me" (*U* 6.76, 77). "Oxen of the Sun" again juxtaposes the Childs murder and infanticide: "the fratricidal case known as the Childs Murder ... miscarriages and infanticides, simulated or dissimulated" (*U* 14.958–62). The association between the murdered Childs/dead child is made manifest in the hallucinatory world of "Circe," when Bloom's feelings of guilt about his child's death translate themselves into a denial of responsibility for the Childs murder: "You remember the Childs fratricide case.... I am wrongfully accused" (*U* 15.761–63).

A pacifist Odysseus-Bloom who acts within the context of a Judeo-Christian morality might have sacrificed his only son to avoid taking part in unjust bloodshed on a wider scale. His action and its consequences would have an analogy in the Biblical story of Benjamin, the darling of his father Jacob's old age and only surviving son of Rachel after Joseph's ostensible death. Jacob's family survives a great famine, and it is made clear by Levenson that "the people of Israel endures [sic], only because [Jacob], like his grandfather Abraham, proved willing to surrender the only son of his preferred wife" (29). The said Abraham, moreover, as Levenson points out, was to have "his multitudes of descendants only because he was willing to sacrifice the son who is destined to beget them" (13)—a paradoxical notion that brings to mind Bloom's equally paradoxical "limp father of thousands" (*U* 5.571). The sacrifice and the reason for it is also echoed in the Christian precept "that one man should die for the people, and that the whole nation perish not" (John 11:50). In *Ulysses*, the sacrificial aspect of infanticide as a ritual of renewal is hinted at in Bloom's observation that "the blood sinking in the earth gives new life. Same idea those jews they said killed the christian boy" (*U* 6.771–72).

Throughout Ulysses, Bloom is connected with Elijah, and the coming of Elijah is associated with salvation through sacrifice: "All are washed in the blood of the lamb. God wants blood victim" (*U* 8.10–11). Elijah is also the prophet about whom it is said that he miraculously resurrected the only son of the widow woman of Zarephath (I Kings 17:17–24), which is yet another version of the plot concerning the symbolic death and resurrection of the beloved son. Throughout *Ulysses*, Rudy is associated with the sacrificial lamb: Molly dresses his body in "lamb's wool" (*U* 14.269), and when he appears to Bloom at the end of "Circe" as "*a fairy boy of eleven*," he is dressed in an Eton suit, and "[a] *white lambkin peeps out of his waistcoat pocket*" (*U* 15.4957, 4967). Levenson argues that among the Israelites, even at the time when child sacrifice was acceptable, the father was always allowed to substitute a lamb or a kid for the child in the actual sacrifice but that when child sacrifice became anathema, the substitution of the animal became *de rigueur*; in the New Testament, then, the death of Christ on the cross involves a return to the origins of this form of sacrifice, as "the dynamics underlying this ritual-mythical pattern come full circle ...: the son takes the place of the sheep who took the place of the son" (208).

In Bloom's mind, sacrifice and bloodshed are associated with the "[s]laughter of innocents"—a phrase repeated later in *Ulysses* as "Herod's slaughter of the innocents" (*U* 8.754, 14.1422–23). In the Greek myths, the concept of the "slaughter of innocents" is almost exclusively associated with the Trojan War. In the Judeo-Christian/Greek framework of the book, the reference associates the Biblical story, in which the infant Jesus was threatened by Herod's soldiers, with the pre-Homeric legend in which Telemachus was threatened by the plough or, instead, by the sword of the recruiting officer, as Lucian's version of the legend has it.[16] It is probably no coincidence that Rudy was born on 29 December, the day after the Feast of the Holy Innocents. His association with the number eleven (he died when eleven days old and would have been eleven in 1904), the number of sin and transgression since the time of Augustine[17] but also the number of renewal,[18] makes him a figure of both death and resurrection.[19] In *Ulysses*, the (metaphorical) sacrificial death of Rudy is also paralleled by the death of eleven-year-old Hamnet Shakespeare who, according to Stephen's theory, "has died in Stratford that his namesake may live for ever" (*U* 9.172–73). Rudy/Telemachus dies so that Bloom/Ulysses may renounce violence. In *Ulysses*, Stephen Dedalus can be regarded as the Telemachus who lived to grow up, as opposed to Rudy, the Telemachus who was killed in the hypothetical scenario. Stephen also repudiates the use of force and refuses to die in battle for his country on those grounds. For his principles, he is knocked down by a British soldier, whereupon he is metaphorically resurrected by a fatherly Bloom (ben Bloom Elijah?) as his metaphorical son—Rudy/Telemachus *redivivus*. As the son, Stephen is, of course, also Icarus, son of Dedalus, but an equally "alternative" Icarus who has resisted death by drowning. With "[c]ouldn't he fly a bit higher than that, eh?" (*U* 3.64), he echoes his father Simon's mocking words in "Proteus" before rejecting them completely in "Circe": "No, I flew. My foes beneath me. And ever shall be. World without end. (*he cries*) *Pater*! Free!" (*U* 15.3935–36).

Stanford speculates about "how much happier Penelope would have been if Ulysses had not won fame by leaving her" (*Theme* 142). *Ulysses* countermands this conjecture by suggesting that the price for staying at home may be equally high. In fact, had Ulysses stayed at home (by killing Telemachus), his relationship with Penelope would have become much like that of Agamemnon with Clytemnestra. Ben Dollard's rendering of "The Croppy Boy" towards the end of "Sirens" leads Bloom to consider his priorities in the light of Rudy's death: "I too. Last of my race. Milly young student. Well, my fault perhaps. No son. Rudy. Too late now. Or if not? If not? If still? He bore no hate. Hate. Love. Those are names. Rudy. Soon I am old" (*U* 11.1066–69). The possibility of another son is a post-Homeric variant that Joyce knew about from Roscher's *Lexikon*:[20] while Homer makes Telemachus an only child, other sources provide Odysseus with "children," while Eugammon's *Telegony* gives Telemachus a brother who, according to Roscher, must have been born after Odysseus's return (4:264). In sacrificial narratives, the second son is often portrayed as the beloved son *redivivus*: examples in the Bible are Seth (Abel *redivivus*) and Solomon. Solomon's case is particularly interesting in the context of *Ulysses*. Levenson argues that "at birth Solomon was not only the sole surviving son of David through his favored wife, Bathsheba, but also the replacement for the nameless offspring of their adulterous union, who had died soon after birth.... [Solomon] ... is the replacement for the doomed son, whose death helps to expiate David's sin and thus to continue his kingship" (29–30). This story may have provided Joyce with yet another ironic layer to his narrative, as he makes the death of the first son one of the causes of Molly's adultery, rather than atonement for it.

Bloom's attitude as a pacifist Homeric hero with Judeo-Christian overtones is put to the test in his confrontation with the hostile citizen in the "Cyclops" episode. As Louis Gillet has, albeit rather incredulously, pointed out, Joyce believed that the etymology of "Odysseus" was "Outis + Zeus," so that "when Ulysses in the cave of Polyphemus says to the Cyclops that his name is *Nobody* (Outis), it is Zeus renouncing himself.... Joyce claimed to perceive here the sacrifice of Calvary!" (194). "Cyclops" is the episode in which the sacrifice of Rudy is, in a sense, justified, for Bloom's newly found insight about love and hate and the hope for renewal through love gives him the moral courage to fend off the citizen's hostility:

> —But it's no use, says he. Force, hatred, history, all that. That's not life for men and women, insult and hatred. And everybody knows that it's the very opposite of that that is really life.
> —What? says Alf.
> —Love, says Bloom. I mean the opposite of hatred. (*U* 12.1481–85)

Bloom's gospel of love does not endear him to the drinkers in Barney Kiernan's, who, according to Budgen, unlike Bloom, "are proud, violent men, willing to kill and be killed for their cause"—at least in theory (165). The accusations leveled at Bloom by the men in the pub are similar to those directed at Ulysses by Ajax in book 13 of Ovid's *Metamorphoses*, after he has raised the issue of Ulysses's pretended madness. The monologic first-person technique of "Cyclops" depicts the citizen as a bigoted zealot and Bloom as a pompous, opinionated outsider. Stanford shows that Ovid similarly depicts neither contestant as a sympathetic figure: "Ajax is too crude and arrogant, Ulysses too suave and self-confident" (*Theme* 141). In the contest over the armor of Achilles, Ajax is allowed to speak first and immediately begins to attack Ulysses's reputation. He accuses his opponent of finding it safer "to engage in wordy battles than in armed combat: for his prowess in oratory matches mine in war and strife" (285). The nameless narrator in "Cyclops" refers to Bloom as "Mister Knowall" (*U* 12.838), and, while the citizen's claim to fame is excellence in the sports arena—he was the "champion of all Ireland at putting the sixteen pound shot" (*U* 12.881–82)—Bloom, like Ulysses, is a talker, and given any subject, "he'd talk about it for an hour so he would and talk steady" (*U* 12.895–96). Ajax accuses Ulysses of being like his father in "thieving and deceit" (286); Leopold Bloom is said to be like "his old fellow before him perpetrating frauds" (*U* 12.1580–81), Bloom's present concern being "[d]efrauding widows and orphans" (*U* 12.1622). Ajax asks why Ulysses is "trying to introduce the name of an outsider into the affairs of the Aeacidae" (286); the citizen denotes Bloom as an outsider by referring pointedly to "strangers in our house" and by asking him what his nation is (*U* 12.1151, 12.1430). Ajax mocks Ulysses by doubting his ability to support the weight of Achilles's helmet, just as "the ashwood spear from Mount Pelion is bound to be heavy and cumbersome for that weakling's arms" (288). The nameless narrator of "Cyclops" makes fun of Bloom "standing up to the business end of a gun. Gob, he'd adorn a sweepingbrush, so he would, if he only had a nurse's apron on him" (*U* 12.1477–78).

While Ovid's Ulysses responds to Ajax's allegations by refuting them and by dwelling at great length on his bravery and physical prowess, Bloom does not deny being physically cowardly and averse to the use of violence. His response to the citizen resembles Ulysses's reply in only one respect. Ulysses denies that he is an outsider on the following grounds:

> "Now, as to race and ancestry, and actions in which we ourselves have had no part, I scarcely call such distinctions our own; but still, since Ajax has brought up the fact that he is the great-grandson of Jupiter, I declare that Jupiter was the founder of my family also, and I am related to him in the same degree as Ajax is. For my father, Laertes, was the son of Arcesius, and Arcesius' father was Jupiter.... Both my parents number a god among their ancestors." (289)

Bloom's parting shot at the citizen is a similar argument of divine affiliation:

—Mendelssohn was a jew and Karl Marx and Mercadante and Spinoza. And the Saviour was a jew and his father was a jew. Your God....
—Whose God? says the citizen.
—Well, his uncle was a jew, says he. Your God was a jew. Christ was a jew like me (*U* 12.1804–09).

Ovid concludes the argument by suggesting that Ulysses's victory over Ajax was the result of rhetoric rather than substance: "it was evident from the result what eloquence could do: for the skilful speaker carried off the hero's arms" (295). Bloom's triumphant apotheosis at the end of "Cyclops" is likewise a triumph of overblown language rather than an actual victory: "And they beheld Him even Him, ben Bloom Elijah, amid clouds of angels ascend to the glory of the brightness at an angle of fortyfive degrees over Donohoe's in Little Green street like a shot off a shovel" (*U* 12.1915–18).

Declan Kiberd has argued that Bloom's pacifism can be regarded as an expression of Joyce's stance against the prevailing themes of the Irish literary revival of the early twentieth century and that, in *Ulysses*, "Joyce was reacting against the cult of Cúchulainn, which was purveyed in poems, plays and prose by writers such as Patrick Pearse, W. B. Yeats and Lady Augusta Gregory."[21] Kiberd continues, saying that the main theme of the tales about the Hound of Ulster "was the skill of Cúchulainn in glamorized combat and his capacity to make violence seem redemptive" ("Bloom" 3). Joyce was familiar with Lady Gregory's *Cuchulain of Muirthemne*,[22] and in *Ulysses* he has Buck Mulligan facetiously paraphrase a line of Yeats's preface to that book and ironically link it with the Greek epic: "—The most beautiful book that has come out of our country in my time. One thinks of Homer" (*U* 9.1164–65).[23] In *Cuchulain of Muirthemne*, Joyce would have read the story in which Cuchulain (Lady Gregory's spelling) kills his only son Conlaoch— information that he would also have gleaned from Yeats's play *On Baile's Strand*,[24] a drama that, as Kiberd points out elsewhere in a somewhat self-contradictory statement, "had shown how self-defeating a commodity heroism can be, and how absurd it can seem when it has outlived its usefulness."[25]

When Conlaoch arrives in Ulster from Scotland and refuses to divulge his name to Cuchulain, the latter challenges him to a fight. The mutual concern of father and son for heroic fame and reputation is stronger than their family bond, which neither of them acknowledges:

> "It would be well for you, young hero of unknown name, to
> loosen yourself from this knot, and not to bring down my hand
> upon you, for it will be hard for you to escape death." But
> Conlaoch said: "If I put you down in the fight ... there will be a
> great name on me; but if I draw back now, there will be mockery
> on me, and it will be said I was afraid of the fight." (238)

Only after Conlaoch has been mortally wounded by his father's spear does
Cuchulain recognize his son, and then he laments being left, Bloom-like,
"'[w]ithout a son, without a brother, with none to come after me; without
Conlaoch, without a name to keep my strength'" (241). Conlaoch's death is
tragic because it is ultimately pointless, an end in itself, the result of heroic
valor without human compassion. Cuchulain's "heroic" killing of his son is
not an act of insanity, pretended or real, nor does it serve to prevent violence:
on the contrary, it leads to madness and further aggression, even against his
own people. Fearing that Cuchulain will go berserk with grief, King
Conchubar tells the Druid to send him to the beach under a magical spell
and "to give three days fighting against the waves of the sea, rather than to
kill us all" (241).

The death of the beloved only son (Rudy, Telemachus, Icarus, Jesus,
Hamnet, and Conlaoch) is a pervading theme in *Ulysses* and, like all themes
in the book, a highly complex and often paradoxical one. In a heroic culture,
violence is an end in itself, one often leading to further bloodshed, or it is, at
best, a means to glory, and there is no doubt that *Ulysses* fundamentally
challenges a culture that fosters the glorification of violence *per se*. Sacrifice,
however, is more ambiguous. Using violence to ward off violence, the
sacrificial act is simultaneously sinful and sacred: there is no question that a
victim is killed (murdered), but the deed is transformed by faith into a
redemptive act (sacrifice). In *Ulysses*, however, any reference to sacrifice exists
entirely on a symbolic, textual level. I have argued elsewhere that it is
precisely such symbolism which transforms "bad" (actual) violence into
"good" (because symbolic) violence.[26] The sacrificial death of Rudy (or, at
one further remove, of Telemachus) in *Ulysses* is redemptive precisely because
it exists only between the lines of the narrative, much in the same way that
the myth of the sacrificial death of the beloved son survived in the Bible long
after the practice of sacrificing children had become unacceptable, in the
form of "narrative sublimations; of the mythic-ritual complex of the death of
the first-born son," as Levenson puts it (52). *Ulysses* blurs the distinction
between history, myth, what might be, and what might have been by
simultaneously realizing the levels of the actual and the possible, so that
different, even contradictory, readings of the text can be generated. Thus, in

the actual-hypothetical-possible world of *Ulysses*, the son is, like the father, "all in all" (*U* 9.1018–19): a mistake of nature, murder victim, sacrificial lamb, and resurrected hope for the future.

NOTES

1. W. B. Stanford, in *The Ulysses Theme: A Study in the Adaptability of a Traditional Hero* (Oxford: Basil Blackwell, 1954), p. 276 n6, quotes Stanislaus Joyce as saying that his brother studied the following writers on Ulysses: "Virgil, Ovid, Dante, Shakespeare, Racine, Fénelon, Tennyson, Phillips, d'Annunzio, and Hauptmann, as well as Samuel Butter's *The Authoress of the Odyssey* and Bérard's *Les Phéniciens et l'Odyssée*, and the translations by Butler and Cowper." Further references will be cited parenthetically in the text as *Theme*.

2. Stanford, "Ulyssean Qualities in Joyce's Leopold Bloom," *Comparative Literature*, 5 (Winter 1953), 125–26.

3. See Hugh Kenner, "Homer's Sticks and Stones," *JJQ*, 6 (Summer 1969), 286.

4. Richard Ellmann, *The Consciousness of Joyce* (Toronto: Oxford Univ. Press, 1982), p. 43.

5. Frank Budgen, *James Joyce and the Making of "Ulysses"* (Bloomington: Indiana Univ. Press, 1960), p. 16. Further references will be cited parenthetically in the text.

6. Georges Borach, "Conversations with James Joyce," *Portraits of the Artist in Exile: Recollections of James Joyce by Europeans*, ed. Willard Potts (Seattle: Univ. of Washington Press, 1979), p. 70.

7. Robert Graves, *The Greek Myths* (Harmondsworth: Penguin Books, 1955), 2:279. Graves cites several sources from which he assembled his version: Hyginus, *Fabula*; Servius on Virgil's *Aeneid*; Tzetzes, *On Lycophron*; and Apollodorus, *Epitome* (2:285 n6).

8. Wilhelm Heinrich Roscher, *Ausführliches Lexikon der griechischen und römischen Mythologie* (Leipzig: B. G. Teubner, 1884–1937). Further references will be cited parenthetically in the text.

9. Ovid, *The "Metamorphoses" of Ovid*, trans. Mary M. Innes (Harmondsworth: Penguin Books, 1955). Further references to Ovid's *Metamorphoses* will be cited parenthetically in the text to this edition. I am greatly indebted to Margaret Musgrove for sharing her insights and her knowledge of Ovid with me.

10. See Horace, *Horace: Satires and Epistles*, trans. Niall Rudd (Harmondsworth: Penguin Books, 1973), 1.2.24, and Fritz Senn, "In Classical Idiom: Anthologia Intertextualis," *JJQ*, 25 (Fall 1987), 41. Further references will be cited parenthetically in the text.

11. Graves, who admittedly sees sacrificial aspects in almost anything, considers the origin of this story to be "the ritual sacrifice of a child at the dedication of a new city" (2:345 n6).

12. Louis Gillet, "The Living Joyce," *Portraits of the Artist in Exile* (p. 192). Further references will be cited parenthetically in the text.

13. See Don Gifford, with Robert J. Seidman, *"Ulysses" Annotated: Notes for James Joyce's "Ulysses,"* rev. ed. (Berkeley: Univ. of California Press, 1988), p. 111.

14. Jon D. Levenson, *The Death and Resurrection of the Beloved Son: The Transformation of Child Sacrifice in Judaism and Christianity* (New Haven: Yale Univ. Press, 1993). Further references will be cited parenthetically in the text.

15. An additional Shakespearean link with the anecdote about Odysseus is that Hamlet also feigned madness or, according to some, really went mad.

16. In Lucian, "The Hall," *The Works of Lucian of Samosata*, trans. H. W. Fowler and F. G. Fowler (Oxford: Clarendon Press, 1905), 4:22, Lucian describes the unmasking of Odysseus's feigned madness when "Palamedes, penetrating his secret, seizes upon Telemachus, and threatens him with drawn sword."

17. According to Vincent Foster Hopper, in *Medieval Number Symbolism: Its Sources, Meaning, and Influence on Thought and Expression* (New York: Columbia Univ. Press, 1938), p, 87, eleven, "going beyond or transgressing the 10 of the law, was known to be the number of sin."

18. As Kenner puts it, in *"Ulysses,"* rev. ed. (Baltimore: Johns Hopkins Univ. Press, 1987), p. 18 n4, "Eleven is a recurrent Joyce-number. Bloom's son in *Ulysses* lived 11 days and would be in his eleventh year if he were alive on Bloomsday.... By one gloss, 11 signifies renewal by inaugurating a new decade." In *Ulysses*, the number is associated with Rudy, Hamnet, who died in his eleventh year, and Baby Boardman, who is eleven months old.

19. Levenson quotes the following verse concerning the proper age of a sacrificial victim: "When an ox or a sheep or a goat is born, it shall stay seven days with its mother, and from the eighth day on it shall be acceptable as an offering by fire to the Lord (Lev. 22:27)" (p. 183).

20. On p. 9 of his *Ulysses* notebook, Joyce mentions "(Arkesilaos / brother of Telemachus—spoken of only in Telegone)"—see Phillip F. Herring, ed., *Joyce's Notes and Early Drafts for "Ulysses": Selections from the Buffalo Collection* (Charlottesville: Univ. Press of Virginia, 1977), p. 16. Herring also mentions Roscher as a source for "the post-Homeric theory of the unfaithful Penelope" (p. 7).

21. Declan Kiberd, "Bloom the Liberator: The Androgynous Anti-Hero of *Ulysses* as the Embodiment of Joyce's Utopian Hopes," *Times Literary Supplement* (3 January 1992), 3. Further references will be cited parenthetically in the text as "Bloom."

22. Lady Augusta Gregory, *Cuchulain of Muirthemne* (1902; Gerrards Cross: Colin Smythe, 1970). Further references to the story of Cuchulain will be to this text.

23. In fact, W. B. Yeats's discussion of the dramatic, lyrical, epical, and romantic temperaments in his introduction to Lady Gregory's *Cuchulain of Muirthemne* may have inspired Joyce's own definitions of the terms lyrical, epical, and dramatic, which he wrote in his journal on 6 March 1903 and later used in *A Portrait* (*CW* 89 n3). Joyce wrote a negative review of Lady Gregory's *Poets and Dreamers: Studies & Translations from the Irish* (Dublin: Hodges, Figgis, & Company, 1903), which appeared in the *Dublin Daily Express* on 26 March 1903—see "The Soul of Ireland" (*CW* 102–05).

24. Yeats, *On Baile's Strand* (Dublin: Maunsel, 1905).

25. Kiberd, *Inventing Ireland* (London: Jonathan Cape, 1995), p. 266.

26. See my "Violence and Sacrifice in Brian Friel's *The Gentle Island* and *Wonderful Tennessee*," *Irish University Review*, 26 (Spring/Summer 1996), 163–76.

JOLEY WOOD

"Scylla and Charybdis" (and Phaedrus): The Influence of Plato and the Artistry of Joyce

The ninth episode of James Joyce's *Ulysses*, "Scylla and Charybdis," is commonly read as a dialogue pitting Aristotelianism against Platonism. This occurs in the context of the positing of a theory by Stephen Dedalus to certain Dublin literati that William Shakespeare actually identified himself with King Hamlet's ghost, rather than with Prince Hamlet. Of interest is one of the texts behind the text; as Stephen argues his theory, the subtle influence of Plato's Socratic dialogue, the *Phaedrus*, can be detected.[1] Joyce's breadth of literary knowledge is notorious—it would come as no surprise to find that the writer with the spider's eye was familiar with this particular work and used it in an episode specifically dealing with Platonic themes. We know from Richard Ellmann's *The Consciousness of Joyce* that Joyce possessed five works of Plato collected in a single volume entitled *Five Dialogues of Plato Bearing on Poetic Inspiration*.[2] The fifth work of this volume is indeed Plato's *Phaedrus*, and it is comprised of a dialogue between Socrates and the boy Phaedrus who discuss the differences among three kinds of rhetoric— writing, persuasive rhetoric, and dialectic (*Phaedrus* 205–77). Of note is the book's introduction by A. D. Lindsay, who treats the *Phaedrus* with particular emphasis on its poetic qualities and treatment of art—aspects that undoubtedly would not have been lost on Joyce (*Phaedrus* xi, xv, xviii).

The question to ask, then, is this: does Joyce use Plato's classical work

From *James Joyce Quarterly* 36, no. 3. © 1999 by The University of Tulsa.

in his own text and, if so, how? Resonances of the *Phaedrus* can be traced
through references to the Platonic dialogue linked with writing and through
parallel examples of persuasive rhetoric and dialectic found in both the
Phaedrus and "Scylla and Charybdis." These resonances, I argue, confront
the reader of *Ulysses* with evidence that Joyce had a deeper familiarity with
Plato than previously known, which ultimately poses the question of why
Joyce uses this particular text to help shape his episode.

The first allusion to the *Phaedrus* occurs when Stephen, while speaking
with the neo-Platonist Lyster, mentally utters, "Thoth, god of libraries, a
birdgod, moonycrowned" (*U* 9.353). The ancient Egyptian god Thoth is, in
fact, a significant figure in the *Phaedrus* and, arguably, a figure familiar to
Stephen, a writer who understands that Thoth represents the failure of
writing to express truth.

In the *Phaedrus*, Thoth (or Theuth) is saluted as the "father of letters,"
who created writing as "a medicine ... both for memory and wisdom" and as
something that will help people learn and remember what they have learned
(*Phaedrus* 271). Socrates relates that Thoth presented this memory facilitator
to the father-god Ammon, but Ammon claimed writing would have the
opposite effect of Thoth's intention:

> Your discovery ... is a medicine not for memory, but for
> recollection, for recalling to, not for keeping in mind. And you
> are providing for your disciples a show of wisdom without the
> reality. For, acquiring by your means much information unaided
> by instruction, they will appear to possess much knowledge,
> while, in fact, they will, for the most part, know nothing at all;
> and, moreover, be disagreeable people to deal with, as having
> become wise in their own conceit, instead of truly wise.
> (*Phaedrus* 271)

Socrates agrees with this statement: in the *Republic*, he explains how poetry
(writing) and painting only offer imperfect representations of things
occurring in the material world, which are themselves only imperfect
representations of the true ideas of things, thus leaving writing and painting
three times removed from the realm of truth.[3] In the *Phaedrus*, Socrates
illustrates this point by comparing writing to painting, both of which suffer
from the same deficiencies: "The creatures of the latter art [painting] stand
before you as if they were alive, but if you ask them a question, they look very
solemn, and say not a word. And so it is with written discourses" (*Phaedrus*
272). One can question a work of writing or painting to learn the truth of the
thing depicted, but the pictures will refuse to reveal anything more than

surface images. Furthermore, when offered up for public consumption, both kinds of work generally suffer from the non-presence of the painter or author to clarify the ideas presented in the work. Socrates here offers two explanations of how writing and painting leave one removed from the truth of the things depicted, echoing Ammon's criticism of Thoth's panacea for memory and wisdom; accordingly, the pupils of writing will only be equipped with a semblance of wisdom, not with truth, and will therefore be incapable of real judgment on the subjects encountered in the writing.

Socrates's ruminations on writing and on Thoth help the discerning reader of *Ulysses* understand this first allusion to the *Phaedrus*. Shortly before Stephen evokes Thoth, A. E. states, "The deepest poetry of Shelley, the words of Hamlet bring our minds into contact with the eternal wisdom, Plato's world of ideas" (*U* 9.51–53). The comment seems misguided since Socrates believed that poetry could not reveal the truth found in the world of ideas. By invoking Thoth, a representation of writing's inability to reveal true wisdom, Stephen arguably suggests that he knows that A. E.'s thesis is erroneous. Were Stephen to make the statement, he might say, "The deepest poetry of Shelley, the words of Hamlet cannot bring our minds into contact with Plato's eternal wisdom but only offer portraits of representations of ideas." Once the reader understands the significance of Thoth as described in the *Phaedrus*, it becomes evident that Stephen's summoning of Thoth undermines the very foundation of the neo-Platonists' philosophy from within, using a Platonic text to prove the neo-Platonic path to truth erroneous.

Later, as Stephen reflects upon Shakespeare's estranged adulterous wife, Ann Hathaway—"Sweet Ann, I take it, was hot in the blood. Once a wooer, twice a wooer" (*U* 9.668–69)—he claims that Shakespeare returned to Stratford "untaught by the wisdom he has written or by the laws he has revealed" (*U* 9.477–78). Again, a relation can be found to the *Phaedrus*. As noted, Ammon believes that writing does not reveal wisdom ("you are providing for your disciples a show of wisdom without the reality"). Socrates shares this sentiment:

> [H]e ... who received an art in writing, with the idea that anything clear or fixed is to proceed from the writing, must altogether be a foolish-minded person, and, in truth, ignorant of Ammon's prediction, as he must support that written words can do something more than recall the things of which they treat to the mind of one who knows them already. (*Phaedrus* 272)

As for laws revealed in writing, Socrates notes as follows:

[If anyone] has ever written, or meant to write, either a private
book, or a public document in the shape of a law, with the idea
that this writing contains a great certainty or clearness; in this
case reproach attaches to the writer, whether people say so or not.
For a total blindness with regard to justice and injustice, to virtue
and vice, escapes not in sooth the charge of being truly
disgraceful, even though it has been lauded by all the world.
(*Phaedrus* 275)

Again we see that writing cannot lead to truth or true wisdom but only
to a false semblance of wisdom ("a show of wisdom without the reality").
Socrates believes that this problem occurs because written views/laws are
subject to the varying and inconsistent opinions of the audience and that,
without the presence of the author, written views/laws cannot possibly be
clear to everyone who reads them. As he sardonically observes,

Moreover, every discourse, once written, is tossed about from
hand to hand, equally among those who understand it, and those
for whom it is nowise fitted; and it does not know to whom it
ought, and to whom it ought not, to speak. And when
misunderstood and unjustly attacked, it always needs its father to
help it; for, unaided, it can neither retaliate, nor defend itself.
(*Phaedrus* 272)

Accordingly, were Shakespeare to return to Stratford instructed by
what he had revealed in his writings, he would leave little room for further
contemplation and interpretation of his own life, thus falling prey to a "show
of wisdom." By remaining "untaught by the wisdom he has written or by the
[human] laws he has revealed" (*U* 9.477–78), Shakespeare refrains from
being "foolish-minded" and avoids the "reproach attach[ed] to the writer."
Shakespeare, like Socrates, is wise because he remains unwise.

A final reference to the *Phaedrus* occurs when Stephen muses on
fatherhood: "A father, Stephen said, battling against hopelessness, is a
necessary evil"; "Fatherhood, in the sense of conscious begetting, is unknown
to man. It is a mystical estate"; and "Well: if the father who has not a son be
not a father can the son who has not a father be a son?" (*U* 9.828, 837–38,
864–65). Stephen is here referring to Shakespeare's and Prince Hamlet's
fathers (and, arguably, his own). Yet this section again recalls the earlier
reference to Thoth and, indeed, shows a deep understanding of the god's
significance within the *Phaedrus*. Thoth, the father of written letters, a signifier
for writing and, thus, a signifier for a signifying system, is actually no father.

Thoth invented writing as a panacea for memory and wisdom. However, as noted above, one can question a piece of writing, but it will only repeat itself and cannot immediately clarify its own implications. In a similar way, the author is rarely present to explain or defend the claims of the work, and a piece of writing cannot present itself only to those who will understand as it is "tossed about from hand to hand" to either the comprehending or the unconcerned. Once ideas are rendered in written form and presented to the general public, they become susceptible to the (mis)interpretations of the audience and cannot guarantee one heightened memory or the revelation of wisdom.

Writing can arguably be seen as an act of fathering ideas, an act of consciously begetting ideas in written form, and, as Stephen declares, fatherhood is also a necessary evil. When writing, the author exists within the sphere of fatherhood and is present to clarify, explain, and support the written ideas, not unlike a father who clarifies, explains, and supports his offspring. However, once the ideas are written and offered to the public, the written work is sundered from the presence of the father/author, the one person who can explain those ideas and guide the audience to the truth of the subject; in other words, the father (writer) ceases to be a father, and the son (writing) ceases to be a son, rendering the offspring/written ideas isolated and illegitimate. Thus a written work, existing without the presence of the father/author, presents the audience with only a semblance of wisdom, not truth. Stephen's "son who has not a father," or written work, can only be an illegitimate son. It is worth noting Socrates's familial language when describing these shortcomings of writing, stating that it "always needs its father to help it" and suggesting its illegitimacy by describing an alternative as a "legitimate brother" to writing (Phaedrus 272). As illegitimate, of spurious origin, sundered *from* the father by the father *through* the very act that brings a written work into existence (writing), the offspring is almost always rendered fatherless. The suggestion is that the act of writing for general public consumption almost always denotes a parallel act of suicide/parricide. Fatherhood, as an act of writing or consciously begetting ideas in written form, ceases to be once the act is finished and the offspring of ideas are offered to the world. Thus, for the writer Stephen, "[f]atherhood, in the sense of conscious begetting, is unknown to man" (U 9.837–38).

All of the above references found in "Scylla and Charybdis" point to the idea of writing and how it fails to lead one to the truth of its subject. Writing is, in fact, one of three forms of rhetoric described by Socrates in the *Phaedrus*, the other two being persuasive speech and dialectic. As we have seen, Socrates holds that writing and persuasive rhetoric cannot lead to the truth of a subject, for only dialectic can accomplish this task. Indeed, in his schema of *Ulysses*, Joyce specified this episode's "technic" as dialectic.[4] As will be demonstrated, all three forms of *Phaedrus* rhetoric play important roles in "Scylla and Charybdis."

The *Oxford English Dictionary* describes rhetoric as "the art of using language so as to persuade or influence others."[5] Indeed, the *Phaedrus* begins with the presentation by Phaedrus to Socrates of a persuasive speech written by Lysias. When Phaedrus asks for confirmation of the speech's eloquence, Socrates replies:

> Are we required to praise the speech for the fitness of its subject-matter, or merely on the ground that every word in it is clear, and rounded and polished off with a nice precision? If on the former ground as well, it is only to please you that I can comply, since for my part my incapacity is such, that I observed no excellence of the kind. For I was merely directing my attention to its rhetorical merit, though this I did not imagine even Lysias himself would consider sufficient. (*Phaedrus* 215)

According to this passage, persuasive rhetoric involves clear, precise, and polished language. Socrates also states that rhetoric is "in general considered as a method of winning men's souls by means of words, not only in courts of law, and other public assemblies, but also in private conversation indifferently on matters great and small" (*Phaedrus* 251). One must note here that Stephen attempts to influence the souls of his interlocutors by using his characteristic polished, eloquent language during a private conversation in a public meeting place.

Stephen initiates his persuasive rhetoric by claiming that Shakespeare identifies with King Hamlet's ghost, implicates Ann Hathaway as Queen Gertrude, and relates the bard's biography within the pages of his plays. His ideas are explained in two particular speech-like sections describing the ramifications of Ann Hathaway's behavior on Shakespeare (*U* 9.450–81, 621–40). The others involved in this written episode/persuasive rhetoric/dialectic find Stephen's views "most illuminating" and "most instructive" (*U* 9.328, 503). Yet despite his ability to persuade the others, Stephen himself is not convinced: "—You are a delusion, said roundly John Eglinton to Stephen. You have brought us all this way to show us a French triangle. Do you believe your own theory?—No, Stephen said promptly" (*U* 9.1064–67). In the *Phaedrus*, Socrates says of persuasive speech, "[T]here is not the slightest occasion ... for people, intending to be competent speakers, to have anything at all to do with the truth ... no one troubles himself in the least degree with the truth of these matters, but only with what is plausible, that is to say, with what is likely" (*Phaedrus* 268). These people are persuasive rhetoricians, who, like Stephen, posit plausible theories to an audience in the hope of influencing their views.

The persuading of others of the truth—or at least of the plausibility—of Stephen's claims is not contingent upon his belief in the truth of those claims. Whether Stephen's disbelief existed from the beginning of the episode or after conversing with the others may only be known by Joyce. However, the facts that Joyce once held the same theory that Stephen posits, that Joyce employs the *Phaedrus* in this episode, and that in Joyce's own lectures, as Ellmann points out (48), he proposes the aesthetic idea that the author is intimately tied to the work, holding that the author is "all in all" (*U* 9.1018–19), provide the reader with a clue as to why Joyce chose to use the *Phaedrus*; these facts can be properly addressed after the significance of dialectic in the episode is discussed.

The idea of dialectic occurs in "Scylla and Charybdis" both as a topic of discussion and as a structural form for the narrative. The concept arises early in the episode when John Eglinton poses the question, "What useful discovery did Socrates learn from Xanthippe [his wife]?" and Stephen replies, "Dialectic" (*U* 9.233–34, 235). Dialectic is also a key concept in the *Phaedrus* and is Socrates's primary method of instruction. Socrates states that the dialectician finds a "congenial soul" and "avails himself of the dialectical art to sow and plant therein scientific words, which are competent to defend themselves, and him who planted them, and are not unfruitful but bear seed in their turn, from which other words springing up in other minds are capable of preserving this precious seed ever undecaying" (*Phaedrus* 274). He also comments that dialectic is a discourse "which is written with insight in the learner's mind, which is at once able to defend itself, and knows before whom to speak, and before whom to be silent" (*Phaedrus* 273). In the *Republic*, Socrates claims that dialectic helps one reach "the summit of the intelligible world" where one is allowed to glimpse "the essential Form of Goodness," the "parent of intelligence and truth" (*Republic* 252, 231).

Alexander Nehamas and Paul Woodruff note that "[t]hroughout the dialogues, [Socrates] insists that he can only discuss matters by means of the short question-and-answer method we know as the elenchus."[6] Hans-Georg Gadamer also asks what dialectic is in Plato and claims that it "began with those talks which direct and guide the interlocutor—the kind of talks for which Socrates is famous."[7] The *Oxford Dictionary of Modern Greek* defines "elenchus" as Greek for "inspection" or "examination," and the *Oxford English Dictionary* defines the Socratic elenchus as "the method pursued by Socrates of eliciting truth by means of short questions and answers."[8]

All of these dialectic definitions share some key elements: dialectic is a discourse intended to produce knowledge of some subject through an examination; it was apparently born in the early talks held by Socrates, as noted by Plato; it speaks and remains silent, meaning one member of the dialectic speaks while others listen, learn, and respond. In short, the Socratic dialectical method can be seen as a dynamic verbal examination of some subject in which the participants hope to gain some knowledge of that subject by questioning and answering each other. This method allows the members involved to gain knowledge of the subject and possibly transfer the knowledge on in the same dialectical fashion in the hope of apprehending "the essential Form of Goodness," the "parent of intelligence and truth." For Socrates, dialectic is the *only* way for one to approach the truth of some subject and thus gain wisdom since writing and persuasive speech (as seen above) actually produce *false semblances* of wisdom. Dialectic is also the method that Stephen uses to present his theory.

As Robert Kellogg points out, since Joyce's characters are assembled in the Dublin National Library discussing Stephen's theory in the hope of gaining knowledge, "Scylla and Charybdis" can be seen as a "mock Socratic dialogue."[9] Indeed, as Stephen presents the evidence for his Shakespearean theory, the prose style even changes for eight paragraphs from a narrative style to something like the dialogic form of a playscript; to reflect this, the lines of prose break, and a character's name is written above the following paragraph, denoting the succeeding paragraph as the speech of the named character (*U* 9.893–934). This style echoes the prose form encountered in plays such as *Hamlet* and reflects the "technic" of dialectic employed in the narrative style of the Platonic dialogues, not unlike the ones in Joyce's possession (*Dialogues* 205–77).

The subject of the "Scylla and Charybdis" dialectic is Stephen's theory that if the biographical Shakespeare is to be found in *Hamlet*, it is with the ghost of the king and not the prince—an idea that "[flies] in the face of the tradition of three centuries" (*U* 9.214) and was first held by Joyce.[10] Stephen's task is to engage his interlocutors and convince them to agree that his theory is at least plausible, which he does in a dialectical manner: he presents his thesis; the others question him; he supports his ideas; and in the process, all involved gain knowledge. Of greater consequence, however, is that by the end of the interaction, Stephen and the others come to an alternate conclusion to the original thesis: "—[Shakespeare] is the ghost [of King Hamlet] and the prince. He is all in all.—He is, Stephen said" (*U* 9.1018–20). This is at once an alternative to the theory that Stephen originally argues and a demonstration that the dialectic was successful—they have all gained knowledge, including Stephen. The new conclusion testifies to the effectiveness of Socrates's dialectical method. One must recall, however, that Stephen does not believe in the truth of his own theory, which, no doubt, contributes to his willingness to accept another conclusion.

Why would Stephen present a theory that even he does not believe is true? Since Joyce once held the same Shakespeare theory as Stephen and the episode gives us an alternative to that theory, it seems that Joyce's idea of who in *Hamlet* represents Shakespeare changed by the time that he wrote "Scylla and Charybdis" to reflect his own aesthetic ideas of authorship. Stephen's disbelief in his theory and his agreement that Shakespeare is "the ghost and the prince" (*U* 9.1018) support this idea, as well as Joyce's very use of the *Phaedrus*. Furthermore, Joyce's theory of authorship is a consubstantial one, meaning that the author shares certain characteristics and/or experiences with the major characters. Ellmann explains that Stephen and Bloom each represent opposite ends of Joyce's own life (*JJI* 365). In *The Consciousness of Joyce*, Ellmann notes that "in middle life Joyce celebrated ... the intimate tie between work and life. He enforced the theory that great literature was necessarily autobiographical," a theory that he developed in his Trieste lectures of 1912–13 (48). Joyce crafted "Scylla and Charybdis" prior to 1918, completing the episode between October 1918 and February 1919, some five years after his Trieste lectures (*JJI* 456). This evidence proves that Joyce's consubstantial aesthetic theory had germinated before writing "Scylla and Charybdis," evidently sometime between 1912 and 1913, and suggests its full development by the time that he penned the autobiographical episode "in middle life."

Joyce may have once believed the theory that Stephen posits but not at the time he wrote the episode—perhaps Stephen/Joyce determine that "they" are able to cease believing/write the theory because "[m]olecules all change. I am other now" (*U* 9.05). When composing "Scylla and Charybdis," and indeed during all of *Ulysses*, Joyce's aesthetic theory of writing was the same consubstantial one he had with his own characters. Applying his aesthetic views to his own theory, then, suggests that Joyce believed in a Shakespeare who identified with both the king's ghost and Prince Hamlet, the father and the son, "all in all," in a way similar to Joyce's own inextricable relationship with Stephen and Bloom.

Further evidence that Joyce's theory had changed can be found in the Platonic text that he utilizes, which may be why he chose to employ the *Phaedrus*. The reader will recall that, according to the *Phaedrus*, writing and persuasive speech cannot lead to truth; "Scylla and Charybdis" is a piece of writing (written rhetoric) depicting a convincing speech (persuasive rhetoric) through the vehicle of dialectic; Stephen refuses to publish his theory: "—Are you going to write it? Mr Best asked. You ought to make it a dialogue, don't you know, like the Platonic dialogues Wilde wrote....—For a guinea,

Stephen said, you can publish this interview" (*U* 9.1068–85). Working from assumptions contained in the *Phaedrus* that writing cannot lead to truth and that a piece of writing presented to the public will lend a false sense of wisdom, two possibilities arise: if Stephen *does* believe his theory, writing it for public consumption would be fundamentally flawed because he would not be able to defend its claims; if he *does not* believe his theory, there should be no problem with his writing something that for him is already a fiction. In fact, for Stephen, it is both; for Joyce, it is the latter.

Two paragraphs before Stephen tells Best that he may "publish this interview," he thinks, "I believe, O Lord, help my unbelief. That is, help me to believe or help me to unbelieve? Who helps to believe? *Egomen*. Who to unbelieve? Other chap" (*U* 9.1078–80). Stephen is unsure what to believe until the final four sentences of this paragraph: "Who to believe?"—the *egomen* or the conscious agents. The only actual conscious agents involved are Joyce himself and Lyster, Best, Eglinton, and A. E., all of whom are real figures from Joyce's life. Stephen is a conflation of fiction and the younger Joyce. "Who to unbelieve?" The other person may be the Stephen from a few pages back or the Joyce from a few years back—both are ostensibly reflections of each other, and both first had the original theory.

Yet we know that Joyce did not believe the Shakespearean theory presented when he wrote this episode; his aesthetic theory of authorship had changed to the consubstantial one decided on at the end of "Scylla and Charybdis" that most readers of *Ulysses* are familiar with. In his confusion, Stephen does not yet have an alternative to his previous theory, for he only agrees with the final conclusion that happens to fit with Joyce's own views of authorship. Having nothing to fall back on and being confused as to the truth of his own theory, Stephen chooses not to publish it for public consumption—and elects not father an illegitimate son, not to participate in the act of suicide/parricide that publishing the theory would require, not to become part of a necessary evil. Joyce, however, did have an alternative view of authorship, his consubstantial relationship with Stephen and Bloom, a concept that also is in accord with the conclusion at the end of the "Scylla" dialectic. Joyce once believed the theory that Stephen originally posits but, having changed his opinions on the subject, finds the old theory no longer true when he writes the episode—and he presents this theory in the manner of a persuasive speech, which the *Phaedrus* claims cannot lead to truth. This speech leads to a dialectic, a medium that, according to the *Phaedrus*, also leads to truth and furthermore leads the reader to the aesthetic theory of authorship that Joyce held. Both of these instances of rhetoric, however, occur in a *written* episode, a form of rhetoric that the *Phaedrus* claims cannot lead to truth. We may assume that Joyce did not share Socrates's disdain for writing, given his breadth of reading and composition. We must also realize that Plato indeed *wrote* the dialogues, which suggests that a written dialectic has the ability to "plant ... scientific words which are competent to defend themselves, and him who planted them, and are not unfruitful, but bear seed in their turn, from which other words springing up in other minds are capable of preserving" (*Phaedrus* 275); even a written dialectic has the ability to lead one in the direction of the truth of some subject—a testament to the power of dialectic. "Scylla and Charybdis" thus exists for us as a performative example of Joyce's progression in his ideas of authorship; the episode enacts the very premises that it discusses, and Joyce's use of the *Phaedrus* allows us to locate and witness this auto-biographical progression.

NOTES

1. Plato, *Phaedrus, Five Dialogues of Plato Bearing on Poetic Inspiration*, ed. Ernest Rhys, intro. A. D. Lindsay (New York: E. P. Dutton and Company, 1910). This is the same translation of the *Phaedrus* that Joyce used. Further references to the *Phaedrus*, the fifth work in the *Five Dialogues* collection, will be cited parenthetically in the text as *Phaedrus* and to the collection as *Dialogues*.

2. Richard Ellmann, *The Consciousness of Joyce* (New York: Oxford Univ. Press, 1977). Further references will be cited parenthetically in the text.

3. Plato, *The "Republic" of Plato*, trans. Francis Macdonald Cornford (London: Oxford Univ. Press, 1945), pp. 252, 321–33. Further references will be cited parenthetically in the text as *Republic*.

4. For Joyce's schema, see Hugh Kenner, *Dublin's Joyce* (London: Chatto & Windus, 1956), pp. 226–27.

5. *Oxford English Dictionary*, 2nd ed., s.v. "rhetoric."

6. Alexander Nehamas and Paul Woodruff, introduction to the *Phaedrus* by Plato (Indianapolis: Hackett Press, 1995), p. xi.

7. Hans-Georg Gadamer, *Dialogue and Dialectic: Eight Hermetical Studies on Plato*, trans. P. Christopher Smith (New Haven: Yale Univ. Press, 1980), p. 93.

8. See J. T. Pring, *The Oxford Dictionary of Modern Greek* (Oxford: Oxford Univ. Press, 1986), s.v. "elenchus," and the *Oxford English Dictionary*, 2nd ed., s.v. "elenchus."

9. Robert Kellogg, "Scylla and Charybdis," *James Joyce's "Ulysses,"* ed. Clive Hart and David Hayman (Berkeley: Univ. of California Press, 1974), p. 147. Further references will be cited parenthetically in the text.

10. As Kellogg notes, "Stephen's theory is based on a reading of the same books that Joyce consulted in 1904.... The two theories, Stephen's and Joyce's, are apparently identical, except that Joyce was less willing to admit that he did not believe his" (p. 151).

SARA DANIUS

Orpheus and the Machine: Proust as Theorist of Technological Change, and the Case of Joyce

Legend has it that when Orpheus sang and played his lyre, not only fellow mortals but also trees and rocks, even wild beasts, were stirred by the sublime sounds he produced. After the premature death of his young wife Eurydice, the grieving hero descended to the netherworld in the hope of rescuing her. He sang so beautifully that Hell was moved; even the Furies were spellbound, shedding tears for the first time. Orpheus was allowed to take Eurydice away with him on one condition, that both of them refrain from looking back until they had reached the land of the living. Walking in silence, they had almost reached the upper world when Orpheus wanted to ensure that his beloved was still behind him. He turned around; his gaze met hers. "See, again the cruel Fates call me back," Eurydice cried, "and sleep seals my swimming eyes. And now farewell!" She vanished from sight, absorbed for the second time by the regions of the dead. For months on end, Orpheus roamed the world voicing his grief, but in vain. His fate was sealed when the women of Thrace tore his body to pieces and threw the limbs into a river. In Virgil's rendering of the myth, Orpheus' head floated down the current, his "disembodied voice" calling "with departing breath on Eurydice—ah, poor Eurydice!" Whereupon the banks echoed: "Eurydice, Eurydice."[1]

The Orpheus myth revolves around love and death, around the powers of the gods and the vanity of humans, but it also tells a story about the eye

From *Forum for Modern Language Studies* xxxvii, no. 2. © 2001 by Oxford University Press.

and the ear: about the all-pervasive desire to look and the deadly power of the gaze, about the pleasures of listening and the animating power of the voice. In short, it is an allegory of the senses and, hence, of aesthetics.[2] Throughout the history of aesthetic discourse, sight and hearing have been privileged over taste, smell, and touch. Sight and hearing are more readily disposed to abstraction, and this is partly why they have enjoyed such prominence in the history of aesthetics. According to Hegel, for example, sight and hearing are essentially *theoretical* senses. For this reason, they are also *ideal* senses. Taste, smell, and touch, by contrast, are *practical* senses. They involve consumption of the work of art in one way or other, and this must not be, for he Hegel thinks of the work of art as an ideal site where spirit (*Geist*) and matter intersect. A privileged blend of pure sensuousness and pure thought, exteriority and interiority, art for Hegel is the sensuous objectivation of spirit. Consequently, only the eye and the ear are capable of respecting the integrity and freedom of the work of art. Of sight and hearing, however, hearing is the most ideal sense. It is the ear, and the ear only, that may establish the ideal correspondence between the inner subjectivity of the perceiver and the spiritual interiority of the object perceived. In this way, the perceiving subject receives and so in a sense corresponds to the object whose ideal, because spiritual, interior is mediated by the sounds it emits. Unlike the eye, then, the ear succeeds in apprehending both material objectivity and interiority, all at once.

Such an idealist theory of aesthetic perception is circumscribed by a long philosophical tradition—the metaphysics of presence. Consequently, it is also marked by a certain historicity. Discussing Hegel's hierarchy of the senses, Jacques Derrida suggests that Hegel could not imagine the machine, that is, a machine that functions by itself and that works, not in the service of meaning [*sens*], but rather in the service of exteriority and repetition.[3] Derrida does not state it explicitly, but it is clear that after the advent of devices for reproducing sound, the sense of hearing can no longer be thought of as *a priori* ideal. Devices such its the telephone and the phonograph strip sound of what Hegel would call its soulful interiority, and the sensory experience of acoustic phenomena henceforth has to resort to an ever-reproducible exteriority. Of course, the same is true of sight: its assumed ideality is exploded in the wake of inventions such as photographic means of recording visual data. In short, from now on the potentially sublime operations of the eye and the ear know an internal cleavage.

Few early twentieth-century writers have dramatised this aesthetic crisis as effectively as Marcel Proust. Describing the advent of modern technology, from the telephone and electricity to the aeroplane and the automobile, *Remembrance of Things Past* (1913–1927) offers numerous reflections on how technology affects human experience, particularly sensory experience.[4] The film-maker Raul Ruiz's adaptation of Proust, *Time Regained* (1999), is particularly sensitive to these aspects of Proust's tale. Ruiz even invents scenes not to be found in the novel: in one sequence, the young narrator operates a film camera, as though the entire novel springs out of a cinematographic vision; in another, Vinteuil's sonata is broadcast over a so-called *théâtrophone*, a popular telephone service that served to transmit music performances to listeners in the privacy of their home.

But Proust's novel more than dramatises technological change; it also delineates a psychology of such transformation, a psychology that may be grasped as a theory in its own right. I am thinking, in particular, of two episodes in *The Guermantes Way* (1920–21), the one revolving around a telephone conversation, the other reflecting upon photography. Read together, these episodes offer a meditation on the historicity of habits of listening and seeing.

Proust its theorist? Such a perspective has been elaborated before. Malcolm Bowle, in his brilliant study of the epistemology of jealousy in *Remembrance of Things Past*, maintains that Proust's novel is "one of the most elaborate and circumstantial portrayals of the theorising mind that European culture possesses".[5] And Siegfried Kracauer, in his widely influential *Theory of Film* (1960), approaches Proust as theorist of photography, basing his ontology of the photographic image in all analysis of the episode where Proust's narrator reflects upon how he beholds his grandmother with a photographic eye.[6] But Proust as theorist of technological change? Surely nothing could be further removed from the great themes of the novel: the primacy of involuntary memory, the priority of subjective time, and the virtues of immediate sensory experience. Yet, such a perspective alerts us to the richness and intelligence that inform Proust's book, demonstrating that vast portions of it hardly fit into that famous cup of tea. The second advantage—and this is what I shall dwell on in this essay—is that the theory embedded in Proust's episodes on telephony and photography yields a convenient point of departure for distinguishing the complex ways in which technologies of perception help reconfigure habitual ways of listening and seeing in the modernist period at large and, ultimately, how such change makes available new sensory domains that open themselves to artistic exploration, particularly in the realm of the novel. James Joyce's *Ulysses* is a case in point. Indeed, to juxtapose Proust and Joyce, as I propose to do in this essay, is to historicise some of the most characteristic formal aspects of Joyce's 1922 epic.

I

Proust's telephone episode relates the narrator's very first telephone conversation with his adored grandmother.[7] Transported across vast distances, from Paris to Doncières, her voice lilts his ear as though for the first time—"a tiny sound, in abstract sound".[8] What amazes the narrator is that although the two of them are spatially separated, their conversation is simultaneous; indeed, despite the spatial distance, they share one and the same temporality. Put differently, the aural impression of the grandmother's voice fails to coincide spatially with the visual impression of her bodily presence. For the narrator, this insight is deeply unsettling, and it immediately acquires symbolic proportions. But it also awakens the theorising mind whose speculative intelligence animates long stretches of *Remembrance of Things Past*. Turning around the dissociation of the eye and the ear, of what can be seen and heard, the uncanny experience triggers a Proustian psychology of telecommunication that stretches over half a dozen pages:

> It is she, it is her voice that is speaking, that is there. But how far away it is! [...] A real presence, perhaps, that voice that seemed so near ... in actual separation! But a premonition also of all eternal separation! Many were the times, as I listened thus without seeing her who spoke to me from so far away, when it seemed to me that the voice was crying to me from the depths out of which one does not rise again, and I felt the anxiety that was one day to wring my heart when a voice would thus return (alone and attached no longer to a body which I was never to see again), to murmur in my ear words I longed to kiss as they issued from lips for ever turned to dust. (*REM* 2: 135 / *RTP* 2: 432)

In short, the narrator discovers his grandmother's voice. Detached and disembodied, it hits him in all its baffling abstraction. Meanwhile, he also realises that he used to identify what he now perceives as "voice" by matching it with her face and other visual features. It is a dialectic moment, for what henceforth appears as having been an organic system of signification has just been sundered; and at the same time, this horizon of signs stands before him, suddenly and visibly revealed, now that it has been lost: "for always until then, every time that my grandmother had talked to me, I had been accustomed to follow what she said on the open score of her face, in which the eyes figured so largely; but her voice itself I was hearing this afternoon for the first time" (*REM* 2: 135 / *RTP* 2: 433).

The narrator discovers not merely his grandmother's voice; now that he perceives her "without the mask of her face", he also hears, for the first time, "the sorrows that had cracked [her voice] in the course of a lifetime". Dwelling inside her is a figure whom he has never yet apprehended, a figure inhabited by time. The narrator realises that his grandmother will die, and die soon, and the psychological impact of this insight is irreversible:

> "Granny!" I cried to her, "Granny!" and I longed to kiss her, but I had beside me only the voice, a phantom as impalpable as the one that would perhaps come back to visit me when my grandmother was dead. "Speak to me!" But then, suddenly, I ceased to hear the voice, and was left even more alone [...]. It seemed to me as though it was already a beloved ghost that I had allowed to lose herself in the ghostly world, and, standing alone before the instrument, I went on vainly repeating: "Granny! Granny!" As Orpheus, left alone, repeats the name of his dead wife. (*REM* 2: 137 / *RTP* 2: 434)

In this remarkable passage, Proust explicitly inscribes the telephone episode in the Orpheus myth, thereby reworking the Greek tale in a number of unexpected yet characteristic ways. Indeed, it is Proust who interprets the myth, adapting it to the cultural imaginary of the machine age, and not the other way around. But there is more to the episode. What the narrator intimates is that a whole new matrix of perceptual possibilities is sliding into place, one that transforms both the perception of voice (forms of audibility) and the perception of visual appearance (forms of visibility). In other words, the narrator perceives her bodily appearance as though for the first time. The experience of the disembodied voice thus elicits a new understanding of that bodily entity front which the voice has been detached.

This, indeed, is confirmed by the episode which follows a few pages later; I shall refer to this passage as the camera-eye episode. Once these two sections are read in tandem, as I believe they should be, and as I believe Proust meant them to be, an interesting pattern begins to emerge. The narrator is on his way to pay his grandmother a visit, compelled to do so by the telephone conversation and its uncanny revelation of a phantom grandmother, shaded by her age and future death: "I had to free myself at the first possible moment, in her arms, from the phantom, hitherto unsuspected and suddenly called into being by her voice, of a grandmother really separated from me, resigned, having [...] a definite age" (*REM* 2: 141 / *RTP* 2: 438). Upon his arrival, the narrator enters the drawing room, where he finds her busy reading a book. Because she fails to notice his presence, she appears to him like a stranger. He, too, feels like a stranger, observing her appearance as he would that of any old woman. To make matters worse, she appears precisely like that ghostly image which he so desperately wanted to banish from his mind: "Alas, it was this phantom that I saw when [...] I found her there reading" (*REM* 2: 141 / *RTP* 2: 438).

The grandmother has become pure image. Why does this stand out to his naked eye? Because she has withdrawn her gaze; indeed, it is her failure to look at her grandson that makes him discover, for the second time, her double. During the telephone conversation, her eyes and face failed to accompany her voice, thus anticipating that eternal separation called death. Here, too, she is shrouded in invisibility, for sitting in the sofa is not the grandmother but her doppelgänger. Disembodied and deterritorialised, she literally emerges as a spectral representation of herself. I stress this point because Proust's episode shares an affinity with Walter Benjamin's notion of the aura. Benjamin approaches aura in two ways: in terms of spatio-temporal uniqueness, and in terms of the gaze; and these perspectives merge in his reflections on photography in the 1930s.[9] In mechanically reproducing the visual real, the photographic image strips the object of its unique presence in time and space; at the same time, photography makes the past look at us, but—and this is Benjamin's vital point—we cannot look back. For this reason, photography is linked to death. Yet there is nothing Orphic in a photograph. In Benjamin, it is not the gaze itself that is deadly; it is the failure to meet the gaze of the other that is deadly. The history of the decline of aura is also the history of an increasing inability to meet the intentional and unique gaze of the other, be it an object, a human being, or history.

It is therefore all the more interesting that Proust's narrator, in order to explain how the uncanny sight of the grandmother was possible, should draw on the language of photography. Not only does he create an analogy between himself and a professional photographer; he also proposes that during those brief moments before his grandmother realised his presence, his gaze was operating like a camera. The photographic metaphor then sparks a Proustian essay which sets out to explain why we perceive our loved ones the way we do, and why these perceptions are always and necessarily faulty. In the process, Proust the narrator is joined by Proust the psychologist. Their dialogue shuttles between experience and theory, between local observations and general laws:

> We never see the people who are dear to us save in the animated system, the perpetual motion of our incessant love for them, which, before allowing the images that their faces present to reach us, seizes them in its vortex and flings them back upon the

idea that we have always had of them, makes them adhere to it, coincide with it. How, since into the forehead and the cheeks of my grandmother I had been accustomed to read all the most delicate, the most permanent qualities of her mind, how, since every habitual glance is an act of necromancy, each face that we love a mirror of the past, how could I have failed to overlook what had become dulled and changed in her, seeing that in the most trivial spectacles of our daily life, our eyes, charged with thought, neglect, as would a classical tragedy, every image that does not contribute to the action of the play and retain only those that may help to make its purpose intelligible. (*REM* 2: 142 / *RTP* 2: 438–9)

In order to drive home his point concerning the alienating vision inherent in the camera, Proust adds yet another example. This scenario, too, rehearses the contrast between what we expect to see, although we may not have realised it, and what we actually perceive:

But if, instead of our eyes, it should happen to be a purely physical object, a photographic plate [*plaque photographique*], that has watched the action, then what we see, in the courtyard of the Institute, for example, instead of the dignified emergence of an Academician who is trying to hail a cab, will be his tottering steps, his precautions to avoid falling on his back, the parabola of his fall, as though he were drunk or the ground covered in ice. So it is when some cruel trick of chance prevents our intelligent and pious tenderness from coming forward in time to hide from our eyes what they ought never to behold, when it is forestalled by our eyes, and they, arriving first in the field and having it to themselves, set to work mechanically, like films [*pellicules*], and show us, in place of the beloved person who has long ago ceased to exist but whose death our tenderness has always hitherto kept concealed from us, the new person whom a hundred times daily it has clothed with it loving and mendacious likeness. (*REM* 2: 142 / *RTP* 2: 439)

In an attempt to explain his grandmother's sudden alienation before his gaze, the narrator splits the category of visual perception into two: the human eye and the camera eye. Marked by affection and tenderness, human vision is necessarily refracted by preconceptions; and such a lens prevents the beholder from seeing the traces of time in the face of a loved one. In effect, the beholder sees not the person, merely his or her preconceived images of the person, thus continuously endowing the loved one with a "likeness". Memory thus prevents truth from coming forward.

The camera eye, on the other hand, is cold, mechanical and undistinguishing. It carries no thoughts and no memories, nor is it burdened by a history of assumptions. For this reason, the camera eye is a relentless conveyor of truth, and so it is that the narrator catches sight of a new person, hitherto unknown and unseen, who now flashes into the present: "for the first time and for a moment only, since she vanished very quickly, I saw, sitting on the sofa beneath the lamp, red-faced, heavy and vulgar, sick, vacant, letting her slightly crazed eyes wander over a book, a dejected old woman whom I did not know" (*REM* 2: 143 / *RTP* 2: 440). The deadly power of the photographic gaze has struck the grandmother, that once so familiar and self-evident being who, like Eurydice on the verge of light, instantly vanishes from sight and disappears into the shadows. All that is left behind is a phantom image. To be sure, the narrator's uncompromising image of his grandmother is bound to evaporate as soon as she lifts her eyes and recognises him. Yet for him those seconds have nevertheless hinted at her impending death. From now on the narrator's perception of his grandmother is scarred by her difference from herself. Her persona is split into two, her uncanny double superimposed upon her seemingly ever-pre-given self.

It should be clear by now just how intricate Proust's treatment of technologies of perception is in *Remembrance of Things Past*. What starts as a reflection on telephony and the discovery of the disembodied voice ends as a meditation on photography and how it changes the perception of visual appearances. In other words, the narrator's effort to grasp the experience of speaking to his grandmother on the telephone motivates a psychology of visual perception as well. Read in this way, Proust offers a germinal theory of how the emergence of technologies for transmitting sound such as the telephone paves the way for a new matrix of perception, in which not only sound but vision also turn into abstract phenomena. What is more, Proust suggests that the perceptual habits of the eye and the ear begin to function separately, each independent of the other, each in its own sensory register.

An episode in the last volume of the novel, *Time Regained* (1927), testifies to the consequences of such technological change. Set in the mid-1920s, the scene unfolds at a social gathering where the narrator is reintroduced to an old friend. The latter expresses delight at meeting again after so many years. A caesura follows, because the narrator, perplexed and confused, fails to identify the person in front of him, although the voice is familiar enough:

> I was astonished. The familiar voice seemed to be emitted by a gramophone [*phonographe*] more perfect than any I had ever heard, for, though it was the voice of my friend, it issued from the mouth of a corpulent gentleman with greying hair whom I did not know, and I could only suppose that somehow artificially, by a mechanical device [*truc de mécanique*], the voice of my old comrade had been lodged in the frame of this stout elderly man who might have been anybody. (*REM* 3: 985 / *RTP* 4: 522)

The gentleman's voice, rising out of the body as though of its own accord, is here rendered as a non-corporeal, hence foreign, element. It is the defamiliarising image of the gramophone that so drastically disconnects the voice from its bodily source. What is more, the mechanical metaphor strips the old acquaintance of human qualities such as consciousness and agency, thus reducing him to a non-human entity, indeed, to a thing. These images serve to underscore the narrator's insistent efforts to match his perception of the voice with his perception of the friend's exterior and, at the same time, they prefigure his utter inability to do so:

> He stopped laughing; I should have liked to recognise my friend, but, like *Ulysses* in the *Odyssey* when he rushes forward to embrace his dead mother, like the spiritualist who tries in vain to elicit from a ghost an answer which will reveal its identity, like the visitor at an exhibition of electricity who cannot believe that the voice which the gramophone [*phonographe*] restores unaltered to life is not a voice spontaneously emitted by a human being, I was obliged to give up the attempt. (*REM* 3: 985–6 / *RTP* 4: 523)

Rich in images and allusions, this passage turns on the tangible discrepancy between the narrator's aural impressions and his visual experience. What marks the representation of this encounter, and what sets it apart from the telephone scenario, is that the dissociation of the eye and the ear, of what can be seen and heard, has already happened. The differentiation of seeing and hearing both precedes and inscribes the narrator's account of the event. Whereas the telephone episode contemplated the experience of an abstract voice and, by implication, how the aural impression of the voice fails to coincide spatially with the visual impression of the speaking body, this scene contains within itself the very experiential effects that the previous one reflected upon. For if the telephone episode ultimately ponders the spacing of production and reception, of sonic origin and transmission, the present scenario both presupposes and enacts that logic of spacing. That is to say, the representation of the narrator's failure to recognise his friend from long ago is organised precisely by that matrix of perception—the dissociation of the eye and the ear, the abstraction and reification of sensory experience—that the narrator, in *The Guermantes Way*, took upon himself to grasp and explain. In effect, then, the representation of the old friend's voice presumes the essential *internalisation* of the very experiential effects that the telephone and camera-eye episodes set out to chart. The phonographic metaphor confirms the implicit dialectics at work. In the telephone episode, the narrator reflected upon the experience of the pure and abstract voice, intimating that it is enabled by a technology for communicating at a spatial distance. To this sound machine we may now add the phonograph, a mechanical device that makes it possible to strip sound not only of its spatial source but also of its temporal origin.[10] From now on, the voice and other acoustic phenomena are, potentially, subject to endless reiteration and exteriorisation.

In this way, then, Proust's telephone and camera-eye episodes articulate a theory of how a new division of perceptual labour comes into play, one that bears on both the habits of the ear and those of the eye. For although each of these two processes of abstraction may be traced back to its own relatively distinct technological lineage, their experiential effects—reification, autonomisation and differentiation—are fundamentally interrelated. Mutually determining one another, the abstraction of the visual is inherent in the abstraction of the aural, and vice versa. Meanwhile, as Proust's own phonographic imagery demonstrates, the new optical and acoustic worlds propelled by such technological change open up realms of representation that readily lend themselves to artistic experiments. From photography to telephony, from phonography to cinematography: technological transformation helps articulate new perceptual domains, charging the modernist call to make the phenomenal world new. Proust's novel thus offers a way of understanding the mediated nature of so many characteristic formal innovations that are to be found in numerous modernist works. Joyce's *Ulysses* offers a particularly rich example.

II

In *Ulysses*, each sensory organ appears to operate independently and for its own sake. What is more, each sensory organ, particularly the eye, tends to perform according to its own autonomous rationality, as though detached from any general epistemic tasks. "His gaze," Joyce writes, "turned at once but slowly from J. J. O'Molloy's towards Stephen's face and then bent at once to the ground, seeking" (*U* 7.819–20).[11] The trivial activity of looking is here rewritten as an event in itself. To look is no longer a mere predicate to be attached to a subject; the predicate has been unhinged from the subject and operates independently, endowed with an agency all its own. By the same token, voices in *Ulysses* also tend to lead an utterly independent life, physiologically as well as syntactically: "The inner door was opened violently and a scarlet beaked face, crested by a comb of feathery hair, thrust itself in. The bold blue eyes stared about them and the harsh voice asked:—What is it?" (*U* 7.344–7). Or, to take another example: "Miss voice of Kennedy answered, a second teacup poised, her gaze upon a page:—No. He was not. Miss gaze of Kennedy, heard, not seen, read on" (*U* 11.237–40).

The dissociation of the visual and the aural runs through Joyce's narrative from beginning to end. Indeed, despite the stylistic variegation that characterises *Ulysses*, this feature persists throughout the eighteen episodes of the novel, coming to the fore especially in the first two episodes, "Telemachus" and "Nestor". The opening of "Telemachus" dwells on how Stephen Dedalus and his two friends Buck Mulligan and Haines rise, chat and have breakfast in the Martello Tower. The first sentence introduces a perky Buck Mulligan and how he, "stately" and "plump", comes down the staircase. Wearing a yellow dressing gown which flutters round his body like a priestly mantle, he greets his half-awake friends with loud cries. A few sentences later, Stephen Dedalus enters the scenario. At the same time, Joyce introduces a characteristic stylistic device, a trademark visualising technique which, in various ways and with varying intensity, will be deployed throughout Ulysses. This is how the implicit narrator details Stephen's visual perception of Buck Mulligan: "Stephen Dedalus, displeased and sleepy, leaned his arms on the top of the staircase and looked coldly at the shaking gurgling face that blessed him, equine in its length, and at the light untonsured hair, grained and hued like pale oak" (*U* 1.13–16).

Within the space of a few paragraphs, the visual representation of Mulligan, whom we just observed proceeding from the stairhead and into the room as though in a full-length portrait, has shrunk to a face. In fact, his face has been turned into a thing which, furthermore, takes on a life of its own. The horselike face is said to shake and gurgle all by itself, even bless a somewhat irritated Stephen. Dehumanised and reified, Mulligan's face floats like a hairy oval before the reader.

Subsequently, Mulligan brings his shaving utensils to the parapet, lathers his cheeks and chin, and begins to shave, meanwhile chatting with Stephen. "His curling shaven lips laughed and the edges of his white glittering teeth. Laughter seized all his strong wellknit trunk" (*U* 1.131–3). Significantly, Joyce does not write that Mulligan is laughing, but that his lips are; likewise, Mulligan is not seized by laughter, but his stomach is. Joyce represents Buck Mulligan's body—that is to say, his lips, teeth and torso—its responding to external stimuli as though its reactions were mere reflexes, bypassing the control of some centrally-operating intentionality. Mulligan's physical appearance turns into a miniature spectacle before the reader.

The aesthetic effect of such passages, so common in Joyce, depends upon the differentiation of the human body, whose various parts are then autonomised and, furthermore, endowed with an agency all their own. In this introductory episode, as so often in *Ulysses*, Joyce's implicit narrator builds upon a narratological aesthetic that aims at defamiliarisation. The narrator, one could say, keeps to what he perceives, not to what he knows is there. In this way, Joyce's aesthetics reveals deep affinities with that of Proust, although Joyce pushes that aesthetic program to an extreme.

When Mulligan is about to descend into the tower, leaving Stephen to ruminate over his dead mother, Stephen's visual perception of his roommate's bodily movement is rendered as it presents itself to his eyes. Temporarily frozen by the entrance frame through which he is disappearing, Mulligan's figure thus appears as all optical outline:

> His head halted again for a moment at the top of the staircase,
> level with the roof.
>   Don't mope over it all day, he said. I'm inconsequent. Give up
> the moody brooding.
>   His head vanished but the drone of his descending voice
> boomed out of the stairhead [...] (*U* 1.233–8)

All Stephen perceives is a head. From a visual point of view, Buck Mulligan's bodily whole has been bisected by the frame through which he passes. There is a striking affinity between Stephen's image and a photographic frame, that instant freezing of time and movement. From a rhetorical point of view, Mulligan's visual *Gestalt* has been substituted for a synecdoche, his thing-like head being the sign that stands in for the whole and whose shape can be observed for a few more moments.[12] But what, exactly, is the whole, the *Gestalt*?

The passage suggests that Stephen's perceptual experience of Mulligan's descent is processed in two different registers. On the one hand there is Stephen's visual impression, and on the other, the auditory one. Each is distinct; indeed, each is separate and independent of the other:

> Buck Mulligan's voice sang from within the tower. It came nearer
> up the staircase, calling again. Stephen, still trembling at his soul's
> cry, heard warm running sunlight and in the air behind him
> friendly words.

> Dedalus, come down, like a good mosey. Breakfast is ready.
> Haines is apologising for waking us last night. It's all right.
> I'm coming, Stephen said, turning.
> Do, for, Jesus' sake, Buck Mulligan said. For my sake and for
> all our sakes.
> His head disappeared and reappeared. (*U* 1.281–9)

What is heard is not joined together with what is seen; and what is seen is in its turn a mere slice of the whole. The multi-sensory hermeneutic horizon, the all-embracing *Gestalt*, refuses to take shape. Aligning himself with a modernist aesthetic that aims to render what is perceived rather than what is known, Joyce challenges traditional ways of describing movement, gestures and action, and with them, the idea of "organic" modes of perception. At the same time, such a pronounced desire to represent what is heard and, furthermore, to represent it in a register that is radically separate from what is seen, may usefully be considered in the light of those late nineteenth-century acoustic technologies that mediate the new matrices of perception, turning the sense of sight and that of hearing into quasi-ideal senses. Indeed, Joyce's mode of representing Stephen's sharply differentiated sensory impressions in the Martello Tower scene is refracted through a perceptual matrix enabled by technologies for transmitting and reproducing the real, acoustic and visual technologies alike.

No wonder, then, that Joyce's novel abounds with reified voices and autonomous eyes. One further example will suffice, drawn from "Nestor", the second episode. Stephen is in the classroom teaching his rather unwilling students history. All of a sudden they are alerted to a sound:

> A stick struck the door and a voice in the corridor called:
> Hockey!
> They broke asunder, sidling out of their benches, leaping them. Quickly they were gone and from the lumberroom came the rattle of sticks and clamour of their boots and tongues. (*U* 2.118–22)

This stylistically sophisticated miniature scene serves to characterise Stephen's sensory apparatus. Beginning with a voice stripped of its author, the passage proceeds to render the students' sudden movements in all their visual purity, only to close with sounds, more specifically, with the acoustic phenomena issuing from the lumberroom. Stephen stays behind with one of the students, Sargent, who needs extra assistance, until

In the corridor his name was heard, called from the playfield.
   Sargent!
   Run on, Stephen said. Mr Deasy is calling you.
   He stood in the porch and watched the laggard hurry towards
the scrappy field where sharp voices were in strife. [...]
   Their sharp voices cried about [Mr Deasy] on all sides: their
many forms closed round him, the garish sunshine bleaching the
honey of his illdyed head. (*U* 2.181–98)

Represented as thing-like and autonomous entities, the boys' voices act on
their own, as though bypassing screens such as the cortex, spreading their
sharp vibrations all the way to the veranda where Stephen is standing.
Meanwhile his visual impression of the boys' appearances fades. Gradually,
they blend into so many optical outlines surrounding the stingy headmaster
whose hair-colour stands out as a sunny exclamation mark.

   A monument to the autonomy of the eye and the ear, Ulysses is both
an index and an enactment of the increasing differentiation of sight and
hearing in the modernist period. Joyce's style thus registers the subterranean
effects of those technological events that Proust reflects upon. Indeed, once
we place Joyce's mode of representing visual and acoustic impressions
alongside the theory of sensory differentiation and reification embedded in
Proust's novel, we realise the great extent to which the very experiential
effects that Proust's narrator contemplates effectively inscribe some of the
most persistent stylistic aspects of *Ulysses*.

   At the same time, the advent of modern technologies of perception
fuels the pre-eminently modernist imperative to "make it new" (Ezra
Pound), and nowhere as palpably as in Joyce. Technology emerges as an
occasion for launching new idioms: it restructures the prose of the world,
yielding opaque signatures that demand to be read and decoded. But this also
means that Joyce's aesthetics of perception comes into being as a solution to
a historical problem—how to recover and represent the immediacy of lived
experience in an age when modes of experience are continually reified by,
among other things, the increasingly powerful emergence of technologies for
reproducing the visual and audible real. In pursuing absolute immediacy,
Joyce's aesthetics of perception seeks to name the everyday anew; and this is
why, in *Ulysses*, the imperative to make you *see* and *hear* is so often an
aesthetic end in itself, utterly divorced from processes of knowledge and
cognition.

   Joyce's aesthetics of perceptual immediacy is thus inscribed by a
historically specific discourse where the empirical materiality of the body is
posited as the privileged site of aesthetics and where perception has become

an aesthetically gratifying activity in its own right. Such a discourse, as I have argued, becomes possible in the period which sees the emergence of technologies for reproducing the visual and audible real. The high-modernist aesthetics of perception I have been discussing in this essay thus feeds on a historical irony that is as palpable as it is inevitable: the more abstract the world of observation becomes, the more corporeal is the notion of the perceiver. And this bodily realm is no longer necessarily of a generalised, transcendental order, as in the aesthetic theories of, say, Baumgarten, Kant and Hegel. Indeed, the sensory body is no longer a universal notion. Rather, the aesthetic now tends to be located in a particular body, a concrete, singular and mortal body.

NOTES

1. Virgil, *Georgics*, with an English translation by H. Rushton Fairclough, revised by G. P. Goold (Cambridge: Harvard University Press, 1999), p. 257. I have also relied on *Bulfinch's Mythology* (New York: HarperCollins, 1991) and *Mythologies*, ed. Yves Bonnefoy, trans. Wendy Doniger (Chicago: Chicago University Press, 1991).

2. Etymologically, the meaning of the term "aesthetics" springs out of a cluster of Greek words that designate activities of sensory perception in both a strictly physiological sense, as in "sensation", and a mental sense, as in "apprehension". *Aisthetikos* derives from *aistheta*, things perceptible by the senses, from *aisthethai*, to perceive. For a full etymological explanation, see H. G. Liddell & R. Scott, *Greek-English Lexicon*, 9th edn (Oxford: Oxford University Press, 1996).

3. Jacques Derrida, "The Pit and the Pyramid: Introduction to Hegel's Semiology", in: *Margins of Philosophy*, trans. Alan Bass (Chicago: University of Chicago Press, 1982), pp. 71, 108.

4. For an inventory of the cultural imaginary of the telephone in Proust's time, see *Le Téléphone à la Belle Epoque* (Brussels: Éditions Libro-Sciences, 1976).

5. Malcolm Bowie, *Freud, Proust and Lacan: Theory as Fiction* (Cambridge: Cambridge University Press, 1987), p. 65.

6. Siegfried Kracauer, *Theory of Film: The Redemption of Physical Reality* (Princeton: Princeton University Press, 1960), pp. 14, 20 et passim. In Kracauer's book, Proust's episode also plays an important role; see *History: The Last Things Before the Last* (New York: Oxford University Press, 1969), pp. 49, 52, 82–6, 92–3.

7. Proust's telephone episode has a rich prehistory. An early version appears in *Jean Santeuil*, in the pages relating Jean's first telephone conversation with his mother; see *Jean Santeuil*, 3 vols. (Paris: Gallimard, 1952), Vol. 2, pp. 178–81. In 1907, Proust published an expanded version of the episode in a piece on reading in *Le Figaro*. He then revised the episode once again and made it a part of *The Guermantes Way*. On the genesis of the episode and its vital role in *Remembrance*, see Paul Martin, "Le Téléphone: Étude littéraire d'un texte de M. Proust", parts 1–3, *Information littéraire* 21 (1969), 233–41; and 22 (1970), 46–52, 87–98.

8. Marcel Proust, *Remembrance of Things Past*, trans. C. K. Scott Moncrieff & Terence Kilmartin, 3 vols. (New York: Vintage, 1982), Vol. 2, p. 432; *A la recherche du temps perdu*, ed. Jean-Yves Tadié et al., 4 vols. (Paris: Bibliothèque de la Pléiade, 1987–1989), Vol. 2, p.

135. Page references, hereafter cited parenthetically in the text, indicate first the English translation (*REM*) and then the French original (*RTP*).

9. See Walter Benjamin, "A Small History of Photography", in: *One-Way Street and Other Writings*, trans. Edmund Jephcott & Kingsley Shorter (London: NLB, 1979), pp. 240–57; "The Work of Art in the Age of Mechanical Reproduction", in: *Illuminations*, ed. Hannah Arendt, trans. Harry Zohn (New York: Schocken, 1988), pp. 217–51; and "Some Motifs in Baudelaire", in: *Charles Baudelaire: A Lyric Poet in the Era of High Capitalism*, trans. Harry Zohn (London: Verso, 1973), pp. 109–54.

10. For a cultural history of the gramophone and its impact on notions of acoustic representation, see Friedrich Kittler, *Gramophone, Film, Typewriter*, trans. Geoffrey Winthrop-Young & Michael Wutz (Stanford: Stanford University Press, 1999), pp. 21–114. See also Kittler's *Discourse Networks, 1800/1900*, trans. Michael Metteer, with Chris Cullens (Stanford: Stanford University Press, 1990), pp. 229–64.

11. James Joyce, *Ulysses*, ed. Hans Walter Gabler, with Wolfhard Steppe & Claus Melchior (New York: Random House, 1986). References cite episode number, followed by line number.

12. Alan Spiegel has usefully related Joyce's visual style to cinematic modes of representation, focusing in particular on Joyce's "method of fractured and cellular narration and description, of rendering wholes by their parts". In Spiegel's view, this feature represents "the characteristic formal procedure of Joyce's modernism" (*Fiction and the Camera Eye: Visual Consciousness in Film and the Modern Novel* [Charlottesville: University Press of Virginia, 1976], p. 64).

ERIC D. SMITH

A Slow and Dark Birth: Aesthetic Maturation and the Entelechic Narrative in James Joyce's Ulysses

In *The Art of Joyce's Syntax in Ulysses* (1980) Roy Gottfried devotes an entire chapter to examining Joyce's implementation of the *entelechy*, what he defines as "the fulfillment of possibilities in matter by the action of form, a realization that [is] achieved by the kinetic process of movement" (81). Though Gottfried confines his analysis to Joyce's use of entelechic syntactic constructions, one need not make too great an imaginative leap to perceive the larger entelechic structure that binds Joyce's four novels (including the aborted *Stephen Hero*) as a conceptual whole, each member of which contains in itself the unrealized potential for the next. *Ulysses* is a unique member of this conceptual whole in that it records stylistically the chain of becoming that precedes it and gestures in true entelechic fashion toward latent stylistic potentialities that succeed it.

To chart fully the trajectory of its own genesis and development, *Ulysses* adopts the metaphor of the human body. In a letter accompanying the now (in)famous Linati schema Joyce writes: "[*Ulysses*] is the epic of two races (Israel–Ireland) and at the same time the cycle of the human body as well as a little story of a day (life)" (qtd. in Ellmann, *James Joyce* 521). The schema itself designates to each episode a bodily organ and an accompanying stylistic *technic*—with the exception of the chapters making up the *Telemachia*, which "does not yet suffer the body" (*Ulysses* 736). The "cycle" which Joyce

From *Modern Fiction Studies* 47, no. 4. © 2001 by the Purdue Research Foundation.

alludes to, however, is not to be found in the disparate (in some cases seemingly random) assignation of organs. Rather, the development of the body (novel) is measured by the progressive sequence of stylistic techniques given to each chapter, a crescent stylistic maturation. Hence, the somatic-literary parallel dramatized in the novel by Stephen's encounter with Bloom is reflective of a deeper conjoining of art and life that serves as the connective hub of the novel's complex thematic-stylistic motifs.

According to the Linati schema, *Ulysses* is partitioned into three intricately balanced movements: *Telemachia*, the first three chapters, concerned almost exclusively with Stephen; *Odyssey*, comprised of the middle twelve chapters; and *Nostos*, the final three chapters. The first chapter of each movement is assigned a technique that situates it in terms of both physical and aesthetic levels of maturation. "Telemachus" is assigned "narrative young," "Calypso" "narrative mature," and "Eumaeus" "narrative old" (*Ulysses* 736). This tripartitioning of physical and aesthetic (narrative) stages evokes another of Joyce's three-part schemes introduced in *A Portrait of the Artist as a Young Man*: Stephen's three stages of aesthetic development.

In delineating his aesthetic for Lynch in *A Portrait*, Stephen claims that "art necessarily divides itself into three forms progressing from one to the next" (213), the lyrical, epical, and dramatic. The three-part division of *Ulysses*, maturing organically from narrative young to narrative old, accords almost exactly in form and concept with the consecutive stages of Stephen's aesthetic; the narrative young style can thus be equated with the lyrical stage of aesthetic development, the narrative mature with the epical, and the narrative old with the dramatic. Yet the three stages are not so clearly divided, for each exhibits vestigial traces of the stage which precedes it as well as (often subtle) glimpses of the stage to come. In this way the style of each chapter may be deemed *entelechic*, hinting at unactualized possibilities latent in the text, subtly undermining to varying degrees the style (and level of aesthetic maturation) of the chapter itself. This gesture forward is the kinesis necessary to actualize linguistic possibilities, create new potentialities, and maintain a perpetual motivation, an inherent restlessness in the text that prevents its ossification by incessantly interrogating its own authority. Such is the true genius of *Ulysses*, a novel which continues to yield with each new reading and generation of readers a fresh perspective, an inexhaustible spring of potential interpretation. Here I will examine the ways in which Stephen's largely disregarded aesthetic may be successfully and instructively applied to *Ulysses*, giving brief attention first to "Telemachus" and "Calypso" before examining more thoroughly the somewhat critically neglected "Eumaeus."

Ulysses opens in narrative young for good reason, for Stephen is as yet the self-conscious esthete, divorced—like Hamlet—from the world of action, subsumed by a numinous world of idea and abstraction, without a fully realized sense of self or identity. Our hero has been abroad, has seen much of the world and more of life, and yet is virtually unchanged from the Stephen we find in *A Portrait*. The chapter's stylistic, maintaining an intimate proximity to Stephen's point of view, is as awkwardly self-conscious as the young artist himself. This can best be perceived in the chapter's predominance of adjective/adjective/noun syntactic patterns, common to young or inexperienced writers: "shaking gurgling face," "light untonsured hair," "long low whistle," "even white teeth" (3). The narrative young style is evident as well in the plethora of weak qualifying adverbs. Almost every verb of action is modified with an adverb—with dubious stylistic effect: "called up coarsely," "blessed gravely," (3); "broke quietly," "looked gravely," "said gaily," "shaved warily" (4); "wiped [...] neatly" (5). Joyce's persistent and distracting use of these "formulaic narrative constructions" has, according to Karen Lawrence, produced an opening chapter of which "no student of creative writing, however inexperienced, would be proud" (45).

Stephen's debilitating egocentrism so infects the narrative that one can scarcely distinguish between the narrative voice and the rendered thoughts of Stephen. The language of "Telemachus" is the hyper-consciously precise diction of an incorrigible *poseur*. In fact, the lyrical style of "Telemachus" may be viewed as Stephen/Joyce's imperfect emulation of William Butler Yeats, the man whom Joyce considered the greatest lyricist ever and whose influence is evident in the affected verse of the young Joyce as well as in the overwrought "Telemachus." In order to achieve personal and artistic individuation, Joyce had to find a way to transcend, to write through his (Stephen/Joyce's) solipsistic and crippling posture, through the egocentrism and subjectivity that characterizes Stephen's lyrical mode. "Telemachus" thus both reveals and recreates the stylistic-aesthetic origins of *Ulysses*, its thoroughly *lyrical* narrative youth.

The style of "Calypso," the chapter which introduces Leopold Bloom, Joyce chose to call "narrative mature." Comparisons between "Calypso" and "Telemachus" abound for good reason: both occur at almost precisely the same time in the novel's chronology—between the hours of 8:00 a.m. and 12:00 p.m.—employ moderately conventional third-person narration, introduce main characters, and even share many of the same objects and images (that is, a cat, a tower, and green gems). However, the nature of such comparisons, particularly in the case of a writer like Joyce who delights in subtleties of style, invariably calls more attention to contrasting features than to comparable ones. "Calypso" is a logical (if subtle) departure from the style of "Telemachus", inasmuch as "Calypso" is in accordance with Stephen's second stage of narrative-artistic development, the epical.

Much has been written concerning the obvious similarities between the two episodes, such as the reappearances of certain distinct objects and images in "Calypso" first seen in "Telemachus." For example, the Martello tower Stephen shares with Haines and Mulligan (the "omphalos") is parallel in "Calypso" to Bloom as seen from the imagined perspective of his cat, itself a benignant manifestation of the black panther from Haines's dream; Haines's green-gemmed cigarette case, a symbol for Ireland, is parallel to the green, gem-like eyes of Bloom's cat. The effect is a general somatizing of the abstract elements of "Telemachus," a firm grounding in all things physical preparing the reader for the bathetic descent from the loft of symbol achieved with Stephen to the gut-level corporeality achieved with Bloom. While this shift in perspective may not necessarily be a stylistic alteration per se, it does serve both to prompt instructive comparisons with "Telemachus" and to prepare the reader for the new stylistic and thematic paradigms occasioned by the appearance of Bloom.

The location of "Calypso" in the novel, shuffling in rather austerely after Stephen's grandiose metaphysical meditation on the strand in "Proteus," is of consequence, for Joyce's growing discontent with Stephen's paralyzing egoism precipitates both the arrival of Bloom and the subsequent carnivalizing of the initial style used in *A Portrait* and—to a somewhat lesser degree—in "Telemachus." Joyce, writing to Frank Budgen after receiving complaints from Ezra Pound about Stephen's conspicuous absence in the second triad of episodes, claims, "Stephen no longer interests me to the same extent. He has a shape that can't be changed" (qtd. in Budgen 105). It is fittingly ironic that Stephen should command center stage for the final time in an episode entitled "Proteus," in which he contemplates the "ineluctable" universal modalities and the signifiers he believes himself ordained to interpret, all symptoms of what Bakhtin calls a monologic sensibility. Conversely, Bloom is, as Kevin Dettmar contends, "Joyce's first truly protean character—ego without boundaries, polymorphously perverse; fluid, he sympathizes, empathizes, melds with all he encounters—cats, dogs, lunatics, women in the throes of childbirth" (117).

Joyce does not abandon Stephen, however, as so many have suggested; rather, by introducing a new character, one who is in many ways Stephen's antithesis (perhaps his complement), Joyce subverts the young artist's ego and calls into question the naivety of his classicist, monologic world view. We recall that the motivation for Stephen's apostasy, his Luciferian "Non serviam," is largely his naive desire to supplant a theocratic monologic worldview with a secular (artistic) monologic one. His effort to be a "priest of the eternal imagination" clearly indicates his lack of ideological distance from both the church and the homogeneic world view it espouses (*A Portrait*

221). The young Stephen Dedalus is unabashedly elitist, and his struggle is, as he suggests in *Ulysses*, one against history (and the authorities which inform it). In order for Stephen to emerge as a true artist, he must free himself from the ossified past and its strict, arbitrarily delimiting forms.

The narrator is decidedly more obtrusive in "Calypso," though still stylistically mimicking the voiced and mental speech of our main character, much as we saw with Stephen in "Telemachus." In "Telemachus," the narrative seems to teeter on the verge of melding wholly and indistinguishably with the mind of Stephen, while in the latter, the narrative voice seems only a half-serious parroting of Bloom's interior monologue, establishing its own position and perspective on both character and action. F. K. Stanzel notes this shift from what he calls "authorial" to "figurative" narrative in both his *Narrative Situations in the Novel* (1971) and *A Theory of Narrative* (1979). Stanzel defines the "authorial" narrative as a way of envisioning "fictional reality from the narrator's spatio-temporal point of view and colored by the authorial interpretation" (*Narrative Situations* 28). In *Ulysses* there is a gradual movement away from this author-centered narrative stance toward the "figurative" narrative, which foregrounds the medium rather than the author and orients the reader to the "now-and-here of the figure [i.e., the novel]" (28). Monika Fludernik has also pointed out that "the juxtaposition of narrative and interior monologue in 'Calypso' sometimes has a distinctly intrusive quality," that the "reader is now frequently reminded of the narrative voice and its external perspective on Bloom" (22).

Another slightly more noticeable stylistic method Joyce employs to draw attention to the narrator is his use of pronouns. In "Telemachus," the pronoun "he" is reserved almost exclusively for Buck Mulligan—reiterating both our narrator's proximity to Stephen and, the "otherness" of Mulligan— while Stephen himself is referred to by "he"—or one of its forms—only sparingly, usually in sentences in which "Stephen" is the clear antecedent. Bloom, on the other hand, is referred to as it he—*excluding* all other forms— approximately 140 times in "Calypso," firmly establishing an exterior narrative perspective in which Bloom, our new central character, is seen as "other."

One notices also in "Calypso" the conspicuous lack of the pronoun "I" in much of the chapter's interior monologue. For example, "Want pure fresh water"; "Wonder is it true if you clip them they can't mouse after?" (54); "Walk along a strand, a strange land, come to a city gate"; "Wander through awned streets"; or "Wander all day long. Might meet a robber or two. Well, meet him" (55). Of course, one effect of the above method is to convey the disjointed spontaneity of Bloom's thoughts, the fragmented stream of consciousness. The question, though, is why Joyce allows Stephen a different, more personalized method in "Telemachus": "So I carried the boat of incense then at Clongowes. I am another now and yet the same" (11); "As he and others see me. Who chose this face for me? This dogsbody to rid of vermin. It asks me too" (6); "He fears the lancet of my art as I fear that of his" (7).

Obviously, the narrative of "Calypso" remains by and large consonant with Bloom's perspective; however, the clearly suggested presence of an exterior narrator, though of small consequence and in no way unconventional, portends the tremendous changes in the novel's dynamics as it slowly leaves egocentric intellectualism in its wake and spreads (or disintegrates itself) to embrace life, as well as language, in all manifestations. This objectification of the character(s) in the novel is in perfect accordance with Stephen's definition of the epical stage of aesthetic development, in which the artist "presents his image in mediate relation to himself and others" (*A Portrait* 213); hence, we recognize the establishment of language (narrative) as medium and narrator as mediator in "Calypso." As the necessary progression from the lyrical form, that in which "the artist presents his image in immediate relation to himself," the epical stage requires just the sort of ego disintegration presented in "Calypso" with regard to both theme/characterization and language/style.

The Linati schema designates "narrative old" as the stylistic technique for "Eumaeus," the chapter that initiates the novel's final movement, *Nostos* (literally "homecoming"). Ignored by critics for decades and dismissed by Robert Bell as the "grandest pratfall of *Ulysses*" (qtd. in Newman 451), "Eumaeus" has in recent years been the subject of a comprehensive re-analysis. In the last two decades, critics, including Karen Lawrence and Edna Duffy, have discovered socio-political and philosophical dimensions of the chapter all but ignored by earlier treatments of the novel and have carefully reappraised the chapter's wearisome prolixity as an ingenious narrative device ahead of its time (like many of the novel's techniques). The "narrative old" technique marks the end of the stylistic progression begun in "Telemachus" with "narrative young." If the exuberantly overwritten, self-conscious style of "Telemachus" represents youth and the end of Stephen's lyric stage of artistic development, "Eumaeus" represents world-weary, *word-weary* senescence and the necessary decline of former linguistic paradigms which facilitates the advent of the dramatic aesthetic stage. However, the uniquely inefficient style of "Eumaeus" not only indicates the end of Stephen's epic aesthetic stage and the arrival of the dramatic but also portends, through various demonstrations of the failure of language and the corollary limitation of human knowledge, the need for a new orientation to language, one without pretensions to Grand Narrative or overtly politicized, exclusivist meaning, one achieved (or attempted in my view) in *Finnegans Wake*.

"Eumaeus" follows its *Odyssey* counterpart perhaps more faithfully than any of the other chapters in the novel (with the possible exception of "Cyclops"). Eumaeus is, of course, the only faithful servant Odysseus discovers in Ithaca upon his return. Eumaeus does not recognize Odysseus, however, as the hero is disguised in the rags of a beggar, the irony being that though he remains faithful to Odysseus, Eumaeus does not believe the truth of the hero's presence before him. Rather, he believes the deceptive evidence of his senses. Not until Athena's dea ex machina descent does Eumaeus assent that the beggar before him is in fact his old master.

It follows that the major thematic and stylistic preoccupations of "Eumaeus" are deception, verisimilitude, and confusion, the first and most obvious example of which is the problem of identity. In "Eumaeus," identity is a most elusive and frustrating quarry. The chapter features a wealth of pseudonyms, nominative coincidences, and cases of mistaken identity that result in a frustrating uncertainty about who is who.

The confusion of identities begins when the speciously titled "Lord" Corley accosts Stephen and Bloom and recognizes (or misrecognizes) the latter as a friend of Boylan. Though there is some possibility that Corley has seen Bloom at the Carl Rosa with Boylan—"Now you mention it his face was familiar to me," says Bloom (575)—the uncertainty of the truth of things is characteristic of every such coincidence in "Eumaeus."

The keeper of the cabman's shelter, "said to be the once famous Skin-the-Goat, Fitzharris, the invincible" (577), an accessory in the infamous Phoenix Park murders of 1882, is never properly identified as such. His identity remains shrouded in rumor and general uneasiness. As the narrator relates, Bloom "wouldn't vouch for the actual facts [of Fitzharris's identity], which quite possibly there was not one vestige of truth in" (577). Despite this disclaimer, however, the narrator continues to refer to the keeper of the cabman shelter as "Fitzharris" or "Skin-the-Goat"—once as "pseudo Skin-the-etcetera" (597)—throughout the chapter's entirety. The narrator is as uncertain as Bloom and Stephen about the keeper's identity: "Skin-the-Goat, assuming he was he, evidently with an axe to grind, was airing his grievances in a forcible-feeble phillipic anent the natural resources of Ireland, or something of that sort ..." (595).

Bloom's sense of national identity, one of the prominent themes throughout the novel, is also brought into question in "Eumaeus." In relating to Stephen the events of an earlier altercation, Bloom explains how he "simply but effectively silenced the offender" by calling into question the ethnicity of Christ: "He called me a jew, and in a heated fashion offensively.

So I, without deviating from plain facts in the least, told him his God, I mean Christ, was a jew too, and all his family, like me, though in reality I'm not" (597). Without deviating from the "plain facts," Bloom makes a claim that is then qualified with an immediate negation.

The salty seafarer, W. B. Murphy, ostensibly recognizes Stephen as being in some way associated with Simon Dedalus:

> You know Simon Dedalus? he asked at length.
> I've heard of him, Stephen said.
> Mr. Bloom was all at sea for a moment, seeing the others Evidently eavesdropping too.
> He's Irish, the seaman bold affirmed, staring still in much the same way and nodding. All Irish.
> All too Irish, Stephen rejoined. (579)

The description, though sketchy indeed, seems to fit the "all too Irish" Simon Dedalus the reader has come to know in *A Portrait* and earlier chapters of *Ulysses*. After all, what are the chances that an Irishman who shares not only the distinctive surname of Stephen's father but the first name as well is in no way related? Yet Murphy describes the Simon Dedalus in question as a crack shot circus performer who can shoot eggs from bottles at fifty yards away, over his shoulder, left-handed. Bloom muses over the "[c]urious coincidence" (579) of it all and comes to distrust the larger-than-life fictions of Murphy's high seas exploits. As he does with most such dubious elements in the chapter, however, Bloom wavers between credence and doubt, ever vacillating between what is possible and what is probable:

> Our mutual friend's stories are like himself, Mr. Bloom, apropos of knives, remarked to his confidante sotto voce. Do you think they are genuine? He could spin those yarns for hours on end all night long and lie like old boots. Look at him.
> Yet still [...], life was full of a host of things and coincidences of a terrible nature and it was quite within the bounds of possibility that it was not an entire fabrication though at first blush there was not much inherent probability in all the spoof he got off his chest being strictly accurate gospel. (590)

Here one can see in Bloom's transcribed thoughts the earnest deliberation, the hesitancy to either believe or summarily disregard as untrue Murphy's tall tales.

Outstanding figures from history and literature are also pulled into the convoluted mix of identities. Never far from the figurative heart of Joyce's Dublin, for instance, is the quasi-Arthurian presence of Parnell: "One morning you would open the paper, the cabman affirmed, and read, Return of Parnell. He bet them what they liked. [...] The coffin they brought over was full of stones. He changed his name to DeWet, the Boer general." Bloom, of course, is skeptical: "Highly unlikely, of course, there was even a shadow of truth in the stones and, even supposing, he thought a return highly inadvisable all things considered" (603). Parnell, one learns, may have also used "several aliases such as Fox and Stewart, so the remark that emanated from friend cabby might be within the bounds of possibility" (604). The effect of the proliferation of aliases and pseudonyms makes it increasingly difficult to affix an accurate identity to the subject in question; thus, Parnell could literally be anyone, and anyone could be Parnell. The bounds of clear identity demarcation are failing.

While debating the existence and characteristics of the human soul, Bloom credits the invention of the telescope first to Edison, then to Galileo, neither of whom contributed to the initial invention of the device (*Ulysses* 589). Bloom also alludes to the controversial theory that Bacon was the author of *Hamlet* (among other works, as the Baconians have it) to illustrate his skepticism concerning the authority of "Holy Writ" (589). The implication is that the *authority* of the written word can never be trusted (presumably in the same sense that "paternity is a legal fiction"), not even, by extension, the book in the reader's hands.

The identity of Murphy (much like that of the mysterious M'Intosh) is likewise a point of uncertainty. He is "Ulysses Pseudoangelos" in the Linati Schema (*Ulysses* 736), the false messenger, a version perhaps of Bloom himself (the merging of identities also being a related motif), wandering the world for seven years before returning to his wife and son. Upon inspecting Murphy's postcard depicting Peruvian cannibals, Bloom makes a discovery: "[He] detect[s] a discrepancy between his name (assuming he was the person he represented himself to be and not sailing under false colours after having boxed the compass on the strict q.t. somewhere), and the fictitious addressee of the missive which made him nourish some suspicions of our friend's bona fides [...]" (582). The narrator, as if to underscore the dubiousness of Murphy's identity, delights in inventing ironically grandiose titles for the sailor. The proliferation of names further fragments his identity as well as draws parallels between him and local, historical, and literary figures: "the communicative tarpaulin" (581), "the doughty narrator," "the globetrotter" (584), "the rover," "the sio-disant sailor" (585), "the old seadog," "[t]he Skibereen father" (586), "Sinbad [...] who reminded him a bit of Ludwig, alias Ledwidge" (591), "Shipahoy" (592), "[t]hat worthy," "the redoubtable specimen" (594), "the impervious navigator," "that rough diamond," "the grizzled old veteran" (595), "the ancient mariner" (612), "the seafarer with the tartan beard, who seemingly was a bit of a literary cove in his own small way" (613).

Murphy's tattoo, done by a certain "Antonio personage (no relation to the dramatic personage of identical name who sprang from the pen of our national poet)," is likewise associated with the question of identity (591). Stuart Gilbert writes, "The tattoo mark on the sailor's chest [...] can be historically associated with the 'homecoming' of a pretender, for tattoo marks have played an important part in the solution of such problems of identity as the Tichbourne case," in which an impostor was discovered because he lacked the identifying mark of a tattoo (Ellmann and Gilbert 364). As Gilbert also notes, Bloom directly alludes to this famous case of fraudulent identity: "And then, number one, you come up against the man in possession and had to produce your credentials, like the claimant in the Tichbourne case, Roger Charles Tichbourne, Bella, was the boat's name to the best of his recollection he, the heir, went down in, as the evidence went to show, and there was a tattoo mark too in Indian ink, Lord Bellew, was it?" (604).

The confusion of human identity, however, is only a small part of the larger convolution, the comprehensive lapse in linguistic efficacy dramatized in the chapter. In "Eumaeus," where pennies are indistinguishable from halfcrowns and Shakespeares are "as common as Murphies," language has lost its power to convey translatable, apprehendable meaning, to delineate accurately the points at which one thing ends and another begins, and as with the chapters examined earlier, style and theme are inextricably bound in representing this point of decline.

The arbitrary semantic, political, and syntactical barriers that distinguish one thing from another are eroded. "Sounds," Stephen has it, "are impostors. [...] Like names, Cicero, Podmore, Napoleon, Mr. Goodbody, Jesus, Mr. Doyle, Shakespeares were as common as Murphies. What's in a name?" (578). If sounds (spoken language) and names (nomenclature, definition) are "impostors," humankind is in a state of epistemological crisis. Meaning, predicated upon the ability to categorize things as separate and definable one from another, is rendered unattainable, and language is reduced to a hoax, a complex game the rules of which are indecipherable. Joyce, it seems, is anticipating the post-structuralist severance of the signifier and the signified.

Notice, for instance, the confusion which attends the problem Bloom has discerning the day: "I met your respected father on a recent occasion, Mr. Bloom diplomatically returned, Today, in fact, or, to be strictly accurate, on yesterday" (574). Bloom, momentarily forgetting that it is past midnight, claims to have seen Simon "today," following the claim with the assertion "in fact." Yet, the fact just stated is immediately qualified upon Bloom's realization that it is "to be strictly accurate," on the day previous that he "in fact" met Stephen's father. A similar confusion occurs in a later exchange between the two characters:

> At what o'clock did you dine? he questioned of the slim form and tired though unwrinkled face.
> Some time yesterday, Stephen said.
> Yesterday, exclaimed Bloom till he remembered it was already tomorrow, Friday. Ah, you mean it's after twelve!
> The day before yesterday, Stephen said, improving on himself.
> (610)

The boundaries of arbitrary (though practical) distinction by which conventional meaning is attained are being carefully, skillfully dismantled. One cannot easily distinguish today from tomorrow or from yesterday. Bloom and Stephen abandon their discussion of the characteristics and existence of the human soul largely because Bloom misinterprets the meaning of "simple" (589), just as he later fails to "[catch] aright [Stephen's] allusion to sixtyfive guineas and John Bull" (615), almost mistaking the musician for the personification of England. Hence, the dominant motif in the chapter is the inability to apprehend truth, primarily due to the inherent insufficiencies and ambiguities of language. As Bloom puts it, "Guesswork it reduce[s] itself to eventually" (603), or, "it is hard to lay down any hard and fast rules as to right and wrong [...]" (597).

The denizens of the cabman's shelter must rely solely upon the evidence of their senses, like Eumaeus, upon the *appearance* of truth. For this reason, the word *evidently* appears (also in the adjective form *evident* and noun form *evidence*) in the chapter twenty-two times. The word's near total absence in the rest of the novel makes its concentrated presence in "Eumaeus" of especially conspicuous importance. Joyce seems to be indicating (with a fairly heavy hand) that appearances, particularly in the form of language, can be, and often are, deceiving.

Thus, though "'Eumaeus' tentatively extends the theme of [homecoming] to include the restoration of linear narrative," as Robert Newman has it (451), the chapter does so only to subvert this convention. Lawrence argues that *Ulysses* follows a progressive course away from the literary, that "literature is destroyed as the book expands" (178); however, "Eumaeus" pushes the boundaries farther than the mere destruction of the literary. "Eumaeus" threatens and perhaps undertakes the destruction of the foundations of human knowledge.

Following the flamboyant narrative pyrotechnics of "Circe" and previous chapters, "Eumaeus" ostensibly offers the promise of safe harbor, a place where narrative is linear, the written word sufficient, the style clear and conventional. Yet, even aside from the overt plot-level confusions enumerated above (the misapprehension of names, identities, and so forth), the style of the chapter, though familiar, ostentatiously exhibits the limitations of language and meaning in a variety of ways.

Pronouns, functioning much as they do in "Telemachus" and "Calypso," serve as a stylistic barometer of sorts, signaling subtle changes in the narrative. In the same way that names and facts are utterly confused at the plot level, the proliferation of ambiguous pronouns in the chapter indicates the limitations of both the narrator and language itself to make adequate distinctions at the stylistic level. A few examples from the chapter's many instances will suffice: "For the nonce he was rather nonplused but inasmuch as the duty plainly devolved upon him to take some measures on the subject he pondered suitable ways and means during which Stephen repeatedly yawned. So far as he could see he was rather pale in the face so it occurred to him as highly advisable to get a conveyance of some description [...]" (569). The first "he" can safely be assumed to be Bloom, as Stephen is the subject of "yawned." The second sentence becomes rather more difficult, for the first "he" has no clear antecedent. Since the former sentence ended with Stephen's actions, however, one might assume the "he" in question to be Stephen, though further reading seems to refute this assumption. At any rate, the narrative inarguably lacks the precision of earlier chapters. One effect of the use of ambiguous pronouns is the conflation of the identities of Stephen and Bloom, who will in "Ithaca" become "Blephen" and "Stoom" (635): "A few moments later saw our two noctumbules safely seated in a discreet corner, only to be greeted by stares from the decidedly miscellaneous collection of waifs and strays and other nondescript specimens of the genus homo, [...] for whom they formed an object of marked curiosity" (577). Two separate individuals are here reduced to a singular "object." Later, the two men, facing each other, seem to become two halves of the same face, "their two or four eyes conversing" (597). Here one perceives the stylistic counterpart to the thematic confusion of identities.

The heretofore omniscient narrator, able to infiltrate the minds of his characters, to speak their language, suffers from an odd deficiency of omniscience. Ignoring the verbose, sententious style proper, the narrator does not even seem to have all the "facts" of the story straight. He is uncertain, for instance, about the relation of "Lord" Corley to the person responsible for his ironic nickname: "Rumour had it, though not proved, that she descended from the house of the Lords Talbot de Malahide, in whose mansion, really an unquestionably fine residence of its kind and well worth seeing, her mother or aunt or some relative had enjoyed the distinction of being in service in the washkitchen" (572). This lack of knowledge would not appear so egregious a deficiency if the relation of the woman to Corley was indeed not a matter of public intelligence, if it is an unproven rumor, as the narrative puts it, however, the narrator interrupts himself one paragraph later in mid-thought, preoccupied with trying accurately to recall the woman's identity:

> He was out of a job and implored Stephen to tell him where on God's earth he could get something, anything at all to do. No, it was the mother in the washkitchen that was a fostersister to the heir of the house or else they were connected through the mother in some way, both occurrences happening at the same time if the whole thing wasn't a complete fabrication from start to finish. (573)

Again, the theme of falsity surfaces, here as a possibly fraudulent fiction within a fiction mediated by a narrator who is himself (while technically omniscient) deprived of the facts. Later, citing Bloom's glorified brush with Parnell, the narrator does not remember the newspaper office outside of which the historic meeting took place: "He saw him once on the auspicious occasion when they broke up the type in the *Insuppressible* or was it *United Ireland*" (604). While this lack of certainty may be ascribed to Bloom, the same misremembrance occurs some four pages later: "He, Bloom, enjoyed the distinction of being close to Erin's uncrowned king when ... the leader's ... trusty henchmen to the number of ten or a dozen or possibly even more than that penetrated into the printing works of the *Insuppressible* or no it was *United Ireland* (a by no means, by the by appropriate appellative) and broke up the typecases with hammers or something like that [...]" (608). Here the false memory is apparently emended with the second title ("no it was *United Ireland*"), followed by a parenthetical aside from the narrator as if to remind the reader that he is present and responsible for the thought.

Perhaps the most obvious stylistic sign of the dissolution of meaning is the chapter's often comic literalization and general misuse of metaphoric language: "Mr Bloom being handicapped by the circumstance that one of the back buttons had, to vary the time honoured adage, gone the way of all buttons, though, entering thoroughly into the spirit of the thing, he heroically made light of the mischance" (570). The appeal to an established maxim or truistic analogy fosters a sense of semantic continuity, of meaning that is literally absent in the text. There is no inherent significance, analogic or otherwise, in the phrase "the way of all buttons," yet the narrator pretends as if there were. The allusion is, of course, to the "way of all flesh." All flesh deteriorates, but are all buttons lost?

Upon leaving the shelter, Bloom pays for the coffee with the last four coppers in his pocket, what the narrator calls "literally the last of the Mohicans" (613), when in fact just the opposite is true; the coppers are merely *metaphorically* "the last of the Mohicans." Another example, "And when all was said and done, the lies a fellow told about himself couldn't hold a proverbial candle to the wholesale whoppers other fellows coined about him" (591), provides a nice illustration of the curious ways metaphors are mixed in the chapter. A final, often-cited example is the following: "The horse, having reached the end of its tether, so to speak, halted, and rearing high a proud feathering tail, added his quota by letting fall on the floor, which the brush would soon brush up and polish, three smoking globes of turds" (618). Here Joyce reverses the conventional order of things by literally applying a clichéd expression to its source of origin, yet allowing the expression to retain its metaphoric tag, "so to speak." The effect is semantic confusion. Is the horse actually or figuratively at the end of its tether? And what are the implications, if any, of either interpretation? These questions, like many others in the chapter, are not answered.

In "Eumaeus," coincidences, verbal or otherwise, are presented as arbitrary phenomena, the meaning of which is either nonexistent or incommunicable, quite a departure from what the early-twentieth-century reader (perhaps even now the early-twenty-first-century reader) had come to expect from a fictional construct. In his fine essay on the subject of coincidence in "Eumaeus," John Hannay postulates that "[t]he art of story-telling is to conceal contrivance so that many small convergences of plot are discovered that portend a culminating revelation of identity. The art of 'Eumaeus' is to parody this function, exposing its own false connections and flaunting the speciousness of its coincidences" (352). The "false connections" and "specious" coincidences of "Eumaeus" are no different, however, from those of everyday life and may easily be interpreted as Joycean realism. In the real world, as Hannay observes of *Ulysses*, "there is no deity or omniscient narrator to uncover the character's disguises or to make manifest the reason for the coincidences" (341). "Eumaeus" lacks the authoritative presence of the conventional omniscient narrator, who, Athena-like, might tie together the loose ends and interpret the web of seemingly chaotic coincidences. As such a presence is absent in the modern real world, Joyce cannot allow such a presence to exist in or bring order to his fictional one. Thus, possible significations are left dangling, uncompleted, undefined, as things are in reality. This concept is applied at the syntactic level as well.

As mentioned earlier, Gottfried examines the relevance of "entelechy" to Joyce's syntactic constructions, finding the perfect realization of the Aristotelian concept in Joyce's half-completed syntactic constructions, those sentences which begin but are abandoned before ever reaching syntactic or semantic culmination. He argues:

> The sentence parts bring with them the seeds of their own fruition, and the motion of the sentences to the actualization of the syntactic form inherent in it is the self-realization of those lexical possibilities. [...] The potential sentences which are imbedded within patterns of language and grammatical parts are brought into being and structured into syntactical form by the sentence's movement. An incomplete sentence only makes this potential emergence more evident. (82)

"Eumaeus" contains eighteen (by my count) of these syntactic culs de sac, more than any other chapter in the novel: "Squeezing or ..." (586); "Still no matter what the cause is from ..." (588); "He turned away from the others, who probably ... and spoke nearer to, so as the others ... in case they ..."; "I don't want to indulge in any ... because you know the standard works on the subject, and then, orthodox as you are ..." (598), and so on. Granted, some of the abandoned sentences appear in dialogue and may merely be representative of the dead ends or stop-and-start rhythms of thought or conversation between extremely tired parties. But what purpose do the same constructions serve when they are rendered by the narrator? The traditional answer (one promoted by Joyce himself) is that the narrator is emulating stylistically the fatigue of his characters. In a letter to Ellmann, Gilbert writes, "The 'Eumaeus' episode—I remember Joyce's insisting on this point—was meant to represent the intercourse and mental state of two fagged-out men" (qtd. in Ellmann, *James Joyce* 372). It is doubtful that anyone would argue the point that the chapter's style is meant to portray the weary mind on the verge of sleep, but is there no other significance?

For Gottfried the entelechic construction implies (by virtue of its incompletion) a gesture forward, "the development and coming-to-be of meaning," each sentence a minute "analogue of life" (167). Gottfried's syntactical theory may in fact be applied to the entire corpus of Joyce's work. As Hugh Kenner has observed in his work on *A Portrait*, Joyce often began a new unit of work by destroying the asseverances (however dear) of the last one. In reference to chapter 5, Kenner writes, "Each of the preceding chapters in fact, works toward an equilibrium which is dashed when in the next chapter Stephen's world becomes larger and the frame of reference more complex" (122). Though Kenner applies this idea only to the chapter by chapter construction of a single novel, one can perceive an analogous development taking place throughout all Joyce's novels, one building upon the experiences and to some degree abrogating the authority of the last while simultaneously forecasting the next. The effect is a steady and crescent growth traceable from Joyce's earliest poems to *Finnegans Wake*—and even to what few clandestine hints he dropped about a fourth novel. To Nabokov, for example, Joyce dismissed his elaborate and painstaking use of Homer in *Ulysses* as merely "a whim" (qtd. in Ellmann, *James Joyce* 616). Whether the dismissal is an affected pose or not, it is indicative of Joyce's fierce singularity of mind, his exclusive concentration on the here and now of his art. His is a literature always in the process of becoming. Thus, the abandoned sentence constructions in *Ulysses*, particularly in "Eumaeus," require the reader to look forward, to anticipate a meaning that is pre-actual, a meaning that is perpetually in the process of becoming, excluding no possibilities.

Upon completing *Ulysses*, Joyce confided to August Suter, "*Je suis au bout de l'anglais*" ("I'm at the end of English"), and to another friend, "I have put the language to sleep" (qtd. in Ellmann, *James Joyce* 559). In the light of Stephen's aesthetic, however, (as well as of the examples listed above), the end of English occurs not solely with Molly's stream of consciousness closing soliloquy but begins at least with "Eumaeus" and the death of functional authoritative language. It is from "Eumaeus" that one may truly mark the end of the epical and the beginning of the dramatic aesthetic stage of which "Penelope" and *Finnegans Wake* are but necessary continuations, actualizations of the potentialities introduced in "Eumaeus," containing in themselves new potentialities.

Stephen defines the dramatic form in *A Portrait*: "The dramatic form is reached when the vitality which has flowed and eddied round each person fills every person with such vital force that he or she assumes a proper and intangible esthetic life. The esthetic image in the dramatic form is life purified in and projected from the human imagination" (214). This definition is vague and perhaps a little mystical, but it may best be understood in the context "Eumaeus" provides, a constructed reality in which authoritative language's own comprehensive failure points the way to aesthetic progress. Revisiting Stephen's assertion that "Shakespeares were as common as Murphies" (587), one realizes that the sentence may contain a variety of implications. First, Stephen may be alluding to the fact that the Shakespeare family name was prevalent in Shakespearean England, much as the Murphy family name is in twentieth-century Ireland. A second interpretation is that Stephen is pointing out the fact that Shakespeare was a common man, that is, not a member of the aristocracy. A corollary to the latter interpretation is that W. B. Murphy, who is not at the time of Stephen's (prophetic) assertion yet identified as such, is the modern equivalent to Shakespeare. He is, after all, a gifted spinner of yarns, "a bit of a literary cove in his own small way" (613), and in a context where fact is indistinguishable from fiction, people of all walks of life are bound by an equalizing absence of authority. Bloom claims that we are all "at the tender mercy of others practically," and one may assume this dependence to include the stories others tell (571). Thus, the ordinary man may become filled with "a proper and intangible esthetic life" as much as the artist. In this way the artist (the authoritative presence) is refined out of existence because life and all its various constituents have become infused with art, with an "esthetic life" or value. This is the philosophy at the very heart of postmodernity: the legitimacy of moral, social, and artistic authorities is called into question, particularly with regard to the languages and forms in which they are manifest. The epistemological uncertainty of "Eumaeus," in undermining authoritative discourse, thus produces two simultaneous, paradoxical effects: nihilism and liberation. The former is a result of the chaos produced by the absence of practical meaning. The latter is the freedom from the outmoded delimiting forms and strictures imposed by authoritative language. It is through this liberation that Murphy (as well as Bloom and all humankind) is infused with Stephen's "esthetic life." Without the dictates of the academy (or other agents of authority) to delegitimize them, Murphy's fictions, never *proven* to be such, are as artistic, as legitimate, as Shakespeare's, and are presented, as Stephen defines the dramatic mode, "in immediate relation to others" (*A Portrait* 213).

In a world without prescribed meaning, without Grand Narrative, language becomes infinitely associational, freed from the constraints of political or idealistic agendas, free to playfully explore semantic and lexical potentialities. Viewed this way, "Eumaeus," as an entelechic construction gesturing toward the unactualized, makes *Finnegans Wake* inevitable. In composing "Eumaeus" Joyce seems to have stumbled upon the same idea that Wlad Godzich ascribes to Lyotard:

> It is the [language] games that turn us into their players and not we who constitute games. Players are immanent to the games they play; as a result they cannot eradicate themselves from these games and cannot produce a metadiscourse that could dominate this plurality. The only option that remains is that of an indefinite experimenting with language games, somewhat on the order of scientific inventiveness that operates by rupture rather than continuous derivation. (127)

"Eumaeus" signals this point of rupture, this break with and from the oppressive history and tradition that Stephen labors under fruitlessly. Stanzel, intimating the narrative subversiveness of the novel, claims that the conventionally unified narrative approach "presupposes a fixed central point [...] which radiates orientation" but that in *Ulysses* "this center of gravity no longer exists" (140). Now freed from the constraints of ego and the authoritative guise of the artistic persona and having completed the necessary aesthetic stages of the artist (lyric, epic, dramatic), Stephen is poised to write (as Joyce has just written) the epic of modern Ireland.

Works Cited

Bakhtin, M. M. *The Dialogic Imagination: Four Essays*. Ed. Michael Holquist. Trans. Caryl Emerson and Michael Holquist. Austin: U of Texas P, 1981.

Budgen, Frank. *James Joyce and the Making of Ulysses*. Bloomington: Indiana UP, 1960.

Dettmar, Kevin J. H. *The Illicit Joyce of Postmodernism: Reading Against the Grain*. Madison: U of Wisconsin P, 1996.

Ellmann, Richard. *James Joyce*. New York: Oxford UP, 1959.

Ellmann, Richard, and Stuart Gilbert, eds. *Letters of James Joyce*. 2nd ed. 3 vols. New York: Viking, 1966.

Fludernik, Monika. "Narrative and Its Development in *Ulysses*." *The Journal of Narrative Technique* 16 (1986): 15–37.

Gilbert, Stuart. *James Joyce's Ulysses: A Study*. Rev. ed. New York: Random, 1952.

Godzich, Wlad. Afterword. *The Postmodern Explained. Correspondence 1982–1985*. By Jean-Francois Lyotard. Trans. Don Barry, et al. Eds. Julian Pefanis and Morgan Thomas. Minneapolis: U of Minnesota P, 1992. 109–36.

Gottfried, Roy K. *The Art of Joyce's Syntax in Ulysses*. Athens: U of Georgia R 1980.

Hannay, John. "Coincidence and Fables of Identity in 'Eumaeus.'" *James Joyce Quarterly* 21 (1984):341–55.

Joyce, James. *A Portrait of the Artist as a Young Man*. 1916. Ware, England: Wordsworth, 1992.

———. *Ulysses*. 1922. Ed. Jeri Johnson. Oxford: Oxford UP, 1993.

Kenner, Hugh. *Dublin's Joyce*. Bloomington: Indiana UP, 1956.

Lawrence, Karen. *The Odyssey of Style in Ulysses*. Princeton: Princeton UP, 1981.

Newman, Robert D. "'Eumaeus' as a Sacrificial Narrative." *James Joyce Quarterly* 30 (1993): 45–58.

Stanzel, F. K. *Narrative Situations in the Novel: Tom Jones, Moby-Dick, The Ambassadors, Ulysses*. Trans. James Pusack. Bloomington: Indiana UP, 1971.

Chronology

1882	James Augustine Aloysius Joyce is born in Dublin on February 2 to John Stanislaus Joyce, tax-collector, and Mary Jane (May) Murray Joyce. He is the eldest of ten children who survive infancy, of whom the closest to him is his next brother, Stanislaus (born 1884).
1888–91	Attends Clongowes Wood College, a Jesuit boarding school. He eventually is forced to leave because of his father's financial troubles. During Joyce's childhood and early adulthood, the family moves many times, from respectable suburbs of Dublin to poorer districts, as its size grows and its finances dwindle. Charles Stewart Parnell, leader of Irish Parliamentary party that sought home rule for Ireland, dies on October 6, 1891. The young Joyce writes an elegy, "Et tu, Healy." His father, a staunch Parnellite, has the poem printed, but no copies survive.
1892–98	Briefly attends the less intellectually prestigious Christian Brothers School, then attends Belvedere College, another Jesuit school.
1898–1902	Attends University College, Dublin (another Jesuit institution); turns away from Catholicism and Irish nationalist politics. Writes a play, *A Brilliant Career* (which he later destroys), and essays, several of which are published. Graduates in 1902 with a degree in modern languages,

| | having learned French, Italian, German, Norwegian and Latin. Leaves Dublin to go to Paris and study medicine. |

1903   Joyce works primarily on writing poems (which will be published in 1907 as *Chamber Music*) and reading Jonson at the Bibliotéque Ste. Geneviève. Receives a telegram from his father ("Mother dying come home Father"). Returns to Dublin, where May Joyce dies of cancer on August 13, four months after her son's return.

1904   An essay-narrative, "A Portrait of the Artist," is rejected for publication; several poems are published in various magazines, and a few stories, which eventually appear in *Dubliners*, are published. Stays for a time in the Martello Tower with Oliver St. John Fogarty (Malachi Mulligan in *Ulysses*). Joyce takes his first walk with Nora Barnacle on June 16 ("Bloomsday" in Ulysses.) The daughter of a Galway baker, she is working in a Dublin boarding house. In October, Joyce and Nora leave for the continent, where they will live the remainder of their lives. Joyce finds work at a Berlitz school in Pola (now in Yugoslavia).

1905   The Joyces (as they are known, although they do not marry until 1931, for "testamentary" reasons) move to Trieste, where Joyce teaches at the Berlitz school. Birth of son Giorgio on July 27. Joyce submits manuscript of *Chamber Music* and *Dubliners* to Dublin publisher Grant Richards. Joyce's brother Stanislaus joins them in Trieste.

1907   After a year in Rome, where Joyce worked in a bank, the Joyces return to Trieste, where Joyce does private tutoring in English. *Chamber Music* published in London (not by Grant Richards). Birth of a daughter, Lucia Anna, on July 26. Writes "The Dead," the last of the stories that will become *Dubliners*. Works on revision of *Stephen Hero*, an adaptation of the essay "A Portrait of the Artist," later to be *A Portrait of the Artist as a Young Man*. Begins writing articles for an Italian newspaper.

1908   Abandons work on Portrait after completing three of five projected chapters.

1909   Joyce pays two visits to Dublin: in August, to sign a contract for the publication of *Dubliners* (not with Grant Richards), and in September as representative for a group who wish to

	set up the first cinema in Dublin. Returns to Trieste with sister Eva, who will now live with the Joyces.
1910	Cinema venture fails; publication of *Dubliners* delayed.
1911	Publication of Dubliners is held up, mainly because of what are feared to be offensive references to Edward VII in "Ivy Day in the Committee Room." Joyce writes to George V to ask if he finds the story objectionable; a secretary replies that His Majesty does not express opinions on such matters.
1912	Final visit to Dublin with his family. Printer destroys the manuscript of *Dubliners*, deciding the book's aims are anti-Irish. Joyce takes the proofs of which he has gotten a copy from his equally unsympathetic publisher, to London, but cannot find a publisher for them there, either.
1913	Joyce's original publisher, Grant Richards, asks to see the manuscript of *Dubliners* again. Ezra Pound, at the urging of William Butler Yeats, writes Joyce asking to see some of his work, since Pound has connections with various magazines, and might be able to help get Joyce published.
1914	Grant Richards publishes *Dubliners*. At Pound's urging, *A Portrait of the Artist as a Young Man* is published serially by the London magazine, *The Egoist*. Joyce begins work on *Ulysses*. The innovative techniques in narrative prose, earlier used in *Dubliners*, will be part of his novelistic scheme. World War I begins on August 4.
1915	Joyce completes his play, *Exiles*. After Joyce pledges neutrality to the Austrian authorities in Trieste who threatened to intern him, the family moves to Zürich, with the exception of Stanislaus, who is interned. Joyce awarded a British Royal Literary Fund grant, the first of several grants he will receive.
1916	Publishes *A Portrait of the Artist as a Young Man* in book form in New York.
1917	Undergoes the first of numerous eye operations.
1918	Grant Richards publishes *Exiles* in London; it is also published in the United States. The American magazine, *The Little Review*, begins serializing *Ulysses*, which is not yet complete. Armistice Day, November 11.
1919	Joyce refuses to be analyzed by Carl Jung. *The Egoist* also

	begins serializing *Ulysses*. The U.S. Post Office confiscates issues of *The Little Review* containing the "Lystrygonians" and the "Scylla and Charybdis" chapters.
1920	More issues of *The Little Review* confiscated. In September, John S. Sumner, the secretary of the New York Society for the Prevention of Vice, lodges a protest against the "Nausicaa" issue. Joyce heeds the call from Ezra Pound to take up residence in Paris. The Paris years will last until the outbreak of World War II.
1921	The case comes to trial, and the *Review* loses, in February 1921. Publication ceases in the United States. Joyce and family move to Paris. Joyce finishes *Ulysses*. Sylvia Beach agrees to publish it in Paris.
1922	Shakespeare and Company, Sylvia Beach's press, publishes *Ulysses* in Paris on February 2, Joyce's birthday. T.S. Eliot's *The Wasteland* is also published. Nora takes children to Galway for a visit, over Joyce's protests, and their train is fired upon by Irish Civil War combatants.
1923	Joyce begins *Finnegans Wake*, known until its publication as *Work in Progress*.
1924	Part of the *Work* appears in the Paris magazine, *transatlantic review*.
1926	Pirated edition of *Ulysses* (incomplete) serialized in New York by *Two Worlds Monthly*.
1927	Shakespeare and Company publishes *Pomes Penyeach*. Parts of *Work* published in Eugene Jolas's *transition*, in Paris.
1928	Joyce publishes parts of *Work* in New York to protect copyright.
1929	Joyce assists at a French translation of *Ulysses*, which appears in February. Lucia Joyce operated on unsuccessfully to remove a squint. She gives up her sporadic career as a dancer; her mental stability seems precarious. To his father's delight, Giorgio Joyce makes his debut as a singer, with some success.
1930	At Joyce's instigation, Herbert Gorman begins a biography of Joyce. Joyce supervises a French translation of *Anna Livia Plurabelle*, part of the *Work*, by Samuel Beckett and friends, which appears in the *Nouvelle Revue Française* in 1931. Marriage of son Giorgio to Helen Kastor Fleischman.

1931   Joyce marries Nora Barnacle at a registry office in London, but refuses to honor the sacrament of marriage. Death of Joyce's father.

1932   Helen Joyce gives birth to a son, Stephen James, on February 15; Giorgio and Helen have the baby secretly baptized so as not to upset Joyce. Joyce writes "Ecce Puer," a poem celebrating the birth of his grandson. Daughter Lucia suffers first mental breakdown; she is diagnosed as hebephrenic (a form of schizophrenia). Bennett Cert of Random House contracts for the American publication of *Ulysses*.

1933   On December 6, Judge John M. Woolsey admits *Ulysses* into the United States, declaring that "whilst in many places the effect ... on the reader undoubtedly is somewhat emetic, nowhere does it tend to be an aphrodisiac." Lucia Joyce hospitalized, as she will often be until her permanent hospitalization.

1934   Random House publishes *Ulysses*.

1934   Publishes *Collected Poems* in New York, and *A Chaucer A.B.C.* with illuminations by Lucia.

1939   *Finnegans Wake* published in London and New York with Joyce stating that what he destroyed in the English language system, he actively reconstitutes a dream language approximating actual apprehension. War declared. The Joyces move to Vichy, France, to be near Lucia's mental hospital.

1940   Herbert Gorman's authorized biography of Joyce appears. After the fall of France, the Joyces manage once more to get to Zürich.

1941   Joyce dies following surgery on a perforated ulcer on January 13. He is buried in Fluntern Cemetery, in Zürich, with no religious ceremony, at Nora's request.

1951   Nora Barnacle Joyce dies in Zürich on April 10. She is buried in Fluntern as well, but not next to Joyce, since that space has been taken. In 1966, the two bodies are reburied together.

Contributors

HAROLD BLOOM is Sterling Professor of the Humanities at Yale University and Henry W. and Albert A. Berg Professor of English at the New York University Graduate School. He is the author of over 20 books, including *Shelley's Mythmaking* (1959), *The Visionary Company* (1961), *Blake's Apocalypse* (1963), *Yeats* (1970), *A Map of Misreading* (1975), *Kabbalah and Criticism* (1975), *Agon: Toward a Theory of Revisionism* (1982), *The American Religion* (1992), *The Western Canon* (1994), and *Omens of Millennium: The Gnosis of Angels, Dreams, and Resurrection* (1996). *The Anxiety of Influence* (1973) sets forth Professor Bloom's provocative theory of the literary relationships between the great writers and their predecessors. His most recent books include *Shakespeare: The Invention of the Human* (1998), a 1998 National Book Award finalist, *How to Read and Why* (2000), and *Genius: A Mosaic of One Hundred Exemplary Creative Minds* (2002). In 1999, Professor Bloom received the prestigious American Academy of Arts and Letters Gold Medal for Criticism, and in 2002 he received the Catalonia International Prize.

RICHARD ELLMANN, formerly Goldsmiths Professor of English at New College, Oxford, was subsequently Research Professor at Emory University. Perhaps the leading modern literary biographer, he is best known for his books on Joyce and Yeats, among them *The Identity of Yeats* (1964), *Eminent Domain: Yeats Among Wilde, Joyce, Pound, Eliot, and Auden* (1967) and *Yeats, The Man and The Masks* (1948).

WOLFGANG ISER has taught English and Comparative Literature at the Universität Konstanz in Germany and the University of California, Irvine. A pioneer of "reception aesthetics" criticism and a founder of the "Poetics and Hermeneutics" research group, he is the author of *The Act of Reading: A Theory of Aesthetic Response* (1978), "On Translatability: Variables of Interpretation" (1995), "Indeterminacy and the Reader's Response" (1997) and an editor of *Languages of the Unsayable: The Play of Negativity in Literature and Literary Theory* (1989)

A. WALTON LITZ has been Professor of English at Princeton University. He is the author of *The Art of James Joyce: Method and Design in* Ulysses *and* Finnegan's Wake (1961), "Lawrence, Pound, and Early Modernism" (1985), and "Dante, Pound, Eliot: The Visionary Company" (1998).

ROBERT D. NEWMAN is Professor and Chair of the department of English at the University of South Carolina. He is the author of *Transgressions of Reading: Narrative Engagement as Exile and Return* (1993), "'Eumaeus' as Sacrificial Narrative" (1993), and an editor of *Joyce's* Ulysses: *The Larger Perspective* (1987).

MARYLU HILL is Assistant Professor in the Core Humanities Program at Villanova University. She is the author of "Learning to Sit Still: The Confrontation of Human Language and Divine Silence in 'Ash Wednesday'" (1995), and "Mothering Her Text: Woolf and the Maternal Paradigm of Biography" (1995).

NICHOLAS A. MILLER is a Professor in the English Department at Loyola College, Baltimore, Maryland. He is the author of "Beyond Recognition: Reading the Unconsciousness in the 'Ithaca' Episode of *Ulysses*" (1993).

WELDON THORNTON is Professor of English at the University of North Carolina in Chapel Hill. He is the author of *Voices and Values in Joyce's* Ulysses (2000), *The Antimodernism of Joyce's* Portrait of the Artist as a Young Man (1994), and *D. H. Lawrence: A Study of the Short Fiction* (1993) and an editor of *Joyce's* Ulysses: *The Larger Perspective* (1987).

JOSÉ LANTERS is a Professor of English at the University of Wisconsin in Milwaukee. She is the author of *Unauthorized Versions: Irish Menippean Satire, 1919-1952* (2000), "Playwrights of the Western World: Synge, Murphy, McDonagh" (1999), and "Brian Friel's Uncertainty Principle" (1999).

JOLEY WOOD is Editor-in-Chief of Garrett County Press. He is the author of "'Scylla and Charybdis' (and Phaedrus): The Influence of Plato and the Artistry of Joyce" (1999).

SARA DANIUS teaches in the Department of Literature at Uppsala University, Sweden. She is the author of *The Senses of Modernism: Technology, Perception, and Aesthetics* (2002), "Orpheus and the Machine: Proust as Theorist of Technological Change, and the Case of Joyce" (2001), and "Novel Visions and the Crisis of Culture: Visual Technology, Modernism, and Death in *The Magic Mountain*" (2000).

ERIC D. SMITH is author of "Johnny Domingo's Epic Nightmare of History" (2000) and "Hegelian Stratagems in Calvino's Invisible Cities" (1985).

Bibliography

Adams, Robert Martin. *Surface and Symbol: The Consistency of James Joyce's* Ulysses. New York: Oxford University Press, 1962.

———. *James Joyce: Common Sense and Beyond*. New York: Random House, 1966.

Arnold, Bruce. *The Scandal of* Ulysses. London, England: Sinclair-Stevenson, 1991.

Arnold, David Scott. *Liminal Readings: Forms of Otherness in Melville, Joyce, and Murdoch*. London: Macmillan; New York: St. Martin's Press, 1992.

Attridge, Derek and Daniel Ferrer, eds. *Post Structuralist Joyce: Essays from the French*. Cambridge: Cambridge University Press, 1984.

Barta, Peter I. *Bely, Joyce and Dublin: Peripatetics in the City Novel*. Gainesville: University Press of Florida, 1996.

Bazargan, Susan. "'Oxen of the Sun': Maternity, Language, and History." *James Joyce Quarterly* 22 (1985): 271–80.

Bell, Robert H. *Jocoserious Joyce: The Fate of Folly in* Ulysses. Ithaca: Cornell University Press, 1991.

Benstock, Bernard. *Narrative Con/Texts in* Ulysses. Urbana: University of Illinois Press, 1991.

———. *Critical Essays on James Joyce's* Ulysses. Boston: G.K. Hall, 1989.

———. Bernard, ed. *The Seventh of Joyce*. Bloomington: Indiana University Press, 1982.

Benstock, Shari. "The Dynamics of Narrative Performance: Stephen Dedalus as Storyteller." *ELH* 49 (1982): 707–38.

Bloom, Harold, ed. *Modern Critical Views: James Joyce*. New Haven: Chelsea House, 1986.

Bowen, Zack R. *Musical Allusions in the Works of James Joyce*. Albany: SUNY Press, 1974.

———. Ulysses *as a Comic Novel*. Syracuse, NY: Syracuse University Press, 1989.

Blamires, Harry. *The New Bloomsday Book: A Guide Through* Ulysses. London; New York: Routledge, 1996.

Boyle, Robert, S. J. *James Joyce's Pauline Vision: A Catholic Exposition*. Carbondale: Southern Illinois University Press, 1978.

Brown, Richard. *James Joyce and Sexuality*. New York: Cambridge University Press, 1985.

Chace, William M., ed. *Joyce: A Collection of Critical Essays*. Englewood Cliffs, N.J.: Prentice-Hall, 1974.

Cixous, Helene. *The Exile of James Joyce*. Translated from the French by Sally A. J. Purcell. New York: David Lewis, 1972.

Curtius, Ernst Robert. "James Joyce and his *Ulysses*." *Essays on European Literature*, translated by Michael Kowal. Princeton: Princeton University Press, 1973.

Davison, Neil R. *James Joyce,* Ulysses, *and the Construction of Jewish Identity: Culture, Biography, and "The Jew" in Modernist Europe*. Cambridge: New York: Cambridge University Press, 1996.

De Almeida, Hermione. *Byron and Joyce Through Homer: Don Juan and* Ulysses. London: Macmillan Press, 1981.

Dent, Robert William. *Colloquial Language in* Ulysses: *A Reference Tool*. Newark: University of Delaware Press; London: Associated University Press, 1994.

Devlin, Kimberly J. and Marilyn Reizbaum. Ulysses *En-Gendered Perspectives: Eighteen New Essays on the Episodes*. Columbia: University of South Carolina Press, 1999.

Devlin, Kimberly J. "The Romance Heroine Exposed: 'Nausicaa' and *The Lamplighter*." *James Joyce Quarterly* 22 (1985): 383–96.

Diment, Galya. *The Autobiographical Novel of Co-Consciousness: Goncharov, Woolf and Joyce*. Gainesville: University of Florida Press, 1994.

Duffy, Enda. *The Subaltern* Ulysses. Minneapolis: University of Minnesota Press, 1994.

Eberly, Rosa A. *Citizen Critics: Literary Public Spheres*. Urbana: University of Illinois Press, 2000.

Eddins, Dwight. "*Ulysses*: The Search for the Logos." *ELH* 47 (1980): 804–19.

Ellmann, Richard. *The Consciousness of Joyce*. Toronto; New York: Oxford University Press, 1977.

———. Ulysses *on the Liffey*. New York: Oxford University Press, 1972.

French, Marilyn. *The Book as World: James Joyce's* Ulysses. Cambridge: Harvard University Press, 1976.

Gibson, Andrew. *Reading Joyce's "Circe."* Amsterdam; Atlanta, Georgia: Rodopi, 1994.

———. *Joyce's Revenge: History, Politics and Aesthetics in* Ulysses. Oxford: Oxford University Press, 2002.

Gifford, Don Creighton and Robert J. Seidman. *Notes for Joyce: An Annotation of James Joyce's* Ulysses, 2d ed., rev. and enl. New York: Dutton, 1988.

Gillespie, Michael Patrick and Paula Gillespie. *Recent Criticism of James Joyce's* Ulysses: *An Analytical Review*. Rochester, N.Y.: Camden House, 2000.

Goldberg, Samuel Louis. *The Classical Temper: A Study of James Joyce's* Ulysses. New York: Barnes & Noble, 1961.

Goldman, Arnold. *The Joyce Paradox: Form and Freedom in his Fiction.* Evanston, Ill.: Northwestern University Press, 1966.

Goldman, Samuel Louis. *Joyce*. New York: Barnes & Noble, 1962.

———. *The Classical Temper: A Study of James Joyce's* Ulysses. London: Chatto & Windus, 1961.

Gordon, John. *James Joyce's Metamorphosis*. Totowa, N.J.: Barnes & Noble, 1981.

Harnkness, Marguerite. *The Aesthetics of Dedalus and Bloom*. Lewisburg, Pa.: Bucknell University Press, 1984.

Hayman, David. Ulysses: *The Mechanics of Meaning*. 2d ed. Englewood Cliffs, N.J.: Prentice-Hall, 1970.

Henke, Suzette and Elaine Unkeless. *Women in Joyce*. Urbana: University of Illinois Press, 1982.

Herr, Cheryl. *Joyce's Anatomy of Culture*. Urbana: University of Illinois Press, 1986.

Hodgart, Matthew J.C. *James Joyce: A Student's Guide*. London: Routledge, 1978.

———and Mabel P. Worthington. *Song in the Works of James Joyce*. New York: Columbia University Press, 1959.

Joyce, Stanislaus. *My Brother's Keeper*. Edited by Richard Ellmann. London: Faber, 1959.

Kelly, Dermot. *Narrative Strategies in Joyce's* Ulysses. Ann Arbor, Mich.: UMI Research Press, 1988.

Kenner, Hugh. *Dublin's Joyce*. London: Chatto & Windus, 1955.

———. *Joyce's Voices*. Berkeley: University of California Press. 1978.

Kimball, Jean. *Odyssey of the Psyche: Jungian Patterns in Joyce's* Ulysses. Carbondale: Southern Illinois University Press, 1997.

———. "Family Romance and the Hero Myth: A Psychoanalytic Context for the Paternity Theme in *Ulysses*." *James Joyce Quarterly* 20 (1983): 161–73.

Kumar, Udaya. *The Joycean Labyrinth: Repetition, Time and Tradition in* Ulysses. Oxford, UK: Clarendon Press, 1991.

Lamos, Colleen. *Deviant Modernism: Sexual and Textual Errancy in T.S. Eliot, James Joyce and Marcel Proust*. Cambridge; New York: Cambridge University Press, 1998.

Lang, Frederick K. Ulysses *and the Irish God*. Lewisburg, Pa.: Bucknell University Press; London; Cranbury, NJ: Associated University Presses, 1993.

Lawrence, Karen. *The Odyssey of Style in* Ulysses. Princeton: Princeton University Press, 1981.

Levin, Harry. *James Joyce: A Critical Introduction*. 2d ed. New York: New Directions, 1960.

Litz, A. Walton. *The Art of James Joyce: Method and Design in* Ulysses *and* Finnegans Wake. London: Oxford University Press, 1961.

———. "The Genre of *Ulysses*." *The Theory of the Novel: New Essays*, edited by John Halperin. Oxford: Oxford University Press, 1961.

Mackey, Peter Francis. *Chaos Theory and James Joyce's Everyman*. Gainesville: University Press of Florida, 1999.

Maddox, James H. *Joyce's* Ulysses *and the Assault Upon Character*. New Brunswick, NJ: Rutgers University Press, 1978.

Manganiello, Dominic. *Joyce's Politics*. London: Routledge, 1980.

McArthur, Murray. *Stolen Writings: Blake's Milton, Joyce's* Ulysses *and the Nature of Influence*. Ann Arbor, Mich.: UMI Research Press, 1988.

McBride, Margaret. Ulysses *and the Metamorphosis of Stephen Dedalus*. Lewisburg, Pa.: Bucknell University Press; London; Cranbury, N.J.: Associated University Presses, 2001.

MacCabe, Colin. *James Joyce and the Revolution of the Word*. London: Macmillan, 1978.

McCarthy, Patrick A. Ulysses*: Portals of Discovery*. Boston: Twayne Publishers, 1990.

McCormack, W.J. and Elistair Stead, eds. *James Joyce and Modern Literature*. London: Routledge, 1982.

McCormick, Kathleen. Ulysses, *"Wandering Rocks," and the Reader: Multiple Pleasures in Reading*. Lewiston, NY: E. Mellen Press, 1991.

McGee, Patrick. *Paperspace: Style as Ideology in Joyce's* Ulysses. Lincoln: University of Nebraska Press, 1988.

McKenna, Bernard. *James Joyce's* Ulysses*: A Reference Guide*. Westport, CT: Greenwood Press, 2002.

McMichael, James. Ulysses *and Justice*. Princeton, N.J.: Princeton University Press, 1991.

Melaney, William D. *After Ontology: Literary Theory and Modernist Poetics*. Albany: State University of New York Press, 2001.

Moretti, Franco. *Modern Epic: The World-System from Goethe to Garcia Marquez*. London; New York: Verso, 1996.

Morse, J. Mitchell. *The Sympathetic Alien: James Joyce and Catholicism.* New York: New York University Press, 1959.

Moseley, Virginia. *Joyce and the Bible.* DeKalb: Northern Illinois University Press, 1967.

Newman, Robert D., ed. *Pedagogy, Praxis,* Ulysses: *Using Joyce's Text to Transform the Classroom.* Ann Arbor: University of Michigan Press, 1996.

Norris, Margot. *A Companion to James Joyce's* Ulysses: *Biographical and Historical Contexts, Critical History and Essays from Five Contemporary Critical Perspectives.* Boston: Bedford Books, 1998.

North, Michael. *Reading 1922: A Return to the Scene of the Modern.* New York: Oxford University Press, 1999.

Parrinder, Patrick. *James Joyce.* Cambridge: Cambridge University Press, 1984.

Pearce, Richard, ed. *Molly Blooms: A Polylogue on "Penelope" and Cultural Studies.* Madison, WI: University of Wisconsin Press, 1994.

Peterson, Richard F., Cohn, Alan M. and Edmund L. Epstein, eds. *Joyce Centenary Essays.* Carbondale: Southern Illinois University Press, 1983.

Pringle, Mary Beth. "Funfersum: Dialogue as Metafictional Technique in the 'Cyclops' Episode of *Ulysses.*" *James Joyce Quarterly* 18 (1981): 397–416.

Raleigh, John Henry. *The Chronicle of Leopold and Molly Bloom: Ulysses as Narrative.* Berkeley: University of California Press, 1977.

Reizbaum, Marilyn. *James Joyce's Judaic Other.* Stanford, CA: Stanford University Press, 1999.

Reynolds, Mary T. *Joyce and Dante: The Shaping Imagination.* Princeton: Princeton University Press, 1981.

Rickard, John S. *Joyce's Book of Memory: The Mnemotechnics of* Ulysses. Durham, N.C.: Duke University Press, 1999.

Sabin, Margery. *The Dialect of the Tribe: Speech and Community in Modern Fiction.* New York: Oxford University Press, 1987.

Schlossman, Beryl. *James Joyce's Catholic Comedy of Language.* Madison: University of Wisconsin Press, 1985.

Schwaber, Paul. *The Cast of Characters: A Reading of* Ulysses. New Haven: Yale University Press, 1999.

Schwarz, Daniel R. *Reading Joyce's* Ulysses. New York: St. Martin's Press, 1987.

Schutte, William M. *Joyce and Shakespeare: A Study in the Meaning of* Ulysses. New Haven: Yale University Press, 1957.

Scott, Bonnie Kime. *Joyce and Feminism.* Bloomington: Indian University Press, 1984.

Seidel, Michael. *Epic Geography: James Joyce's* Ulysses. Princeton: Princeton University Press, 1984.

Senn, Fritz. *Joyce's Dislocutions: Essays on Reading as Translation.* Edited by

John Riquelme. Baltimore: The Johns Hopkins University Press, 1984.

———. *Inductive Scrutinies: Focus on Joyce*. Baltimore: Johns Hopkins University Press, 1995.

Shechner, Mark. *Joyce in Nighttown: A Psychoanalytic Inquiry into* Ulysses. Berkeley: University of California Press, 1974.

Sherry, Vincent B. *James Joyce's* Ulysses. Cambridge: New York: Cambridge University Press, 1994.

Sicari, Stephen. *Joyce's Modernist Allegory:* Ulysses *and the History of the Novel*. Columbia, SC: University of South Carolina Press, 2001.

Steinberg, Erwin Ray. *The Stream of Consciousness and Beyond in* Ulysses. Pittsburgh: University of Pittsburgh Press, 1970.

Storey, Robert. "The Argument of *Ulysses*, Reconsidered." *Modern Language Quarterly* 40 (1979): 175–95.

Theall, Donald F. *James Joyce's Techno-Poetics*. Toronto: University of Toronto Press, 1997.

Thomas, Brook. *James Joyce's* Ulysses: *A Book of Many Happy Returns*. Baton Rouge: Louisiana State University Press, 1982.

Thornton, Weldon. *Voices and Values in Joyce's* Ulysses. Gainesville: University Press of Florida, 2000.

———. *Allusions in* Ulysses: *An Annotated List*. Chapel Hill: University of North Carolina Press, 1961.

Tucker, Lindsey. *Stephen and Bloom at Life's Feast: Alimentary Symbolism and the Creative Process in James Joyce's* Ulysses. Columbus: Ohio State University Press, 1984.

Ungar, Andras. *Joyce's* Ulysses *as National Epic: Epic Mimesis and the Political History of the Nation State*. Gainesville: University Press of Florida, 2002.

Van Caspel, Paul. *Bloomers on the Liffey: Eisegetical Readings of Joyce's* Ulysses. Baltimore: Johns Hopkins University Press, 1986.

Warner, John M. *Joyce's Grandfathers: Myth and History in Defoe, Smollett, Sterne, and Joyce*. Athens: University of Georgia Press, 1993.

Weinstein, Philip M. "New Haven, New Earth: Joyce and the Art of Reprojection." *The Semantics of Desire: Changing Models of Identity from Dickens to Joyce*. Princeton: Princeton University Press, 1984.

Wicht, Wolfgang. *Utopianism in James Joyce's* Ulysses. Heidelberg: Universitätsverlag C., 2000.

Wollaeger, Mark A., Luftig, Victor and Robert E. Spoo, eds. *Joyce and the Subject of History*. Ann Arbor: University of Michigan Press, 1996.

Acknowledgments

"The Backgrounds of *Ulysses*" by Richard Ellmann. From *James Joyce*: 367–390. © 1959, 1982 by Richard Ellmann. Used by permission of Oxford University Press, Inc.

Iser, Wolfgang. *The Implied Reader: Patterns of Communication in Prose Fiction from Bunyan to Beckett*: 179–195. © 1974 by The Johns Hopkins University Press. Reprinted with the permission of The Johns Hopkins University Press.

"Ithaca" by A. Walton Litz. From *James Joyce's Ulysses: Critical Essays*: 386–405. © 1974 by The Regents of the University of California. Reprinted by permission.

"Narrative Transgression and Restoration: Hermetic Messengers in *Ulysses*" by Robert D. Newman. From *James Joyce Quarterly* 29: 315–337. © 1992 by The University of Tulsa. Reprinted by permission.

"'*Amor Matris*': Mother and Self in the Telemachiad Episode of *Ulysses*" by Marylu Hill. From *Twentieth Century Literature* 39, no. 3:329–343. © 1993 by Hofstra University. Reprinted by permission.

"Beyond Recognition: Reading the Unconscious in the 'Ithaca' Episode of *Ulysses*" by Nicholas A. Miller. From *James Joyce Quarterly* 30: 209–218. © 1993 by The University of Tulsa. Reprinted by permission.

"Authorial Omniscience and Cultural Psyche: The Antimodernism of Joyce's *Ulysses*" by Weldon Thornton. From *Bucknell Review: Irishness and (Post)Modernism* 38, no. 1: 84–102. © 1994 by Associated University Presses, Inc. Reprinted by permission.

"Old Worlds, New Worlds, Alternative Worlds: *Ulysses, Metamorphoses* 13, and the Death of the Beloved Son" by José Lanters. From *James Joyce Quarterly* 36, no. 3: 525–540. © 1999 by The University of Tulsa. Reprinted by permission.

"'Scylla and Charybdis' (and *Phaedrus*): The Influence of Plato and the Artistry of Joyce" by Joley Wood. From *James Joyce Quarterly* 36, no. 3: 559–70. © 1999 by The University of Tulsa. Reprinted by permission.

"Orpheus and the Machine: Proust as Theorist of Technological Change, and the Case of Joyce" by Sara Danius. From *Forum for Modern Language Studies*. © 2001 by *Forum for Modern Language Studies* xxxvii, no. 2: 127–140. Reprinted by permission.

Smith, Eric D. "A Slow and Dark Birth: Aesthetic Maturation and the Entelechic Narrative in James Joyce's *Ulysses*." From *Modern Fiction Studies* 47:4 (2001), 753–773. © 2001 Purdue Research Foundation. Reprinted with permission of The Johns Hopkins University Press.

Index